D0938492

ghetto celebrity

CROWN PUBLISHERS | NEW YORK

Donnell Alexander

ghetto celebrity

SEARCHING FOR MY FATHER IN ME

Copyright © 2003 by Donnell Alexander

All rights reserved. No part of this book may be reproduced or transmitted in any form or by any means, electronic or mechanical, including photocopying, recording, or by any information storage and retrieval system, without permission in writing from the publisher.

Published by Crown Publishers, New York, New York.
Member of the Crown Publishing Group,
a division of Random House, Inc.
www.randomhouse.com

CROWN is a trademark and the Crown colophon is a registered trademark of Random House, Inc.

Printed in the United States of America

Design by Barbara M. Bachman
Line drawings by Josh Sheppard
Lettering in graphic interlude by Lisa Zahra

LIBRARY OF CONGRESS CATALOGING-IN-PUBLICATION DATA
Alexander, Donnell.
Ghetto celebrity: searching for my father in me: a memoir / Donnell Alexander.—1st ed.
1. Alexander, Donnell—Childhood and youth. 2. African-American young men—Ohio—Sandusky—Biography.
3. African-Americans—Ohio—Sandusky—Biography.
4. Fathers and sons—Ohio—Sandusky. 5. African-American fathers—Ohio—Sandusky—Biography. 6. Absentee fathers—Ohio—Sandusky—Biography. 7. African-American youth—Ohio—Sandusky—Social life and customs—20th century.
8. City and town life—Ohio—Sandusky—History—20th century.
9. Inner cities—Ohio—Sandusky—History—20th century.
10. Sandusky (Ohio)—Biography. I. Title.
F499.S22 A43 2003
944.1'21400496073'0092—dc21   2002015801

ISBN 1-4000-4602-5

10 9 8 7 6 5 4 3 2 1

FIRST EDITION

(Boogedy)

To B.L.G. and A.M.O. and Jetoye

—D.E.A.

WARNING!

   Constantly I got niggas tryna act like I ain't ghetto—white muhfuckas as well as black ones—but that's alright yo. It's not like I'm proud of the shit. Rather, I'm on this topic strictly to score the comfort that's derived from being recognized for who one is.

   See, I got a ghetto name, so suckas don't know how to play me. They act like I'm ahistorical, like I dropped in from space. To complicate matters more, I'm from the hood in small-town Ohio. Niggas always accusing Buckeye niggas of acting white, but that's a small-town thing. The little, out-of-the-way hoods are actually, like, extra-ghetto. In the sticks it ain't like Brooklyn. There you just marinate, 'cuz if you're in a burg and have to live life like underground, public transit ain't <u>tryin'</u> to come through and lift you up and out, on some <u>Fame</u> shit.

   This is what kills me the most, straight up: Hardly a goddamn person who don't live in the ghetto sticks can even see you. And yet they want to speak on how you be. That's why that ignorant shit keeps poppin'. All these black-ass alleged stars up in the sports and entertainment spotlight, and y'all still don't know ya niggas.

   <u>If you don't see it, then it can't be . . .</u>

   Y'all think that shit and y'all hate that shit, here in America, Land of the Free, Birthplace of the Nigga. It's the fact that's the wellspring of my spite.

At the end of the day, muhfuckas gonna acknowledge me though. I know this like I know my dick size.

It's like pussy, to me. The word pussy, that is, and the way girls tend to it. In this end-of-the-millennium time of mine, a whole buncha girls wanna act like they can't know the word, like they don't want to know it. But if you get caught up in the 3 a.m., down-on-all-fours of a contemporary female's soul, most will tell you all that's more real to them than their pussies is what comes out of it. My dream is that one day women will love their pussies like they love their niggas. And if you ain't got a nigga to love, well, that's on you.

I'm talking about America's most prissy aspect, this thinking that if you don't name something, it will go away. The same people who don't want to hear the word nigga wanna fuckin' put a buncha us up under flawless modern jails. As long as only African-Americans are what they see, the growth of prison culture is just unfortunate.

Shit, I'ma say nigga until I stop seein' niggas.

All y'all book-learnin' muhfuckas should hear some real nigga stories. This here is one. **Ghetto Celebrity** is a story of me—for sure not the story of me—just a story of me. I left out crazy wild shit. You aren't even knowing.

Listen up, I got a brand-new invention: me. 'Cuz yo I gotta ghetto name and suckas don't know how to play me. I mean, a black-ass writer named Donnell—who gets good reviews. And I'm in the game. As that nigga X put it, I went from underrated to now most anticipated. There were hella dues to pay, but I did that shit. It was not supposed to happen. You were not supposed to read this line.

There are rules against me.

Back toward the end of the eighties, around when Baldwin died, Marsha Warfield had an Uptown Comedy Express routine about niggas like me. She said, "Let's face it, you're never gonna have a president named Donnell!" The first time this bit entered my world, all half dozen people in my girlfriend Robin's living room about fell on the floor laughing, 'cuz niggas know who's ass-out. Robin lost half her curl activator, shaking her head and stomping her feet. I laughed, but burned, too, as I had just pretty much stopped doing hard drugs and focused on being all I could be. Part of me went:

Awfuck.

I couldn't be president?

Not to politick, but a little after that I embarked on proving to Marsha Warfield and every other comedian/critic that news of my doom was exaggerated. There was too much evidence of my fate's unpredictability.

I could be president yo. Maybe one day I'll be in D.C., under an umbrella and holding a Bible, looking into the camera and saying:

"Joke's on you, motherfucker!"

Who am I to be talking to you, gentle-ass reader, in such impertinent tones? Why, it's me, that dope guy. The one who gets the rest of the room high through presence, that old ghetto presence. I am quoted by others who make things that move a great many others. I enrich the lives of old squares in the hills, even them without no cable. Ad people use me to get their kids fed and you shop to me in your malls. I'm almost like an artist.

Yet I come covered in wild shit, dysfunction and disarray. Maybe, gentle-ass reader, beyond this layer you aren't able to see.

Hey yo I gotta ghetto name, so suckas know they can't slay me.

This is a book about my life, not the book about my life. Just some perspective on a few dominant themes, a travelogue of America beyond the experience of TV's obligatory colored cast member or corporate thug cliché. And I left shit out because the purpose of this project isn't purely to quantify who I am. (Is such a thing even possible? How do you recount the days, their effect on you? And how can you put your finger on just one thing, one day that spooned the next or an hour that turned you askew? How do you sketch the shape of your life?) For years I've known that I'm nothing more than the sum of those who raised me, the dope people I got to be around. This book is a tribute to dopeness by osmosis. Regardless, what follows is tangibly real. So real, in fact, that some conversations are accurate only in essence. And to heighten realism, I have, wherever possible, referred to related tapes, transcripts, and articles. But that's just really another kind of distortion, as these devices put recorded events on a higher plateau than those countless private developments.

I've also made up a bit here and there, if only for brevity. (Contrivance is so useful it's disgusting, like putting another finger up in there.)

If my take on reality already has you bugged, maybe this isn't the book for you. Think the purchase through. (Shit, take **Ghetto Celebrity** home and chances are I'll be all up in your ventilation, fuckin' with your family.) If you're one of those people who's going to become angry halfway through and huff and puff and think about starting a watchdog organization whose purpose is to eliminate the likes of me—but you won't do a thing because you're too damn shook—then don't take my shit home. 'Cuz I'm a wild card. And most don't know how to play me.

But, say you're feeling me. Then know that the shit is real as fuck. Read on, get open, but don't act like you don't know.

Donny Shell, Brooklyn, NY

i'ma keep doin' me unfortunately.

—S. CARTER

act 1

SOWN

1.

Stroh's genius

OCTOBER 1978

AS IT HAD BEEN THE HANDFUL OF TIMES I HAD DECLINED THE DOOBAGE, at my side was a French horn—in its black, generation-old, Adams Junior High carrying case. My friends, some of whom I'd known throughout grade school, would wave the snub-nosed, sweet-smelling marijuana cigarettes under my nose like " 'Ere," and I'd decline and they'd not push, because I was a good boy and there was nothing wrong with that.

They'd do it in the park, smack-dab in the middle of pistachio- and emerald-colored leaves and the vacantly staring buckeyes or sometimes in a cold, gray alley as we walked that circuit from our downtown school, just blocks off the dock of Sandusky Bay, to our homes, scattered about the East Side. Windchill diminished so that the closer you got to the East End, kids forgot the bracing snap coming off the water. That morning, I didn't wear a coat.

I don't remember there being any potential witnesses, which is weird because the last bell at Adams rang in midafternoon, and, even though most adults were still loading and unloading machines at the factories that kept the town on the map when tourist season wound down, there ought to have at least been cars moving to drop off helmets and lads at practice fields, so that boys could lay pads into each other. Columbus Avenue traffic aside, the coast seemed pretty clear.

All there was were huddling seventh-graders at the downtown open space outside Erie County Common Pleas Court. Spread across an acre of naked green space, we hung in cipher-sized cadres, with most kicking it the way fake-hard twelve-year-olds did in those days: white boys in denim jackets, with greasy hair and Kool cigarettes hanging from their lips like straight and opaque lunchroom straws aflame; nappy-headed niggas having wind-induced ashiness, ostentatiously imitation pleather, and maybe a lunchbox-size ghetto blaster cradled in their arms. Present also is the girl who might be pregnant but doesn't know for sure.

I stood underdressed and on the perimeter—a shade over five feet, not yet one hundred pounds, havin' freakin' black buckshot for hair—with that ridiculous French horn at my side. It was about the size of a baby hippo, and not even a sax. And this being just an open space, sans trees or other high-wind blocker-outers, my shit fairly whipped about, like a little black flag. I was getting ashier by the minute.

There was no agenda when I smoked weed for the very first time. I was just bored and cold, thinking, *maybe, this joint will warm me up.*

The funk had gone out, and I had to light it. Fire beyond my fingertips formed a furnace in the palm of my hand. High up on the doobie, I pinched the paper and leaned in and sucked it past my lips.

"Don't nigger-lip it," someone said.

Was there any other way? This was a new one on me. By the joint's next time around though, I'd figured out what was meant, and pillow lips got pursed.

Italian-ass Jeff (aka Biscuit Head Jed) was there, but he didn't say *nigger-lip.* Neither did Victor, although he *could* have. Victor was one of those five-o'clock-shadow-havin' niggas who looked eligible for the draft even when he was in seventh grade. Talked a lot of shit, but he didn't say it. I can't say who else was in the circle, except a bunch of white boys, but I know that after the command to keep the joint off my tonsils, I took it out, eyed it stem to stem, and then hit the fuck out of that weed.

Someone said, "Aw, he didn't even inhale."

This I ignored, since all I knew was that some smoke had gone up in me. As the real temperature hovered just above freezing, I exhaled a languid line of mildly laced carbon dioxide and was indeed warmer when the joint had made its way back around.

The next one had me coughing. I could practically feel the blood vessels in my lungs expanding. From the fulcrum of my waist, I pulled over double. *Hack, hack. Phlegm, phlegm.* Explosions on my brainstem. The French horn case now lying sideways on the sidewalk. If this were a movie, now I'd be straightening my clothes and checking slyly to see if anyone had noticed that little, er . . . snafu.

A thump came on my shoulder. It was my turn again. This hit went less harshly, more enveloping.

The act of smoking a joint was beginning to make sense. Inside me something bloomed that was clearly different from the effect of the cigarettes I had smoked during the summer of two years back, behind a Farrell-Cheek Dumpster with my neighbor Mike. Those only cooked my lungs and reinforced Mama's warnings against drugs and booze. Based on tobacco, I could only wonder why anyone would purposefully smoke anything.

Well, what I was feeling this autumn day downtown was clearly more rewarding. By the time the cipher broke up, I wasn't coughing. I was floating. The cold no longer hassled, it invigorated. The nip against my skin seemed the urge to life itself, no lie. And Jed and them and me laughed until our bodies wouldn't let us anymore. Jed's every misstep was like a Walter Lantz cartoon. He cracked up at me, too, and I didn't mind. "Pimple forehead," he observed of the white-peaked, hella rugged terrain residing above my eyebrows. We both broke down, tears streaming along our cheeks. Now my bad skin was an in-joke. We cursed, debated who we'd fuck, *gimme just one chance goddammit.* And at Tim's house, a pit stop on the way to our East Side abodes, we read the letters in *Hustler.* We read and critiqued. Tim said, "I like when they be havin' them organisms!" Jeff and I were speechless. Was it us or him who had paid insufficient attention in biology class?

A lot of things happened that fall—not the least of which was this brilliant dawn of hashish—things that would make me all serious and ethereal, as though my body were strictly a rental apartment. Soon that French horn would be cast aside as would the entirety of my beloved North Coast, dissed nationally as the Mistake on the Lake, but home all the same.

But I felt good. You knew that I would now.

People ask me, from time to time, whether I'm in bed with criminals. I tell whoever puts this question to me that my mother was when she conceived, so the answer may well be moot.

YOU COULD ACTUALLY STILL HEAR FRANKIE VALLI SONGS OVER TRANSISTOR radios in the day when the whole thing started. On the summer Saturday in 1961 when Brenda Graham, my mother, joined DuJuana from downstairs and some of that girl's friends for a day at Cedar Point, she was still young enough and country enough to have never kissed a boy, to have never had a date. Brenda was first off the steps and led the charge to the park's ferryboat, downtown at the docks. She led with a skip and skipped with a bop.

They had been neighbors for years, but DuJuana was older than this oldest Graham girl and talked back to boys, provided they approached respectfully. Her discretion eliminated her most wolfish suitors, but, regardless, DuJuana had boys after her. Like Billy, that big pretty boy with a stutter. Billy ran with a crew who all wore their hair in slicked-back conks, and if they didn't see the inside of a jail until around their eighteenth birthdays, they'd be lucky.

It took five minutes for the girls to get from the Bay View Arms apartments to the dock, and just as Sandusky Bay came into sight, DuJuana confirmed what Brenda suspected was the plan: Billy and the boys would take a later ferry to the amusement park and meet them at that icon of a roller coaster, the Blue Streak. From front to rear the line leader fell.

Brenda didn't mind Billy—he had proper Southern manners and he spoiled DuJuana silly—still Brenda didn't come out to get caught up in her friend's fast-girl ways.

"You sure take your time letting everybody in on things," Brenda complained, nearly to herself, making eye contact with no one.

DuJuana shrugged, "It's a big park." Then she called out back, without turning around:

"Grow up girl. See who you want, ignore who you don't."

That smart remark made Brenda mad. Earlier, back at the apartments, Brenda's five siblings had looked at their fifteen-year-old sister like she was grown. She was going to Cedar Point *without Mother and Daddy*. She'd pulled off a caper incalculable to them.

Brenda had convened a parental conference of great subtlety and stood with humbled shoulders just outside the door of the Grahams' converted hotel unit and begged Mother and Daddy's permission, but only after detailing her daily list of chores and quasi-matronly responsibilities. She was shady with her histrionics, and built to a precariously developed crescendo.

She said, "So I can take care of these kids all the time, but can't just *one time* go to Cedar Point and have *one day* to myself as a reward? Oooo, that's just not right."

Brenda got her way.

In this scrap of northern Ohio, an amusement park could matter enough that a teenager might wield its name with searing melodrama. Otherwise industrial and approaching anonymity, Sandusky kept the Cedar Point name so tied up in local identity that its high school sports teams were called the Blue Streaks. The very fact of Brenda's going was a big thing.

But even before DuJuana had brought up Bill, a malaise had set upon the girls. The problem stemmed from Brenda. Cedar Point was real live—not just a way of getting back at Daddy and Mother—and its thrill rides weren't at all to her taste. She found nothing fun about fear. As Brenda was the brainiest, her filibustering and coaxing had everyone sticking to the tame stuff: bumper cars, swing rides, games of chance. By noon, the day had slipped into the mundane.

Near the saltwater taffy stand, DuJuana, with authority, threw away the paper cone from her second bag of cotton candy.

"Look, the Blue Streak line ain't that long. Let's get *on* it."

Brenda forced her eyebrows together and asked, "Have you *seen* the Blue Streak, up close?"

"You can just cool your heels, Brenda. Eat another damn bag of popcorn for all I care, but we didn't come here to ride like five-year-olds!"

"And that's fine with me," Brenda said. "But do you really want to risk your hair? Messing it up I mean."

DuJuana smoothed back her hair, right above her straightening-comb tan, where the do was starting to kink up some.

"And those nice shorts," Brenda continued, "why you even wanna put them on, much less iron them, if you're going to have them get all wrinkled?"

DuJuana brushed down the material covering her thighs.

Brenda went in for the kill. "I understand though. You don't want Billy to think you're too interested in him, hunh? That's smart." With a wave at the hem of her friend's floral fabric, Brenda dismissed the matter.

DuJuana *hated* when her protégé tried to play slick.

"Ungh. Brenda Lee Graham, you get on my last damn nerve."

The flow of tourists on the midway pushed them to the crowded fun-house entrance. DuJuana pointed up, then put her foot down. All in favor said aye, and it was agreed that this was a much more reasonable choice than the Blue Streak.

Brenda abstained from voting and cursed her fortune. She was more scared of the fun house than the coasters. The girl walking at a distance behind her friends improvised excuses all the way.

DuJuana, who all morning had let Brenda's open cowardice cover for her own fear, said, because she could:

"You scurred."

"Scared," Brenda whispered as correction, then said, "No, I am not."

The quartet latched onto the turnstile mosey, her friends acting all cool and straying behind clusters of Bermuda shorts and lobster-red legs. Soon the gang would be separate in the dark.

Inside, Brenda lingered before the most pleasing in a series of warped mirrors. For once she was stretched tall. Not as pretty as her younger sister Sherry—or Mother, for that matter—but Brenda could see even in the curvy metal that she was doing alright. Her palms did not sweat here. Hands on hips, in fists, then wrapped around her shoulders in a Dorothy Dandridge pose. Too long a look, too dreamy, then she was alone, scouring the passageway for her friends.

In the mock-horror darkness, Brenda kept one friend between herself and the railing, always. Beyond the distorted mirrors, piped-in spookiness, and calibrated lurching of plastic skeletons, the haunted house offered genuine elements of fear. There was a sound of shuffling feet, too real to have come from a speaker so tinny. Brenda wanted to wrap her trembling hands around DuJuana's fingers. Were those heavy whispers in the middle distance for real or a joke? When the clomp of about four pair of unseen hard shoes hit the floor, DuJuana's digits were vised.

And then there were hands on Brenda, all over. Much of the feeling was below the belt and behind, expert and powerful. She grabbed both groping hands, before she even screamed, and felt an energy ignite. It was different from that time Daddy's friend had put his hand down her pants. That was wrong. This felt wrong too, but, for that pause before she screamed in the fun house, there was fascination where disgust ought to have been.

Her oversize rear end, breasts, and thighs had been investigated roughly by small, wiry hands, and when she finally wrestled free and said, "Stop!" she heard DuJuana yell the same thing.

'Cept DuJuana was laughing. Everyone was, except for Brenda.

Now Brenda's labored vision revealed DuJuana hugging Billy. The attack had been only a mating ritual. There were four boys, all older than Brenda.

On the walk toward flittering daylight beneath the fun-house Exit sign, Brenda nicked glances at the one who had picked her. She glimpsed a sneer in his smiling profile, then poked out her bottom lip, looked at her shoes, and softly mumbled, "These guys are lowlifes."

He had nice hair though. Not greasy, but clearly straight and shining in the minimal light.

Brenda was silent the rest of the day, playing the blitz over in her head. Each time the footage unfurled behind her eyes, Brenda's mind perked up at the picture's start, before she screamed.

There was no getting away from the fact that the one who had groped her, sexy lurking in the damp darkness, was a little mug, just a bit taller than her five-foot self.

He lagged behind, next to the girl, down the ramp to the turnstiles and back out into the midway, and through the day's remains loitered, telling Brenda corny jokes. Brenda received each effort coolly. Sometimes she even declined to acknowledge them with a dim smile. But when curfew came, at the ferryboat landing, the miniature kid's lips were on hers. He kissed her, and she kissed back. Awkwardly, excitedly, scared. Brenda's kiss was that of a child in passion.

BILLY AND THEM WERE DELBERT ALEXANDER'S SAFE, SQUARE HOMEBOYS.

He had just come back to Santown from down South. Anderson, South Carolina, to be precise. His parents, the closest thing Erie County had to monied colored people, had all but given up on trying to change Delbert's trifling ways, but the real reason for Delbert's absence from the hometown picture was legal: the law had promised to lock him up if he had remained in Sandusky with the grown criminals he called friends.

Charlene Rice Alexander and her husband, Gospie, known among the coloreds as Mr. Hots, had really thought that a summer with the boy's Rice relatives would help sever Delbert's underworld ties. Instead, he had just refined his penchant for sniffing out action. In South Carolina he would hitchhike to the next town over if word was it had get-highs and cards, women and music. Delbert accomplished half his missions undetected. When he didn't, Charlene's sisters whipped his butt. But that didn't mend him.

Before the summer was done, Delbert was ducking certain down-South gangsters with a vigilance he had once reserved for the police.

Five-four and sinewy, with delicate cheekbones and wavy hair, Delbert won folks over before he opened his mouth. Those compelled by the looks were pulled through that threshold into his confidence. Anyone venturing that far was done.

Delbert manipulated words like Junior Walker worked the saxophone and charmed like a radio minister. He was a hustler to his marrow. The cousins and aunts in the Alexanders' extended Sandusky family—the Rices, Prophets—passed around the story of how, when Delbert was twelve, he got a route delivering the *Chicago Defender* and the *Pittsburgh Courier.* Within two weeks, the boy had conned his big sister Barb into distributing the Negro weeklies onto doorsteps across the South Side. He paid Barb a fee, and you couldn't be mad at him.

Soon Delbert's rascally ways wouldn't come across so cute. He left his dirt in the street, but the unexplained money and new clothes tipped off family. The Rices talked, so did the Prophets. Charlene and Mr. Hots denied plain evidence until cops got to be regular callers at their Clay Street address, always asking to talk with their son.

The resulting humiliation drove Mr. Hots to unknown levels of fury. And Delbert's indifference to his father's pain touched off epic chase scenes. Late nights when Hots came home from his railroad job and found Delbert's bed empty, he would get on the phone, putting out word that the boy was MIA. Then Hots would call out the window to reach every residence not hooked up. These episodes ended most neatly when Delbert came home to take his beatings straight up, but the act got messy on occasions that Hots caught wind of his son's presence at one house of ill repute or another and had to hand out an ass whipping on the spot. Many times Hots just missed Delbert and drove back down Clay Street to find his son in bed, eyes closed, faking and hoping.

Delbert was fleet of foot, but quit track when the coach insisted on practice before competition. His ease in classroom discussion was canceled out by a deep-seated disdain for homework. Girls Delbert's own age flipped for him, stopped just short of calling him Daddy. But he messed with older, looser women because he wanted sex, fast. He openly, endlessly coveted, adjusting his means to get what he wanted, and after the fun-house episode he had a ripe brown country girl in his sights.

BRENDA WAS SEVENTEEN WHEN SHE WENT WITH DUJUANA TO BILLY'S Christmas party. Sherry, Brenda's much faster sister, teased Brenda as if the girl had not been out one time in her life. There had been parties—so what if it was just a handful—and Brenda secretly felt superior to Sherry for not being so out there in the world.

Art and Geneva Graham hadn't raised Brenda to be exceptionally naive or introverted or consumed with denial; it just turned out that way. Blame it on this oldest of six children coming while Geneva was only fifteen, back when home was Kimball, fifteen hundred people living off coal and farmland in a southeastern nook of Appalachia. Sherry would come next, then Roger and Marlene and the rest. One on top of the other.

Down in the holler, Brenda grew to be reticent.

Up North, she exemplified the Grahams' outback clannishness, sticking to the home base as though afraid of being tagged "it." And the quality did not dissipate even after that crude kiss on the Cedar Point ferry landing. Brenda holed up in hallways outside the Bay View Arms apartments when she wasn't cooking and cleaning or going to school. For a while though she had been itching to do like DuJuana.

THE RECORDS THAT PLAYED AT HER FRIEND'S PARTY WERE HER favorites: James Brown, Aretha Franklin, the Supremes. It took more effort to be still than to groove alone in the corner. For big bundles of minutes, Brenda's friends, as well as boys she knew from school, boogied with her. Donald, the lunchroom flirt and that other cute one, the

Stovall boy, they gyrated into the circle of girlfriends and made Brenda think about doing this more often.

From the kitchen doorway, then from the living room corner, Delbert watched the girl's easy stabs at the watusi and the mashed potato. Brenda was oblivious to the gaze. When she loitered by the record player to gossip with DuJuana, Brenda felt a rough hand clutch at her elbow and heard above the happy wail of Motown her name stuttered in Billy's Alabama timbre.

Billy might be old enough to vote. He has a process. He's over six feet tall.

Billy couldn't get what he wanted to say heard above the party din. He yanked Brenda gently and said, "Y-Y-You come here.

"You remember my friend Delbert?"

"Yes," she answered, pinching the word off at the end to make sure it got told that the memory was not pleasant.

"Well, he l-l-likes you. He r-right over there."

"So?"

"So why don't you give him a chance?"

Brenda psh-awed and rolled her eyes.

"He's a lowlife."

Brenda snatched her arm from Billy and went back to the cleared-out space in the living room where DuJuana was by herself, doing the jerk.

AFTER THAT, DELBERT SEEMED CONSTANTLY ON THE PERIPHERY OF Brenda's social life, hanging with clumps of other not-so-recent graduates, on the blacktop behind Sandusky High and in the hallway outside Blue Streak basketball games. Brenda kept him at arm's length. She knew his reputation for being out of control. Shoot, the reasons behind his being sent to South Carolina were secret to nobody. And she'd heard Delbert had been in reform school, too, for sticking up the ice cream man.

It wasn't Brenda's bag to pretend she'd been around. But she liked romance and, while maintaining her distance, soaked up the danger in

Delbert's aura. It was fascinating having a lowlife liking her. The Grahams had lived in Cleveland for a while, on the way up from West Virginia, and Brenda remembered the walks to school, the East Side sunrise, and dope fiends on the block. A junkie got close up once and took her lunch money. She was ten and with Sherry. The way Delbert insinuated reminded her of how that mugger had approached.

Here is what Brenda could not get over: he was an obviously likable guy who paid people back for being attentive by treating them like crap. It was well known that he had one girlfriend, Juanita, who let him beat her butt for breakfast, lunch, and dinner. Even a naive colored girl from Ohio knows that's what happens to a girl who's been turned out.

JUST THINKING THESE THOUGHTS MIGHT HAVE BEEN CRACKS IN BRENDA'S facade. The moment she started liking Delbert was a bigger surprise than the day in the dark at Cedar Point.

Little by little, occasion by occasion, Brenda began reciprocation. When he and his whipped hair happened upon her at the White House, a diner hangout that Brenda thought cool and her mother found seedy, Delbert paid for the sodas. She told him to phone her while Art and Geneva were at work, and when he did, he said gentle things. Surprise.

Delbert began to remind Brenda of boys from her trashy novels, the reading she fell into just after the Lois Lenski books got tired.

Brenda's favored breathless prose told the same story: Girl meets bad boy. Bad boy rubs girl wrong. Girl learns boy has depth beyond what the world can see. This was just like that. Nothing in Brenda's life so far had been half as thrilling. She had never had a boy, none of any kind, and here was someone so special that the world couldn't take him.

He sang in a band, too. Brenda imagined the music showed the positive inside Delbert. They—that amorphous and nameless "they"—*made* him act so bad. Each time she politely declined to go out with Delbert on a date—how would she ever have swung that?—her suitor's braggadocio seemed to Brenda a shield. He posed cool to keep

Sandusky from seeing too much. It made her want to watch him sing, on a stage.

Time passed between them in crowded White House booths (no, Brenda lied to DuJuana, she was not talking to him) and via gymnasium convos in which Brenda found herself carried away to beneath the bleachers. Brenda admired how Delbert never appeared sly.

He was skilled. Delbert was someone, and after he sent her a box of chocolates for New Year's Day, 1964, Brenda decided to give him a chance. When they kissed, she secretly wanted more, but Delbert did nothing to suggest he wanted her to go any further.

WELL, GENEVA GRAHAM WASN'T FALLING FOR ANY OF THIS. BRENDA'S mother knew what Delbert was, because she had seen him before. Saw his kind in Cleveland, glowing red in Arthur's "rockin'" gambling circle, talkin' mess. Delbert wasn't nothin' but a sawed-off ghetto celebrity. She knew this from his little criminal reputation, knew it from the Perry Street men's rooftop card games, and knew it from the whorehouse next door. How could she not know? Sandusky just wasn't that big.

And he had a band. A band? That "James Brown Junior" bullshit? Nuthin' but some nonsense. Geneva hadn't heard that blasted noise, but sensed this kid was on the scene for something other than music. Geneva was not naive, not after being married to Arthur for all these years.

Such a person's becoming close to Geneva and Arthur's firstborn made them more than a little distraught. Steady Brenda was turning into a dirty liar now, just as the family was about to buy its first home. Geneva, then Arthur, yelled at their daughter. Spanked her, tore that ass up. They forbade her from seeing Delbert.

But they couldn't watch the girl every day, and after a while Brenda wasn't even trying to conceal her actions. The open secret hung heavy among siblings Sherry and Roger, even among the younger ones. Geneva's whippings with switches went from sure-fire threat to worn-out gesture in the space of months, and a sense of inevitability bore down on the bond between her eldest and this thug.

Geneva was thirty-one. Life had so sauntered on that the years spent with Arthur had matched up even to life before his arrival. Only rarely did Geneva question how she was living. The fact of Arthur hitting her was no longer heavy trauma, just something to steer clear of. That's no question when you live in an apartment full of kids who are quick to say they're hungry.

There was no room for bruised feelings or extratender emotion. West Virginia wasn't hardly in the rearview anymore. Arthur demanded none of the spouse-swapping that went down on other floors of the Bay View Arms. And while Geneva did clean houses, it was Arthur's home-repair work that put food on the table and kept up rent. The youngest, Ricky, was actually on his way to being spoiled. Eavesdrop on any church social, and if a brother or sister knew them at all, they'd tell you the Grahams were doing alright. They'd say the family came up quick.

In the spring of '64, seven out of eight Grahams at the Bay View Arms received, with muted glee, news that Delbert's dirt had caught up with him. Police busted his gang for a drugstore robbery. Mr. Hots posted bail, but the prison stretch in Mansfield would be long this time.

The girl's infatuation reminded Geneva of how Arthur had dazzled her down in the holler. But Geneva could not afford to show much sympathy. The Graham females folded clothes at the laundromat, and Geneva swore out loud that the arrest was a blessing in disguise. Delbert got convicted, and whether packing the youngest boys' lunches or plodding with her mother through the aisles of A&P, Brenda moped.

"You'll forget him," Geneva said.

A funny thing happened on the way to Brenda's forgetting. She wrote Delbert winterlong, at dusk and dawn and for pages on end. For Delbert, correspondence and visits from Hots and Billy and all the girl-friends dwindled away. But there were letters with that Perry Street address weekly, coming as sure as his mama's cookies. The writing was passionate and personal and, isolated as they were, elicited from the captive responses in kind.

Geneva didn't find out about the letters until spring.

She had worried a bit when her daughter didn't get serious with the one named Donald, who called a lot, or the Stovall boy. And then Geneva learned Brenda had been accompanying Charlene Alexander to the reformatory where Delbert was housed, about an hour down the road.

Enough was enough. She and Arthur had planned the first ever Graham family vacation for that summer, but Geneva emptied the savings account, shipped a money order off to Malden, Massachusetts, and bought a bus ticket to Boston. Relatives would watch over Brenda, and maybe that suburb would show her a big, wide part of what lay out beyond the fringes of ghetto celebrity.

CONSIDER THESE PICTURES OF BRENDA IN BOSTON:

1.

SHE'S IN THE KITCHEN, FIXIN' CHICKEN, PLATE NUMBER TWO, GREASE stains spreading across the quicker-picker-upper. Brenda's freckle-faced aunt Ella is at the table, and what she's eating is making her sing all high and joyful.

"Oooh, chile, this is some good chicken! Did Geneva teach you how to cook like this? Girl, I wish my own child would try to get down like *this*. Brenda, you are getting down!"

Lorna, Ella and Uncle Dan's adopted, college-bound daughter, is present, sitting with her rear up against the countertop. The girl's arms are crossed so as to appear angry, but she's putting on a show. A tall, soft-featured, coffee-and-cream beauty, Lorna is awed by Brenda's reckless quandary and habitually struggles to thwart her roomie's secret long-distance phone calls. Also, she occasionally bullies Brenda, who's short, dresses loud, and is willing to take guff.

This time Lorna lets the girl have a moment to shine. She knows that Brenda preps meals daily back home. She knows that there her chicken is received with nothing approximating fanfare.

Dancing with an apron on, the Malden houseguest grooves through tunes that buoy the grease-fried air, having Saturday-night fun in the middle of the week. *It's like thunder / and lightning / the way you love me is frightening . . .*

Lorna harrumphs exaggeratedly when her mother asks for seconds, and Brenda doubles over, slapping her legs and laughing.

2.

NOW SHE'S GOTTEN HER RUMP INSIDE THE DOOR. THE GIRL STANDS tightly packed on a train. She carries boxes in bags. Outfits, makeup, magazines, and a paperback, all just purchased from Cambridge shops with pay from her candy-factory job. Brenda reeks of chocolate. The car is full of commuters and bags are spilling out of her arms.

She needs the map of subway routes that's on the wall. A scrappy, fair-haired college type—a wee bit taller than she—stands between Brenda and directions. Privately the two share a subway moment. They smile intimately.

The girl has no idea where she's going. As she scans the obscured walls for alternate presentations of the way she needs to head, the white boy slides his grin back into view. Reverb from the loudspeaker's compromised articulation suggests a connection stop that might be hers, might not. Oh, good, it's repeating. The grin is not without charm. Brenda needs to stay, but might want to go. Or something like that. She searches overhead as if vision might produce clearer sound, and the route update ends. When Brenda shoots back to where a map should be hanging, all she can look at is an inquisitive smile, a smile she hasn't seen in a while, a smile that's actually entirely new.

Brakes suddenly begin setting, and a box pops free from her collection of sundries. The boy bends floorward, quickly, when the doors hiss open. Brenda snatches information from the subway car wall, then edges in reverse off the train.

She reaches ahead for her packages as her feet backtrack onto the platform.

"Thank you. That was so sweet"—she smiles—"of you."

Her cheeks are heated at the sight of the boy's flush red visage. And when the package is clutched close to her chest, the warmth reaches her neck.

3.

CHURCH LADIES RETURN HOME IN THE HEAVY AIR OF SUNDAY. BRENDA and four friends of Lorna's are sitting on a row-house stoop in Roxbury. Lorna is next to Brenda, who's getting her hair rollers taken out by a girl up two steps higher. On the far side of Lorna is her best friend, and this girl is bad-mouthing white people, with a passion. She is on them like Daddy and the Bay View Arms men when they've had too much to drink. But Brenda has never heard anyone, much less a girl, talk this way about the races. The girl is talking about how crackers will never treat us fair and black people—black!—might need to get guns.

The funny part though is that at first the girl struck Brenda as a person who acted white. She spoke perfect grammar that fell forward in a furious swirl. Again, Brenda's face feels hot enough for someone to witness the chemical change. With her hair in fat, unbrushed curls, she thinks, what kind of Negroes are these?

"YOU DO KNOW THEY DID IT TO GET HER AWAY FROM YOU?" DELBERT'S mother asks.

"Of course. She wrote me that."

"I thought nobody sent you letters. I can't believe that girl still talks to you."

"Why wouldn't Brenda talk to me? She says she loves me."

"That girl is so clean."

"*Clean?* I'm supposed to be just filth?"

Charlene's pause is reasonable to her, cataclysmic to her son.

"I'm your mother, of course I think you—"

"Damn, Mama. Are you ashamed of me?"

In five minutes Charlene will leave her son so that he can return to his cell and study for a hog-butchering exam. Other mothers in the faux-comfy visit room seem as hardened as their sons. Charlene feels out of place. She will go home to Hots, and her husband will not want to hear how she spent this Sunday.

"You might be in prison, but you better watch your mouth around me."

"Sorry Mama."

Hots never wanted the boy. A year before Delbert's birth, his first son, Gospie Junior, out of nowhere died in his crib. Charlene had wanted Delbert. She got a lot of what she wanted out of her husband.

Late nights when Hots was at his most drunk and vulnerable, back when Delbert was just a rascal who could be sent to bed early, he would rail at the framed photograph of baby Gospie on the wall, cold in his coffin and dressed for eternal rest.

"I never wanted no replacement baby any damn way." And Hots would slam his liquor.

The replacement baby has a number on his back.

"It's not so much shame as sorrow," Charlene answers to her son, "what I feel."

She recognizes Delbert as a bad boy and has understood this about him for ten years now. Yet this is still her baby boy. The only one.

"More than anything, it's the feeling that this"—and here Charlene spreads her arms wide enough to encompass the waiting room—"this is not what you are. You're spoiled, but you ain't all bad. I know this in my heart. It's something I can see. Other people see it and they want to be around you. They want to be close to you, not close to jail or crookedness."

Charlene doesn't even know about the mess he puts in his arm.

"If you didn't draw people like you do, I'd have cut you off a long time ago. I like that girl up in Boston. She's a sweet thing and I can't see how she would want to be close to you if you were something shameful. She makes me trust those feelings. I wish you'd marry that girl and make something of yourself. 'Cuz you have so many things others won't ever have."

SOMETIMES PEOPLE ASK ABOUT WHERE I'M COMING FROM. AND THIS IS it right here. I mean, I did yoga for years, did all the drugs and subversive art the straight crowd said not to do. I have no illusions about where I'm coming from. The origins are a naive silence, that still force at home in a young country girl. Run that vibe through with an immovable object, hard-ass, low-down, and married to beef. It's like an accident, kinda tragic in a way. Yet at the same time it's beautifully impossible, a bad miracle. Grand. Fucking "James Brown Junior" gets the hillbilly girl pregnant.

About all I'm ever nostalgic about from my first days of existence is the language. "Outtasight!" my aunts and uncles used to say. It was more obvious in that scene that amazing stuff happens outside plain view. Just beyond where things get born is where the action lies. We used to know this better.

Because you can bus a girl a thousand miles, but that won't change her heart. She'll still love like a young person. She'll still let romance rule the day. Then there will be cherry bombs and whistling fire, out of sight, just soft conclusions and unexplained tremors that make folks twist their heads. These would-be spectators cluck about the mess, the waste, the trash that's left behind, because they missed that thing so bad and true.

Delbert and Brenda had no idea what they were doing.

TURN THE CALENDAR OVER TO 1966.

The leaves were going brown when the wedding took place. Brenda was nineteen, Delbert twenty-four. His pompadour shined deep as eternal reflection. Were he able to hide the hint of sneer in his smile, the groom would have looked princely in his tux. Brenda, a baby's mama dressed in white, did little but giggle, overwhelmed by the fuss. She held her chubby preemie as often as she could, which wasn't much. Marlene and Sherry led the charge of women fighting for the right to hold little baby Donnell. The boy was on display almost as much as Delbert.

The Grahams paid for the liquor, the Alexanders everything else. The reception hall overflowed with shows of Delbert's parents' largess: flower arrangements, a congratulatory banner, a stage that implied another level of gaiety to come. An ice sculpture stood at the center of everything. Not even this ravenous crowd could eat all of the chicken, roast beef, and rice pilaf that the catering truck brought through.

Freeloaders, Geneva thought.

Watching strangers gulp down whiskey, she stuck to wine herself. Geneva loved Donnell, but didn't see much to celebrate. Last winter— before Brenda admitted to being pregnant, and the whole house knew she was with child—Geneva beat her on the porch of their first rental house. Brenda had borrowed her mother's blouse without asking, and everything spilled out. It wasn't one of those extended whuppings Papa, Geneva's daddy, used to hand out, but a violent burst of slapping across the face, ass, and back. Now the girl was tied to that evil little man.

Delbert's mother and sister made their way over. They seemed fine. Them she wanted to know. Geneva sipped the red grapes and pondered: Would she trade the life that gathered around her to start all over from Appalachian scratch? This no doubt had been the biggest colored wedding in the history of Sandusky, and every Negro with the audacity to crash the reception party had put on their Sunday best. Yet Geneva wasn't feeling it.

The night seemed to be about reclaiming Delbert, and Geneva definitely wasn't feeling that. Geneva only observed, her smile tight, smooth, and impassive. Arthur glad-handed all of his gambling cronies and the white men who gave him work. Aging hookers exchanged looks with him on the sly. These were the same women she ran into at the A&P, acting so sincere when they congratulated her on the marriage. They were lying then and they were lying now.

Still, the party was impressive, and that she couldn't deny.

Charlene was much better at playing the part. Of course, this was all her day anyway. Everyone knew this, and it became viable that the velocity of the party might transform Delbert into the son his mother desired. Geneva tried to picture Mr. Hots there, knocking back glass after glass of bourbon and showing no effect. He would have acted like one of those Don King crime dons from Cleveland, and she respected him for it, secretly. She had to imagine the presence of Delbert's father; a stroke had dropped Hots dead in his backyard garden the summer before Donnell was born.

There was no denying now that the Alexanders were in the family.

While uniformed women covered food tins with foil, four men, all conked and wearing matching tuxedos, stepped onto the stage. One mounted the drums and another strapped on an electric bass. Young girls with bright dresses and fresh perms crowded at their feet.

Delbert leapt behind the mic, counted off, and then bent until his knees nearly touched the floor.

"This is a maaaan's world!"

Brenda was standing at her husband's feet, being sung to for the first time ever. She enjoyed the show of it, of everything, though less than her husband. With that first driving chord of the James Brown song, this crystalline attention the singer lived for focused on him in a way unprecedented. Delbert couldn't really sing much. Brenda grinned at the spectacle, but not her role in it. She saw DuJuana shimmy with her eyes shut.

A half hour later, the band broke. Brenda waited for her husband to wade his way over, kissed him, stepped back, and then told him she was ready to go.

Delbert looked past her.

You stay, of course, she said.

He pulled her in for a picture, then sent the bride on her way. The band was already working out an instrumental when he got back to the stage.

Brenda, who did not drive, rode with her mother to the new

Harrison Street apartment, a renovated Alexander property behind the house Delbert had grown up in. Brenda toted Donnell. The women relived the night a little, then Geneva drove home.

In her gown, nudged gently away from sleep by the murmur of day, Brenda Alexander forced on toward calm and struggled to drift off. Her light went out after the sun came up, and in a fashion that was becoming rote, she awakened to an infant's cry. She would change Donnell's cloth diaper and hush the boy down. As the wailing fell, she heard beyond the wall bets being called and the fits and starts of three-part harmony.

MAYBE TEN NIGHTS PASS, MOST RESEMBLING THAT WEDDING-NIGHT living room party, low-budget style. The high life rolls home with Delbert when he gets in from a cheap gig twenty miles away, in Lorain. Brenda's youngest sister, Marlene, is asleep on the made-up couch. Downstairs, carelessly, a car door slams closed on a long night's drive, and the baby starts up in that full-blast way he's perfecting. The father clomps down the hall in a pre-nod stagger.

Donnell is screaming.

The father slurs an offer of aid. The mother snaps that she'd settle for no help at all: "Just don't sabotage me every time."

Their bedroom flickers to life with shadows that bruise. Thrown in the gray fall light, Delbert's punches come furious, sloe-eyed. At first the blows glance, cuffing Brenda's scarf, making her scream, "Stop!" Then one really connects. Eyeteeth are buoyant in the blood at the back of her mouth. Marlene rushes from the living room. Brenda flails past her sister, gurgling molars. Marlene cowers in the bathroom and Brenda dials with a passion, seven rapid tones over the phone lines— Mother!

Doors slam consecutive in pop Pop POP!

Time stills, recedes into a towel soaked burgundy, and wakes up in a flash, rubber on gravel. The wooden steps tap quick and dull as Arthur and Geneva stalk two flights up to the scene. Delbert comes into focus through the metal-framed screen door. Geneva rushes past him, to her daughters; Art walks back out, holding a smoke out for his son-in-law. The two go down to the just-parked car.

Geneva catches a short glimpse of the two men through the bathroom window, her fingers on the .38 in her pocket. She considers squeezing off one shot. This happened to me, she's thinking. It won't happen to her.

Instead she does what she needs to take her family across town, home.

I WAS THERE, NOT YET THREE MONTHS OLD, SCREAMING MOST OF THE while. Of course the memory can't be mine, but I've spent much of my cognizant life recollecting that night. Just after the fun-house story, it is the most vivid of what I have to go on about my father. For the longest, both tales sounded the same to me.

My actual first memory is a memory by committee, a story repeated so many times I can't say whether what happened is something I recall, or if the reminiscence is a script that's been impressed upon my mind.

Late in an afternoon, about fifteen months after the big wedding, I toddle into the bathroom of my grandparents' place. The two-story home where half the Graham children would spend their adolescence is cozy, made warm by the handiwork Arthur and Geneva put into every upgrade and meal. This is the place my mother ran to with me in her arms and, beyond her knowledge, my sister Gaye in her belly.

The house on First Street, with all my mother's siblings around, is a joyous place to be. Everyone treats us babies like God's greatest invention. Constantly we are tended to. Anyway, baby Gaye is being bathed by Marlene when I walk into the bathroom. On the back of the toilet sits a can of Stroh's, the official beer of working-class Ohio. My grandfather has been here. Only the faint smell of Camels or a folded-up copy of the *Sandusky Register* on the linoleum would better confirm this fact.

Pointing tentatively, I blurt out an observation:

"Stroh's!"

Marlene calls down the stairs, and half her five sisters and brothers run up to the bathroom. Ricky, the youngest, holds me on his shoulders while Marlene displays the can.

"Say it again," Marlene goes. "What beer is this?"

"The boy is a genius," Ricky announces after he hears me repeat the brand. *He's a genius,* it is seconded.

Okay now. I am fully aware that the beer's name and logo were likely branded in my mind through advertising and/or snatches of conversation. But from the Graham family perspective, my outburst was proof that one undeniably positive thing had come from the Delbert imbroglio. From here on, just about everything I did served as confirmation of my exceptional brightness.

Over the years they said "That boy's a genius" so many times that I thought it was my middle name.

Donnell Ellis That Boy's a Genius Alexander.

And I was glad they said this. It's not the sort of thing you can put on an application to Harvard, but I wasn't headed for that particular situation anyway. Repetition forced me to believe. I had the best self-esteem of any toddler in Santown.

2.

extra people

I TALKED BEFORE I WALKED, AND AT A CRUCIAL STAGE THAT ESCAPES recollection, I decided my words and thoughts were so valuable they should not be directly expressed to the world. *Can't talk now, conjuring.*

I stockpiled metal bottle caps and cut lengths of drinking straws. These I fished from a niche in the sock-and-underwear drawer. Out of our kitchen cabinet I pinched aluminum foil. Press at the fingertips, roll with palms, and there's a perfect baseball, marble-size. The first Topps card was always Silent George Hendrick. The Hostess? Bill Madlock. Creased at the knees, players lined up for selection. Draft time arrived when Mom and Gaye trudged off on some religious outing or I'd faked sick to get out of school.

This was my personal time. Out came the blanket, thrust flat with a snap that would provide my arena its roof. An alarm clock and a jewelry box would weight the top, which spread across the one double bed and a dresser. Poised on haunches beneath the linty ceiling, I directed the action as coach, umpire, and color commentator.

"Play ball!"

"And we're here *liiive* at the Astrodome for the 1973 Major League All-Star Game!" I'd announce, Herb Score–style, into a megaphone fist, lit monstrously by a lamp that had been liberated of its shade. "And as always here in Houston, it's a *bee-eautiful* day for baseball."

Those stand-up trading cards made the game. A pencil bat held to their paper shoulders, they were to be manipulated around the bottle-cap base paths. Heavy hitters like Hendrick slugged the foil ball over a fence made up of Jehovah's Witness literature balanced spine-side up.

Shit, I loved being alone. Solitude to me was water from a deeper well. For hours on end, halfway autistic, my curiosity and introversion found new ways to be transgressively intimate.

Around the time that I was perfecting escapism, my father was learning that a person ought to relish real life's highlights. All his big moments were apparently behind him.

ON A SMOLDERING JULY NIGHT, DELBERT DROVE THE HALF MILE FROM HIS mother's crib to that ground-floor bar inside the Murschel House, a hooker haven. He wore a trench coat and it was not raining.

Sandusky hadn't been too cool to Delbert in the months since he'd returned from Akron, having fronted his last band. After so much time away, trying to be a star, he'd lost all his Lake Erie 'hos. But there were girls here willing to sleep with tourists for money. They would always need managers, Delbert just needed to buy some time.

Lots of musicians hustled, but he had crossed that line between necessity and criminality. The trife life was no longer a sidelight. Delbert hardly did music anymore. His connections were just as tangentially linked to the scene as he, and if the nigga didn't see that other nigga, Willie, at the Murschel House, the night might just break him.

This guy Willie, who Delbert knew from grammar school days, had run up an unforgivable debt on his *her*-on tab, and the made men Delbert reported to told him he had better come back with Willie's dough or send dude a message in a bullet. He'd assume Willie's debt and lose more than cash in the deal if he returned without accomplishing this mission.

Willie was a big, rough bully, even when he and Delbert were boys. He'd shown Delbert a lot, truth be known.

Delbert saw his man at the bar, talking to a tender, and approached.

"We've got some shit to talk about," he said. The young girl got scarce.

First, Willie came all familial in explaining his deal, intimidating with his size. Delbert demanded with polite menace to be paid.

Then Willie laughed, hectoring fiercely into the shorter man's face. Delbert did not back down. In fact, he reciprocated Willie's intensity.

"Gimme my six hundred dollars, nigga!"

In almost any other Sandusky gathering, the way Delbert said this would have attracted attention, but not at the Murschel House, which was only known for being low down. He told Willie to get up and, through his trench-coat side pocket, swatted sideways, firmly, so that Willie could feel the barrel of the sawed-off shotgun Delbert held alongside his body.

The power was turned around. Who's bossin' who now?

And Willie begged.

He didn't have the money, just didn't have it! But he could get it. Come on, Dell!

He said it like the man's name was Dale.

Don't you remember, Willie backed away and asked, how your mother used to put leftover biscuits in your lunch for you to share with me?

Mention of Charlene Alexander, the woman who had spoiled him beyond repair, ordinarily soothed Delbert. But he was a junkie under pressure much heavier than jonesin'. Willie's plea telescoped the inevitability inside a gangster's price to pay.

"Outside," Delbert said. "Let's deal with this outside." The fog in his head was very dark.

He urged Willie off his barstool, then, at the door, moved from behind and crowded the exit. *This cat dead will feel like hell.* Within the tight, flaked-paint frame, he let loose a blast that landed in Willie's hip and leg.

This is what the newspaper reporters would call a cheap shooting, a colored underworld crime, not the sort of thing that made page one. Delbert ran and ran and rode and hid. When the police tracked him down, the charge was attempted murder.

DELBERT WOULD HAVE PLEADED GUILTY TO ANYTHING, HAD IT MEANT A shot of that pain-numbing *her*-on. It got that raw in the Erie County jail. There had been a time when homesickness was the worst thing about being on the inside.

In this midnight hour, on a sheetless cot that stank of urine, Delbert could not deny his insignificance. Around Sandusky they called him Showdown Shorty, but really he was just a rank-and-file gangster with a terrible hankering for smack. Delbert was a reflection of something lost, a smeared reflection of what he'd seen time and again. He'd seen it when he toured down South with Buddy Miles's band and when he'd hustled in Chicago. All he possessed was illusory.

The jonesing got to Delbert so bad that deputies put him in a straitjacket. Stew Williams, a star fullback when Showdown Shorty was really poppin' in the street, was one of them that did the honors.

Here was doubly repressed nowhere, just like the music scene. He was in jail, but his criminal career had moved faster than the one that had him onstage. Not even that Del Savage Band the white boys in Akron cooked up would see light. Here was the answer to the question "How low can you go?" A fix would feel as good as God turning back time.

If he could cop that fix, Delbert would turn over what 'hos he had left in the stable. Had they gotten him anywhere? He was a popcorn pimp—presto!—a street-life sidelight who put as much money into maintaining the facade as making serious bank. Were it not for Mama putting the house up against a bond yet another time, he would have been stuck inside until the trial started. For sure, the facade was crumbling.

When Delbert made bail, he straight went to score. He shot up in a house that was hot. The generous hit calmed his nausea and nerves, but a familiar paranoia came creeping along the back of his buzz. This time, the paranoia didn't come across the least bit distorted. Shit was real, for real: Out on the street, how much longer would it be before he got done like Willie? How long before he was under the gun, held down by a leveraged dookie fiend? The night's yearning humidity brought his skin to a polish wherever he touched.

On the street, Delbert understood now, it was all over for him.

OUR REC CENTER WAS WHEREVER WE SAT THE CLOSE-N-PLAY. GAYE AND I shared this miraculous invention, this plastic red suitcase of a record player. You placed a vinyl 45 in the Mattel product and sound came out. Magic. No needle visible. Sometimes Mom's Sly Stone and Philly soul singles carried the day, but we tended toward the *Sesame Street* oeuvre. My sister, being ten months younger than me and—let's just fess up— immeasurably less mature, would play a cut like Bert and Ernie's "Rubber Ducky." Most often I selected something advanced, like the criminally underrated Roosevelt Franklin's "How Old Are You?" featuring Rosey's inimitable *basso profundo.*

It went:

(Girls:)

Roosevelt Franklin, how old are you?

(RF:)

Well now I used to be one but now I'm goin' on two.

Genius. We listened to records until all evidence said time stopped.

The Graham household grew as Sherry, the second oldest, deposited first Leah, then Marlon into the scene. Four years separated all in this next generation. Gaye told stories. Feety and Flanky were her main characters, and by the time we were primary graders she could gather and hold a crowd. I could never figure out how Gaye improvised on the spot, a new story every day. The crowds got bigger as we made neighborhood friends, and Gaye reveled in her popularity, hoarding it. By first grade I was relegated to playing my sister's hypeman or being her bitch.

That's mostly because I couldn't hit her. Gaye did the dirty deed of stealing my attention, and I was inclined every so often toward giving her a smack. But the one constant within our hurdy-gurdy household—aside from a flowing seventies sound track—was that I couldn't lay a hand on Gaye or everything stopped and I got a whipping. And I didn't get many beatings.

Mom referred to my viscerally hot temper as the Delbert in Me. Gaye actually had the fire worse, but mine was taken as a menace to be exterminated with extreme prejudice.

Any alleged inequity in the not-hitting thing was explained away as relating to our new religious philosophy. We were now Jehovah's Witnesses. Sandusky was littered with a few dozen families like ours: weird white people and poor blacks who had joined this obscurely self-exiled Christian sect. Our whole lot was ascetic and earnest in preaching the gospel. The taboos on "being worldly" were as ingrained in me as pacifism and the necessity of door-to-door fieldwork.

Discounting the periodic bout of baseball-card reverie, my attendance at worship was above reproach. If Mom was tired and couldn't make a meeting, Grandma or Uncle Roger or someone else from among the First Street clan would cart along me and my sister. The part I liked best was when we sang Witness songs from a little mauve book, although all the data we called spiritual food was also quite agreeable.

Sometimes, I'd give talks, and people seemed to have sat forward. These presentations racked my nerves. The music helped to assuage the anxiety.

After we finished singing, there was coatrack fellowship, at the back of the Kingdom Hall, rugrats running waist-high among the baptized faithful. Tag games in and out of the hall's rear auditorium might steer me back to the crush, forced to hold my mother's hand or go sit in the car. The risk of restriction was worth the chance I might find myself head to chest with teenage Lisa, whose daddy might have been the ranking black brother. Lisa had big titties, pointy ones, and so adventures in the coatrack rear, braced in the winter by a frequently opening exit, put a great capper on the spiritual songs.

Mom made being a Jehovah's Witness fun; ritual Pledge of Allegiance abstinence aside, the marginalization hardly registered. Brenda Graham's becoming religious seemed a whimsical, dark-times decision that never went away. I believed, oh Jah did I believe, and any effort Mommy made toward making the material less dry easily turned the good times better.

Wednesday was Bible study night, an oven-fresh companion to Sunday, Tuesday, and Thursday worship outings. Gaye and I waited all week to engage our assigned scriptures on this night (mine? Matthew 5:37—"Let your yes mean yes and your no, no") as well as to choose dinner. Q&A's from *Listening to the Great Teacher*—the Witnesses study book for kids—went down a lot easier with mashed potatoes, corn on the cob, and other soft cell comfort foods. Mac-and-cheese was to *Great Teacher* studies as Wednesday evening overall was to the three nights of mandatory meetings at the Kingdom Hall. If religion is the opiate of the masses, then mac-and-cheese is a gateway drug. This may make my mother my first dealer.

Being a Witness involved a load of reading and legwork, tools real crucial for beating Sandusky. As we walked to our top-shelf, East Side grade school, it seemed the town's most remarkable aspect was how, regardless of layering, the winter cold managed to get inside your clothes and bite! Lake Erie whipped ice darts and otherwise menaced worse than the most tireless playground villain.

There was a lot more to Sandusky. Sure it was the county seat, but for five months out of the year it was sleepy, obsessed with sports and hoping some sort of mall or multiplex would arrive. Then, with spring, throngs of tourists from all across the Midwest descended upon us on the way to Cedar Point. I mean "us" specifically because a main route into the amusement park passed right by the Graham house on First Street.

Mom and us were way too broke to go more than semiannually, but we got a lot of mileage out of watching the cars line up for entrance, counting the out-of-state plates. If you didn't focus much on being excluded, if from the front porch you tried to figure the family that had traveled the greatest distance to visit Cedar Point, the tag parade went a long way toward fleshing out the overall transformation of Sandusky during sunny season.

Ohio had a dozen cities with more than one hundred thousand people and was second to no other U.S. state in this category. Sandusky—pop. 32,000—wasn't one of them, but big-small-town flavor was lavished onto our shitty little burg, thanks be to Jehovah, through the presence of Cedar Point. By the middle of the decade all these municipalities had seen better times. Bruce Springsteen was singing about us and we ain't even know.

One upside: factory towns like ours tended toward a quasi-inclusive racial environment, at least as far as the assembly-line workers could see. Both races—and all that was more rare than seeing a Spanish person was seeing an Asian—worked side by side, like coal miners. A stand-alone abode in the aluminum-siding petri dishes of Sunnyside or Larchmont marked the highest aspiration a working-class black could have. If you had some sort of degree, you probably weren't from round Santown.

The environment was such in the early 1970s that white boys on the East Side might now call you nigger for having too much attitude, rather than shiftlessness. Real niggas weren't so easy to see. They lived away from us, on East End or outside city limits, in Searsville or the original Sandusky colored section, the South Side.

WE ALEXANDERS ON GRAHAM TURF LOVED OUR BLOCK. EXCEPT WHEN sent to school or the corner bar by Granddaddy for cigarettes, we never ventured far from the property, as the JW lifestyle obliged. And bully for us, because all the teenage kids in and around the house brought home wonder. Ricky, Mom's youngest brother and seven years older than me, would play the big-brother role, clarifying NFL rules, taking me down the block to fish and convincing me that ketchup is blood.

Across the street were the Denslows and to the left we had the Gambrells. In the backyard of the lot on our right was a clubhouse. It belonged to the Aldermans, the white couple with kids Ricky's age. A shared back-alley entrance turned this garage into the neighborhood head spot, featuring rock-and-roll music and drinks and drugs. It had glory holes and bashful wusses. In the garage were seventies leisure activities of the kind that could make a gay, Haitian IV smack user say it's all good.

Ricky and our next-door neighbor Kenny, the only other black boy who was official, dominated the clique. On more wholesome days, an Italian member from Larchmont named Dino brought his little brother Jeff. These things made it easy for me to be in the mix.

All the members knew me. Shrimpy, sensitive, and covertly fiending for attention, I entertained the whole bunch whenever they let me hang. It took next to nothing to make me laugh or cry. One weekend in the factory parking lot adjacent to the spot, a clubhouse regular mentioned pimping and I got caught giggling out of turn.

Ricky said, "Boy, you don't even know what pimpin' is."

My grin showed gums. "Yes, I do."

"What is it then?"

I stood up. And I started walkin' down the gravel alley. I maintained a stiff leg, swinging the left forward with a hip swivel. Left, limp. Left, limp. Step, pimp, with my arm out firm to the rear. I was July black, with red high waters on and hair all beady.

About ten yards out, there were snickers, and that struck me as a good thing. But then, maybe a little quicker than planned, I wheeled as though that hard leg was a kickstand, and on the way back toward the fellas, I showed more limp than pimp. Half the crew was lying on the asphalt, dying. I stopped right there, uncocked my hips, and announced to a bunch of stoners who were now howling and clutching themselves as if awaiting medical assistance, "That's pimpin'!"

Ricky looked at me like I was a retard.

I shouldn't have taken their reaction personally. But it did bother me when Dino said that even his little brother knew about mackin', and he was white.

If there's an exact middle point between genius and goofball, I'd nailed it before I had hair on my balls. I bedeviled my grandfather and my uncles, asking for precise explanations of how to figure ERA or the car's inner workings.

I was otherwise so much inside my head that coordinating my body was hopeless. The understanding that I'd drop the dinner plate I was carrying to my space in front of the TV was the first I learned of self-fulfilling prophecy.

My sister called me Blacky, and most everyone else referred to me as the white boy. I wouldn't have minded aside from the failure implicit in the accusation. The older I got, the more still my expression became. If people were going to get me wrong, they wouldn't get me at all.

DELBERT DIDN'T HIDE A DAMN THING. HE HAD A WAY OF PUTTING HIS promise on display. Lawyers worked harder for him than their other clients, because there was just something about the man.

Charm helped get the attempted murder charge reduced to felonious assault by the morning of his date at the Common Pleas Court. An assault conviction meant that if he had to do any time, it would be nothing life-altering. But Delbert wanted his world rocked. So he walked into the judge's airless and moldy courtroom with a very special plan.

"Now, Mr. Alexander," said Judge McCrystal, who was a known inmates' rights advocate, "has anybody made any promises to you that you would receive probation on this case?"

"No, they haven't, because I don't wish to consider it."

"Pardon?"

"No one has, because I wouldn't consider probation."

Judge McCrystal paused, confused. "I am going to refer the matter over to the Probation Department for at least a presentence investigation."

"Sir. I am not asking for probation. I don't want to be in Sandusky, but I got stuck here three years ago. I came back and got hooked up again. For me, it's an extremely negative situation to be in your town."

"Now, Delbert, are you aware that there is criticism all over the place about conditions in penal institutions?"

Delbert started to laugh, but caught himself. "Yes, I've been there."

The judge scribbled into the pile of papers before him. "And in view of that, you want to go?"

The accused thought about his past bids. Ducking dicks, ducking death. He considered the merits of the duck option.

"I don't like those words 'want to.' But at this time, I have decided to go. To me, the society in there is not that much worse than out here."

As simple as that, he was property, a ward of the state. It would be Delbert's last time in prison, but his first as a grown-ass man. Koran discussions on the yard now took the place of jailhouse boxing, and he completed essay assignments when sent to the hole. He signed his writing *Delbert Bilal*.

EVERY EIGHTEEN MONTHS OR SO, MOM HOARDED HER NURSE'S AIDE'S pay, moved us out of Arthur and Geneva's house, and took a stab at raising us alone. We would shuffle into some dumpy one-bedroom, where we lived without a television or car. Weekly, with Gaye and me on either side of her, our mother would march downtown to the library, where we'd round up as many books as we could carry. The two-mile walk might have benefited us most.

At each new school, prospective friends were bound to ask, and ordinarily I said I didn't have a father. (Except for Mike, the blond kid from First Street whose father had been in jail, too. In a minute, he'd have cigarettes.) About the only regular reminder of Delbert was at the barbershop. While I'd sit in the oversize, hydraulic chair, Charlie the barber would ask whichever cat was waiting to be served:

"Do you know who this boy's daddy is?"

"Naw, who?"

"Del-bert Alex-AN-der!"

"Aw shit!" they would shout, every time.

The source of my father's fame was such that they could never really convey to me what the fuss was about, so the conversations trailed off into vague allusions. And the customers would pitch forward from their chairs and envelope their waxy, big hands in mine.

"Yeah, your father was somethin' else . . ."

Handshake pump here. *Was?*

"Some-thin' else!"

Since he'd broke camp when I was two months old, I had no recollection of my father, not even a face. Actually, that last part's not true. Grandma Charlene kept a black-and-white portrait of him in her beauty parlor. His grin was tight and insincere, and his spiraling pompadour tested the boundaries of the frame. On the few occasions that the picture didn't function in the pure abstract, it scared me. Jesus drawings were discussed with greater realism.

So imagine how surprised I was when he showed up at our apartment during my eighth year of life. I answered the door to a handsome, copper-complexioned man of modest height and chiseled features. He was wearing a skullcap and a dark green, one-piece work suit. Then Mom took over. The two mumbled not so quietly in the entranceway and then my mother turned toward me and said, "This is your father. He wants to spend some time with you."

My stomach felt jumpy as we left. All I knew about Delbert insisted he was a bad man. He had done crimes and been in prison. This man was not like us.

He drove me to Lorain, where he introduced me to a woman and her daughter.

"That's your sister," he said. I had no concept of what he was talking about. He might as well have been pointing to the bookcase in the corner of their living room while making the comment.

But Delibra turned out to be cool, and we played until nightfall. Then Delbert told me it was time to go back to Sandusky. I think we stopped for fast food along the way.

At this point I'd become very interested in the idea of having a father. Delbert was forceful, rougher than anyone among the Grahams, and he seemed to have a genuine interest in me. On the road he told me about a program he was starting for people who had been in prison—so that they'd not have to go back again. It sounded nice. Maybe he'd want to get baptized and become a Jehovah's Witness, no?

We talked sports, obsessed as I was by the games. I was gonna be a wide receiver when I grew up. My father's history didn't matter.

Talk turned to boxing. Delbert asked if I liked Muhammad Ali in the upcoming fight against George Foreman. I said no, that I liked Foreman, and proceeded with the glee of a child who still believed wrestling was real to outline the many ways in which Foreman would kick Ali's butt.

Almost immediately, my father cooled toward me, shut down. After a few minutes I noticed that only I was talking, and eventually I climbed into the backseat, feigning sleep until we got back to Sandusky

For a couple of decades it occurred to me that if I'd answered differently, I'd actually have had a relationship with my father.

3.

it's either the best
or it's the worst

(and since I don't have to choose,
I guess I won't)

IS IT A MATTER OF HEIGHT AND WEIGHT? OR IS IT THE TIME-HONORED realization of what I'm set to become? It's in the eyes of the bait shop salesman and the counter lady at the library. I am no longer cute. I am not wholly wanted or desired. No plans are in my head, but I know what becomes of dudes like me in this town. They get broke down or mean or they get totally gone. And where is gone, exactly? I've never seen it. I've seen Granddaddy dead to the world after coming home from a double shift. I've seen Alexanders work themselves invisible so they can dangle their Caddie or golf club membership or the hovel they rent out as the ultimate existential proof.

One year, me and Gaye saw Ann Arbor, when Mom tried her most ambitious solo flight. She forgot to make sure Michigan hired nurse's aides. And I saw my mother just flat-out crash. She put us on her back though and staggered back to Santown.

I'd seen disconnection: phone, lights, and beyond. But I'd never seen gone.

"ARE YOU READY TO PLAY THE FEUD?"

The boy mutters, "Of all the stupid new shows, this here might be the stupidest."

Donnell has officially passed onto the surly side of reticence and sometimes sneers as warped as the wooden floor he's stretched across. Seems like he's crafting witty comebacks to strike at the game show host, as if the two were in conversation. Or debate. Brenda hardly recognizes the pubescent boy as anything that might have come out of her. Where in the bloodlines does this sarcasm come from?

Is that Richard Dawson cute, or what? she wonders, and she plops into the recliner, half-groggy, just up from the slumber that's relegated the day's just-passed sunlight to an unconfirmed rumor. Brenda's ride to her job at Good Samaritan Hospital arrived at this new old apartment and honked at ten-thirty last night, dropped her back home at seven forty-five this morning, and will do so again tomorrow.

Just beneath the surface, she's amused by her son's curmudgeonly ways.

"Survey says!"

The rolling of his eyes is almost audible.

Brenda asks, "What don't you like about the *Feud?*"

"Mama, think about it: they give you points for saying what everybody else is saying. Why would anyone wanna play a game like that? Worse, why would you want to *watch* it?"

Against her will, Brenda bursts out laughing. Beneath a big Aunt Jemima scarf, her plum face releases a moist snigger, jettisoning eye mist and saliva, juvenile, and she no longer looks old for her age. All at once, Brenda's a goof, and maybe it's not the end of the world if she doesn't know him. Too much of what she knows is all messed up.

"... ahh ha ha ... ha," winds down her laughter. "Whoohoo boy ... my goodness, oooh ... where's Gaye?"

"School probably. Or with Dawn. I didn't go. My stomach didn't feel so good."

"Unh-hunh."

This, for him, is a long and giving verbal exchange. The boy might as well have stayed back at the old place, with the mildewed basement furniture. *One of these niggas just doesn't belong here.* Brenda senses this not just because Donnell's woolly hair is skipped-school matted or because he's angry and forever dressed in sweats. And it's not because as a Tom Snyder/Phil Donahue truant he's in the apartment at all the wrong hours.

What's strange is how his presence is so spectral and elitist, while so bony and bumpy.

At two in the morning, Brenda can call home from the nurses' station and he'll be up, watching Showtime. Now, that's great for the ward-wide trivia contests, but it's not what she imagined coming of the little boy she dolled up for her wedding.

Brenda no longer takes away TV privileges, grounds, or whups. Not for him or for Gaye. And the boy seems indiscriminate in his passions.

"Survey says!"

"I'd like to give y'all something to feud about," he growls at the television.

Then he pops up. He must be six feet now.

"I'm going down to Ricky's car, Ma, and listen to some Rick James."

Brenda, too, has heard car keys dink across the kitchen table. Her youngest brother, out of the Navy and holed up in the apartment indefinitely, arrived a minute ago.

"Okay, see ya."

Brenda might not see either of her children tonight.

GRANDMA GENEVA'S DIVORCE FROM ARTHUR GRAHAM BROUGHT ABOUT THIS change in residence. All of a sudden Grandma didn't live in the big house on First Street. We guessed the spate of visits from our long-rumored aunt Dawn had something to do with it. Ricky was Grandma's last child, but my half aunt was just a few months younger than me. Guess it was good for Granddaddy that all offspring except my mother and us had cleared out of the First Street homestead. He faced only a narrow range of outrage before he could sell the place and light out for California.

Me, Mom, and Gaye moved away from the mouth of Cedar Point to this apartment as deep as you can get into the South Side, way past Camp Street. Grandma Charlene gave us a deal on the apartment around the way from her, and there was this weird move-in déjà vu when I stomped up the straight-shot, two-story staircase on the South Side and, particularly, when I peeled back the metal screen door.

Mom told me and Gaye last winter that we were moving back to Harrison Street, and there was confusion. *Back?* In time we figured out that our new residence had ties to that period when she was married.

That was last year, after New Year's. Now I snag my uncle's keys from my sweatshirt's belly pocket and twirl them around my ring finger and spit over the unpainted, unsanded railing. Plans involve Ricky's eight-track stereo. Tonight's selection will be Richard Pryor's latest, *Wanted,* again. But Mom doesn't want to hear about that. Besides, the real reason for making the trip into the October crispness is to burn this half joint I've scored off my man.

Skitting down the wooden stairs, I slow to peek in the bathroom vent. Maybe I'll see Dawn with her top off again. Nope, she's dressed. Fuck.

Ricky's parked car: Thunderbird, '79. Burgundy.

Sitting in the T-Bird is the bomb, especially if I'm getting high and listening to tapes.

By now I've quit smoking, mostly because I don't know anyone in this new South Side neighborhood who's got greenery. But today this white boy Steve from track had some to share, so I'm treating myself. It was white boys who put me on to herb, during that autumn when Ricky's ride had the new-car smell. We smoked out on the way back to our East Side houses. But on the South Side? Shit, they didn't even have sidewalks, how could they have anything as advanced and beautiful and special as weed?

Mostly though I put smoking out of mind. Track season was coming and I became increasingly preoccupied with cultivating the loneliness of a long-distance runner.

But here I'm sparky, sparking up below window level. This Richard Pryor mess is the funniest I ever heard. I like comedians, Benny Hill and the stuff from Ricky's day, Bill Cosby, George Carlin, and Cheech and Chong. I've already read *Lenny*, the Bruce bio, but this shit right here sounded like my life. Rich was from Peoria, a downscale Sandusky two states over, and clearly had a rough, loving childhood. The folks across the street, the ones with twisted-wire fence and grass grown to the windows, would be right at home in Pryor's bit on tasty roaches in rice pudding. Laughter from the live crowd shoots out of the speakers and up my spine.

Everything goes better when I'm smoking. My radio stays tuned to the rock station, but because Ricky's around and the downstairs neighbor jams loud records, I am hearing the future sounds of "Rapper's Delight" and "Jamaica Funk."

The blend of music and marijuana makes me high enough to feel like I'm not even there.

The smoke, the jokes, the music, all of these things are part of my running life. Stretching out, changing my voice, getting deeper into who I am. I'm not old enough to drive, so this is the best I can do, traveling in a manner wholly unconfined by my Santown boundaries. The most external my trippin' gets is when I write on my bedroom wall.

From our new old digs my father lived one flight of a mega-hocker down and away, in a shabby, shedlike dwelling between our place and Charlene's home. Delbert keeps a perpendicular line of pit bull cages between his pad and ours.

On the far side of Delbert's place, beyond Grandma Charlene's and across Clay Street, was the ranch house and two-car garage belonging to Aunt Barb, Delbert's sister. It might have been the nicest crib on the South Side. Barb's kids could be picked out and separated from her brother's even before you got close enough to spot the brand names on their clothes.

My father and I didn't speak much. More than anyone else I talked with on the block, but certainly not much. We'd chat awkwardly about how my sister, the worrisome Gaye, was doing or about dogs, which I hardly cared about enough to pretend. The man's uniform seemed the same as when I was a little shaver and he'd taken me to Lorain. He had the mustache and the skullcap. There was the baggy, drab olive, one-piece work suit, which seemed like prison clothes. The thought occurred: Did these make him feel at home? I was much taller than him now, awkwardly taller. He carried himself like a fighter and used his body to advantage. Delbert would crowd me to get his point across.

He called me Son. I addressed him by name and rearranged conversations so that his role in my life might be without title. Really, who was he anyway?

We discussed running. Delbert had competed in high school, still ran, and caught wind of how I'd won my first race.

At the second one, my father was up in the bleachers, pulling for me. Telling all the other track kids' parents. I caved in to the pressure of being consciously watched and ran nearly last. That nigga was gone before I even crossed the finish line. I saw it from the back stretch. Our conversation faded.

It wasn't just Delbert I wasn't talking to. I hated the South Side, even though half the people over there were supposed to be my cousins. I didn't *know* these motherfuckers. The South Side felt almost rural, but ghetto, like a mix of how the family described the West Virginia holler and their old Cleveland neighborhood. You could see women in bedclothes beat their daughters in the street. Dogs ran wild, and especially after dark, safety wasn't guaranteed.

We got on food stamps, but Mom swore that was temporary, just until she got her nursing degree. Life felt balanced on a trapdoor. Gaye was thirteen and fell right into the fast-girl lifestyle, smoking Newport cigarettes now, hooking up with ghetto boys and keeping her distance from me. Without her big brother's nerd baggage, it was easier faking like she belonged.

AT FIRST I REFUSED TO ACKNOWLEDGE THE MOVE, MAINTAINING MOST OF the long after-school walk to First Street with next-generation crew grandfathered in from the Alderman clubhouse. Upside: I saw San-town to the fullest, ranging around as though those last year's dope days were pure destiny. The sun would drop from our late-winter sky, and I'd be farther from home than when I first started. To beat the elements, I ran. In motion this way, I felt reality get live. A runner hits his stride, an internal rhythm that becomes a high, and everything outside is revealed for what it is: just an option. I traversed Sandusky, from just shy of East End to the crib on Harrison Street. And that was all the new neighbors knew of me—Delbert Alexander's son, running long distance. My breath pulsated and seared in my throat, in my chest. I was gone to a world where I could explode out of my body. Inside there were no stupid questions about the D's and F's on my grade card and no uneasy waiting in the free-lunch line. Inside was worldly, home.

WE DWELLED IN THE MOST OBSCURE ENCLAVE. TO DITCH, I MANEUVERED 120 yards—behind an apartment building, across its lot of cars—to a shortcut through a dozen acres of overgrowth even longtime South Siders thought impenetrable. But between an abandoned factory and the railroad tracks lay a clearing two yards wide, and it meant passage to Camp Street—mid–South Side—where the neighborhood grocery, barbers, and damp underpass to other parts of town lay. My dilettante friends from the South Side periphery, my baseball buddies who thought they lived in the heart of the hood but didn't know my area, called this route The Path.

But before you could step onto this trail, you had to get past Choo-Choo, the dirty, rabidly territorial Afghan that the Prophets kept on their spread behind the factory. Choo-Choo—speedy, relentless, and probably crazed—got your heart beating, no question, but I kept a half step ahead of him.

Choo-Choo, the Afghan warm-up.

Alone in the emerging a.m., I got drunk on the otherness of The Path's isolation. These autumn mornings called for meandering toward Jackson Junior High School, and the way came clear through a full range of darkness. By around Halloween, light was scarce enough to hide the walkway's origin and trip me up over wayward railroad ties hidden in the brush. It was worth a dirt sandwich or two to feel as though inertia could be cheated.

High weeds, low bushes, and the occasional overhanging branch. It was a new way to be gone, better than herb. On mornings that school was unavoidable, I removed my shirt, pants, and jacket. Then once tree boughs blocked the Prophets' place, I peeled off my T-shirt and drawers and stuffed everything into the Blue Streak duffel bag alongside my textbooks, *Mad,* and certain Topps All-Pros.

I got butt naked.

The frame of wild weeds completely hid my city, excepting brick and broken windows from the factory next door. I wondered what this meant. Was there anyone there who could see me? Could secret streaking be a crime? Inside I was feeling myself. The Path was too short, so I ran through tomorrow, and onrushing bushes beat me like Grandma's backyard switches. Each stride brought a scratch and excited my mind. *How can there be one true God? Why is Sean Connery a better Bond?* My escape lasted less than a quarter mile. Too soon Camp Street would come up and this would be no more.

I blew through ideas like they were would-be tacklers, but there was one concept that stuck: **The Theory of Ultimate Selfishness.** Oh, it got deep, deeper with every ding-a-ling flip, with every flop of my uncircumcised penis. And I thought: *Everything an able-bodied person does comes about because, to one degree or another, they want that. If you lie around the house watching TV, it's because you want that. It's your desire acting, whether you rob banks or serve the Lord, feed the poor or work yourself to death. Every deed is ultimately selfish. I'ma be selfish. The real deal is that I'ma admit it. Because we're all selfish when you get down to the nitty-gritty.*

The notion came as top speed approached the dawning of an idea I couldn't comprehend, but found inviting, overwhelming. Something visceral, a sudden introduction. I was in over my head, Blue Streak bag strapped between my shoulder blades like a long-ass backpack, giving gravity the finger.

Here is where I let go of my mother.

The world ain't ready for me. (Full sprint now.) *I'm not even s'posedta be. I should be.* (All out now.) *I'ma be.*

I ran like this until it got too cold, past when it got too cold, to where my thighs and ass tingled and then felt bitten by hot grease. Not much distance, but plenty of reps.

Nekkid in the hood, approaching Thanksgiving, it seemed the rabbit looks at me funny.

Then, in the vegetation cluster about ten yards from Camp Street, I'd land the plane, get dressed, scan from Perkins Avenue to the underpass, zip up, and go back to the business of halfheartedly flunking out of school.

"MAN, YOU SHOULD HAVE SCORED!"

I'm hunched over in the huddle, wearing hard shoes and dress trousers, gulping for air. The Kingdom Hall remains in radar range, albeit faintly and near the perimeter.

On the way to the Lawson's minimart of our post-food-stamps hood, the one in the sticks, these kids asked if I wanted to play. The only one I knew was Boo-Boo, son of my father's best friend Billy, but he didn't recognize me, probably because of my new Jheri curl. Seconds ago, at the end of a long-gaining pass play, Boo-Boo had tackled me from behind. Maybe he remembers me now, because he'd tackled me extrarough and let out a jungle holler before he gave me a hand up.

"How'd you let that fool catch you?"

Back in the huddle, a Sandusky High freshman, the younger brother of the girl I've had a crush on since third grade, is quarterbacking and giving me shit.

I peruse the play area, a rolling jade chasm between newish apartment buildings, up and down. I wipe the misting sweat off my glasses, on my Greg Pruitt jersey.

"Yo, don't even try it," I said. "Boo-Boo is fast! Besides, this field's too short for me. I'm a long-distance runner. If this thing was five thousand meters, I'd be scoring touchdowns all day."

The freshman quarterback looks at me like I'm berserk, but a thick teammate in sweats that hang low off his ass falls to the ground, howling in delight at what I've just said. He's rolling around and making enough noise for people in the apartments beyond the goal line to peer out windows and wonder what's up.

The guy on the ground is called Sensation.

THE FIRST KIDS TO GRANT ME EXIT FROM THE RITUAL CONFINES OF SMALL-town black life were white kids whose daddies got laid off from the assembly line as often as niggas and whipped ass at home. They taught me to smoke and cuss, that it was a better deal to be bad than to be nothing. I tripped first with them. Then the slow seepage of hip-hop culture into northern Ohio let me connect with something exotic and old, familiar and new. One day there were rap songs blaring out of ghetto blasters, the next members of my smoking circle—the U.S. Dueling Team—were in mobile DJ crews. Cold Crew, our boy Stokes's group, made a novelty song that WZAK in Cleveland played at Christmastime. When the snows came, on the high school bus home to suburban Fox Run, that tune, taped off the radio, blared from a boom box as though looped: "I don't care what the white man says, Santa Claus is a black man."

Even with this subtle sense of something in the air, Sensation, whose birth name was Darrick, stood out. Not a lot of genuine b-boys were calling Sandusky home. It might be fair to call this New York transplant the first one in town.

Jet-black and stocky—tightly muscled at five-eight, 175 pounds—Sen-Dog walked with his sweatpants butt-crack low and his boxers showing. He rolled with that pimp stroll that I'd dug even as a child.

The year we met, George Clinton's "Atomic Dog" was black America's youth anthem, bigger than "Billie Jean," and as was the fashion with a lot of guys then, Sensation would bark to hammer home a point. But when he made the sound, it convinced enough to make you want to dial up the pound. Sensation really sold the bark.

From the first days I knew him, Sensation was at our apartment well past what would be bedtime for most SHS students.

"Who's this boy's mama?" my mother would whisper in the hallway.

"Well, George Clinton's my father," an eavesdropping Sensation answered, his face gravely serious. My mother believed Sen-Dog until he feinted: "Psyche!" Mom found him endlessly entertaining. So, he could hang out past when Mom put on her uniform and went to Good Sammy's.

Sensation called me Dee-zon-eezell or Donny Shell and only went to class when he felt like it. Chicks gave him license. One day off the bus, he put the rim of his crème-soda bottle up to one of Dawn's breasts.

"Nipple to the bottle, Dawny," he sang, biting the Grace Jones song.

And she laughed. I was dumbfounded. The girl *laughed*. There wasn't a girl in town who wouldn't have slapped me behind that shit. With Sen-Dog a simple walk through the SHS halls was like honors class at audaciousness school.

The boy beat grown playground stars at basketball, but declined to play varsity. He introduced me to older neighborhood cats, like Julio and Dino, who sold drugs and packed heat and pulled back the facade from our quasi-bucolic new digs. Through Sen I met Troy, a pimp nigga who used to clown Steve Arrington for being "Weak at the Knees." And there was Robbie, who let me watch while he fucked a white girl, Jennie, who was stunningly into being watched. Previously, I didn't even jerk off.

Boo-Boo was the one who took me to get my ear pierced, and Chris showed me how the rich Caucasians on Causeway Drive did their thing, but Sensation was my best friend. He might not have known this or felt it reciprocally, but I saw him as my best friend in the purest sense: top dog, most potent, uncut dope. He was the first raw nigga I ever met. Not counting my father, of course.

———

MOM'S NURSING DEGREE HAD BEGUN REAPING BENEFITS, AND SHE GOT the family into a two-bedroom unit too small for the volume of company her kids drew upon arrival. Dawn and Gaye attracted more friends than me, but even I was moved to chill in the outside hallway. Ol' Jed from the Alderman clique, the omnipresent Sensation, and Boo-Boo and Chris and Robbie and my nerd friends Don, Brian, and Mike— some strange sampling of the lot—sprawled out to talk shit and debate all up the hall and across two layers of stairs.

"If you could have one wish, what would it be?"

"Man that's a hard one."

"Two bitches at the same time?"

"The ability to run really fast and not feel pain."

"I know," I said.

"What?"

"I know the very best one. Trumps every wish."

"Say it, man!"

"Okay. Peace on earth, goodwill toward men," I said slowly and demonstratively, as though delivering covert information.

Nobody says anything for a few seconds.

"You are such a dork."

"Naw, for real. If you did peace on the planet—or the galaxy or whatever—you wouldn't have the need for the wishes you mentioned. One wish erases the need for the rest."

Silence.

"See that's what I'm talking about," says Sensation. "It's like having some goddamn professor around here with this guy."

THE MIXED HOUSING OF FOX RUN WAS BRAND-NEW, PROMISING TO BE A much-needed middle-class enclave in our less-white-than-formerly-imagined Santown. And the development did serve strivers, resting as it did on the municipality's country edge, Perkins Township. But the apartments were already harboring dope dealers and sex traders. A lot of their clients lived in the ranch homes and town houses that rimmed the development. Markets for the illicit emanated toward the city.

Dawn's mother and the chocolate-and-vanilla couple and every neighbor on our end of the building knew how we got down, out in the hall. Sometimes they left their doors open and turned up the stereo. The atmosphere was cool.

"When you gonna show me how to party with the white boys?" Boo-Boo asked one night. His father had a good job at Ford and a house on the Santown side of Fox Run, but Boo-Boo felt cheated because he hadn't yet cracked the race barrier.

"What?" I said. "You definitely sick in the head, man."

"For real though, 'cuz I wanna get drunk on some Canei and eat me some white bitch pussy and be, like, 'Unh, uhn, uhn!' "

Doors sometimes closed on our conversations.

And then the girl, the one whose apartment traffic would start around the time Mom went to work, smiled at me special when she walked past.

"Go 'head, Donny," Sensation nodded, "knock that."

"Man, she's not givin' me no booty."

"Sheee . . . Yvette be 'hoin' though. We should go in on her."

You could all but see the lightbulb go on in his head, and the idea got Sensation proselytizing. He pulled a wad of bills and started waving around for contributions.

"Fiddy dollas for a prossy. Fiddy dollas for a prossy. Come on, y'all, bet! *Shell?*"

Boo-Boo looked out the window though nothing was visible for miles, except fields at night.

"Shell!"

"Nigga, I ain't got no money. Told you she wasn't *givin'* me no booty."

There was a lot of that. Trying to get me laid, make me cool. Boo-Boo and my earring, Robbie rockin' Jennie. Niggas would get girls drunk and skip out on me at these lonely chicks' cribs. I was never with that random shit, and now motherfuckers wanna set me up with 'hos.

Sensation stuffed his dough back into his sweatshirt.

"Aww," he whined, "y'all a buncha punk muhfuckas."

I ONLY KNOW THIS FONKY-ASS BAR, MY FIRST, IS CALLED THE BUCKET OF Blood. It's near the old Bay View Arms, and feels the way I always imagined Detroit nightlife. Smoky, like in that Tina Turner video. I'm as much contemplating the elements as trying to be shadowy while I loiter at the bar. Darrick and that other nigga named Troy are off in the car or something and I'm here alone, trying to act like I belong. Maybe if I hold my new mustache toward the light . . .

The man who has sidled next to me and is looking up with amusement is my father. Peeping down, I say what the deal and then turn my head away like, yeah, it's great to see you, too, Old Boy.

Delbert offers to buy me a drink, but I tell him I'm straight. He asks about running, and I say I do seven miles a day.

Delbert grins, too broad, like *That's my boy!*

"It's funny," he says, "you got the kinda eyes where you can tell real easy that you're high. I got those too."

"I wouldn't know. Do you?" And I look all down in his face.

He asks about Johnnette, this grown woman who's on the outskirts of the Graham family circle.

"Has she sucked your dick yet?"

I almost spit out my beer. "No!"

"Yeah, well, don't worry, she will. That bitch will suck your motherfucking dick!"

I make a mental note on that one. *Will suck . . . my . . . motherfucking . . . dick.*

Coming back into focus, I catch a glimpse of Yvette's Asian eyes as I look past Delbert. She averts the look catlike, and her plump ass is so fly in those Jordache jeans. She's shiny, the color of cocoa butter, with a round, shapely nose and that gap in her top front teeth. A gap in her jeans. That short, wavy hairstyle is done up like the bomb. She looks like she smells good. Delbert is, as usual, talking. But I'm not listening. I tell my father I have to find my friends and split. Yvette was walking toward a table full of dudes, and I was floating after her when Sen tugged me the other way.

"Ain't that your old boy right over there, at the bar?"

"Yeah. I already talked to him."

It was a weeknight at maybe half-past one and the place was getting packed.

"Woo. There go Yvette," Troy said. "That nasty bitch is fine."

THE NEXT TIME I SAW YVETTE, A FEW WEEKS LATER, I WAS READING *Hit Parader* in the stairwell and she had to step over me. Then, from over the second-floor rail, she called my name, and for what seemed like the very first time, I glimpsed her youth. She was scandalous young, no older than me or Gaye. I could see, too, that her left eye was bruised. Her mouth looked swollen on the side. Yvette said she saw me walking over to Lawson's when I was supposed to be in school, that I should come up and visit someday.

I saw her apartment before the next time I saw homeroom.

Yvette came to the door with her robe tied haphazardly. Up close, the eye looked purply. Her moves were sluggish, like Mom's on mornings after her fifth shift in a row.

But Yvette still looked sexy.

I was about to pull up some couch when she stepped to me, seeming self-conscious and uncertain. Then Yvette asked:

"Would you go to the store for me?"

(Awfuck.)

I came back from Lawson's with a pack of Newports, and Funyuns and root beer for myself. Yvette had a joint waiting for me on the dining room table. The robe was off, the curtains closed, and there was a bounce to her now. Yvette's bronze body, faintly covered by a chemise, seemed the generic apartment's only illumination.

She lit up a cigarette, turned, and sorta skipped to the kitchen, then popped back.

Yvette threw an ashtray onto the tabletop with everything else.

When she folded down to tuck a bare leg in under the cheeks of her loose booty, Yvette's right one came free from her scant top. This small brown orb—and its spacious, amorphous, and ebony areola—just hung there wobbling, casting a pendulous spell.

In the conscious world, Yvette was talking to me, asking what grade I'm in. I didn't remember. She was pulling out another Newport.

If Yvette knew she was showing, she ain't care. So, while she lit the Newport, I softly palmed that warm dumpling, pulling down so that the tip pointedly coalesced.

Yvette shut her lids for just a measure. Pull nipple, thumb and forefinger. Then she jerked back and slapped my hand away.

"That's not why you're here," she said. "That's *not* why you're here."

She handed me the joint and matchbook, then popped up to turn on the radio.

That semester I had a first-period study hall, so many late mornings through the rest of the year I hung out at Yvette's lonely apartment, being her conduit to peer life, providing the scoop on the teachers she'd never know and the classmates who once populated her universe and maybe, secretly, still concerned her. A parade of morphing bruises and Yvette's shy teenage giggle fascinated. Our spectral exchanges zoomed me each time. But I could never touch her. Only warm visuals of this hands-off hooker served as the take for my talk.

Still, in a way, she was my first girl.

IN THE SUMMER BEFORE MY SENIOR YEAR, I'D MADE A GOAL OF JOINING the cross-country team's 750-mile club. SHS had won the state championship the fall before. All Coach Logue promised was a jersey, but if I could make myself run 750 miles by September—seven and a half miles a day—I might get that scholarship to Eastern Michigan University, a couple of hours away in Ypsilanti.

Academically ineligible most of high school, I regarded EMU and its tantalizing 2.0 admission standard as the only hope. Mr. Cox, my guidance counselor, had begun telling me to aim for a job at Ford.

Sensation and I were hanging tough. After the Old Girl went to work, we'd ride around town in the cars of associates who weren't getting up at 7 A.M. to run. They were on the run right now.

FROM MY ROOM ON THIS ONE SATURDAY NIGHT, ABOVE THE STRAINING guitar solo from "Lady Cab Driver," I can hear Mom getting ready in the bathroom, her rubber-soled nursing shoes maneuvering across the tile. The all-in-one stereo is parked on a chair, which, too, is visiting from the front part of our crib. I'm up on a puny cabinet, formerly a towel cupboard from our old First Street john, both knees together, like I'm praying. Instead I'm toking, peering out my window onto the flat landscape and lying head tilted in the crook of my arm. Out in the darkness, trees line up perpendicular, getting smaller before they are no more. We live a half mile from the mall, a bit farther from the drive-in. Little separates us from the two.

I finger my earring. It hasn't changed my life. There's this one kid, Darrin, from the wrestling team, who punches me in the chest every day before homeroom. It's supposed to be a game. I'm supposed to hit back.

The smoke doesn't always go out over the balcony like it should, so I wave my arm. But I wave the joint. A total fucking idiot.

I put my ashes in the tracks where the window glass rides. Mama yells good-night. See ya in the morning, I singsong back. We maintain the illusion that we're close. Gaye is somewhere else, maybe dancing, probably gossiping, with a baby in her belly.

Hoist the stereo, then the chair and speakers back to the apartment's less private space. On the way back run my hand along the connecting wall. I'm dirty funky from a late-day run and my hair is dry and crinkly like I don't care. Untie the bandanna, press to face, and inhale the aromatic blend of sweat and curl activator. There's a shower in my future because adventure awaits. Cartoon-ishly so.

I STOOD IN FRONT OF THE MIRROR WITH A PALMFUL OF CAREFREE CURL. THE HAIR SOLUTION LOOKED LIKE JISM. MY MOUTH SAT EFFORTLESSLY CLOSED BECAUSE MOMMA CONVINCED ME AT A YOUNG AGE THAT WHITE FOLKS HATED TO SEE A NIGGA WITH HIS MOUTH HANGING OPEN.

THAT CREASE BETWEEN MY EYEBROWS GETS DEEPER EVERY DAY. I GOTTA STOP THIS. BY THE TIME I'M 20, IT'S GONNA LOOK LIKE SOMEONE TOOK A HATCHET TO MY FACE.

SATURDAY NIGHT LIVE WAS NOT YET ON WHEN I HEARD THAT KNOCK AT THE DOOR...

"Y'ALL DON'T EVEN KNOW. I CAN SCRATCH JUST LIKE THAT FOOL. YOU WATCH. I'MA BE ON MIXMASTERS."

WHY DO PEOPLE GET MAD WHEN THE WORD "BITCH" GETS SAID? ARE THEY MAD AT THE IDEA OF IDENTIFYING THE EXISTENCE OF BITCHINESS?

IT COULD HAVE BEEN A LOT OF PEOPLE, BUT IT WAS SEN-DOG. HE HAD A SACK OF WEED, ACAPULCO GOLD. A PRE-DRUG WAR EIGHTH.

"I GOT THE FUNK, SHELL. ATOM BOMB. YO, TURN THAT SHIT OFF, MIXMASTERS IS ON!"

WE SAT ROLLING AND SMOKING JOINT AFTER JOINT. SEN WOULD BUST THE BUDS DOWN TO FINE BITS AS I QUESTED TO THE KITCHEN FOR POPSICLES.

SUCH WORLDLY HERBAL AWARENESS WAS A RARITY ON OUR LITTLE PATCH OF THE NORTH COAST, AND THE BUZZ WAS EXQUISITE.

I HAD SWITCHED THE RADIO TO THE DEEP MIX SHOW OUT OF CLEVELAND, TO OBSCURE 12-INCH JAMMIES AND ADVANCED TURNTABLE TECHNIQUES. DJs CUT UP RECORDS UNTIL THE DAYBREAK PUBLIC AFFAIRS SHOW.

"ALL THIS WEED WE SMOKIN' AND YOU STILL CAN'T CHILL LIKE I CHILL. LOOK HOW I CHILL, DONNY. LOOK: COLD CHILLIN'."

HE'S RIGHT, WHY WOULD GOD MAKE ME LIKE THIS?

"SOMETIMES I THINK GOD'S RETARDED. LIKE OUR GUY IS THE STUPID KID IN THE CHEMISTRY LAB AND HE CAN'T GET HIS PROJECT RIGHT, AND THEY KEEP MAKING HIM DO THE SHIT OVER AND OVER."

"SHELL, YOU CRAZY."

"I LOVE THE WAY THAT TRUE ATOM-BOMB TAKES YOU DEEPER INTO WHO YOU ARE."

SANDUSKY

"YOU WOULD REALLY PUT MIDNIGHT STAR ABOVE CAMEO? YOU SICK IN THE HEAD!"

"BESIDE, ROGER TROUTMAN WOULD SKATE ON ALL THEM NIGGAS."

THE ICES WERE LIKE EPIPHANY RESPONSES TO THE JULY LAKE ERIE AIR, EACH ONE MORE TANGY AND DELICIOUS THAN THE ONE BEFORE IT. OVER THE NIGHT WE EMPTIED A BOX OF 20. EACH SLURP-DOWN POP ACCOMPANIED A STICK OF THE FINEST MARIJUANA WE'D HAD IN OUR VETERAN POT-SMOKING CAREERS.

"TO THE SUCKA MC'S WHO DID NOT LEARN..."

ON AND ON TO THE BREAK OF DAWN.

AT THE HEIGHT OF THE NIGHT, WITH OUR CHESTS SEEMINGLY TRANSOMS FOR THE BEATS BURSTING THRU THE SPEAKERS AND OUR MOUTHS SPITTING THE RHYMES WE LIKED, SENSATION STOOD UP AND BEGAN POP-LOCKING, SHOWING WHY YOU WEREN'T REALLY A B-BOY WITHOUT THE SKILL.

"IF YOU DON'T NEXT TIME WE SHALL RETURN!"

"DANG MAN, YOU HAVE TO SHOW ME HOW TO DO THAT!"

"JAM ON IT" BEEPED HARD PERCUSSION INTO THE ROOM. WHILE SEN-DOG'S LEFT HAND POPPED THE LOCKING MOVEMENT THRU HIS SHOULDER AND DOWN TO HIS ANKLE, HIS RIGHT HAND PASSED OVER THE MOVEMENT, LIKE A DEVICE TO MEASURE RADIATION.

"CATCH THE FLOW. IT'S LIKE ENERGY. FEEL IT? LIKE A BALL OF LIGHT."

"FEEL THE CURRENT AT THE TIP OF YOUR FINGERS, MOVE IT UP JOINT BY JOINT THROUGH YOUR HAND TO YOUR WRIST."

SENSATION PULLED HIS BODY INTO THE VISCOSITY OF A CHARGED STARFISH, SPINNING AND LOCKING, FREEZING AND DEFROSTING. THE HERB MADE IT SEEM LIKE HE DANCED ACROSS TIME.

I AWAKENED TO SUNLIGHT SO YOUNG IT WOULD ONLY SHOW ITSELF TO HALF MY ROOM. WHO KNEW WHETHER I'D SLEPT ONE HOUR OR FIVE? "GOTTA RUN" I THOUGHT, REFLEXIVELY. REGARDLESS, MY BELLY NEEDED FILLING. I PULLED OUT SUPPLIES FOR TOASTED CHEESE SANDWICHES AND TURNED THE OVEN UP HIGH. I STOOD UP LIKE A SOLDIER, THEN NEARLY SWOONED. IF I DIDN'T LAY DOWN QUICKLY, I WOULD FAINT.

THAT'S THE LAST CONCRETE RECOLLECTION. FROM HERE ON, IT GETS BLURRY.

MOM FINDS ME LYING IN THE HALLWAY.

"WHAT'S THIS HOLE IN THE WALL? I'M NOT ASKIN' YOU AGAIN! BABY WAKE UP!"

I TELL MOM I ONLY HAD TOO MUCH TO DRINK. ...MORE POPSICLES PLEASE...A SUNLESS SKY... VOMITING... MY EYES LACKED FOCUS AND I COULDN'T STAND. I HAD A STEWY MENTAL STATE, SLUGGISH AS ANALOGUE TAPE BEING CHEWED BY THE INNARDS OF A PLAYER.

MOM PUTS ME IN HER BED.

DON'T TELL... MOM... DON'T TELL... MOM...

SENSATION STRIDES INTO THE ROOM, MORE OR LESS WITH THE IDEA THAT WE'D BE DOING THE SAME THING TONIGHT.

"DAAAMMN, DONNY! YOU FUCKED UP!"

GAYE'S BACK HOME. SHE'S SIX MONTHS PREGNANT AND SLEEPS IN THE ADJACENT SINGLE BED.

"UNH-HUNH. NOW SEE. YOU MESSED UP. MAMA KNOWS YOU DID SOMETHIN', AND YOU GONNA GET IT!"

"SHUT UP GAYE."

MOSTLY, SHE'S MAD BECAUSE I ATE ALL THE POPSICLES.

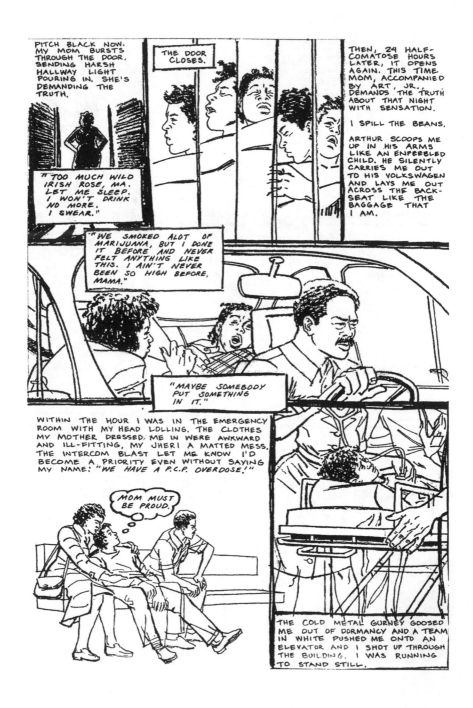

OVER WEEKS I GAINED COHERENCE, BUT TALKED LITTLE. I COULDN'T WALK. MOM HELPED ME SHUFFLE DOWN THE HALL, FIRST HALFWAY AND THEN THE FLOOR'S FULL DISTANCE.

THE WALKS WERE WARM-UPS FOR THE EXERCISES THAT WOULD BE OVERSEEN BY MY PHYSICAL THERAPIST, A BEAUTIFUL PUERTO RICAN GIRL, WHO, PREDICTABLY, I FELL HARD FOR.

TO BE CLEAR OF ANY CHEMICAL BOOGIEMEN, DAY AFTER DAY, DOCTORS ARRIVED WITH ANOTHER TEST TO DETERMINE THE CAUSE OF MY INCAPACITATION.

"NO TRACES OF P.C.P. AND YOU DIDN'T HAVE A STROKE. TOMORROW WE'LL DO A SPINAL TAP TO CHECK FOR MENINGITIS."

NEAR THE END OF MY STAY, THE COLD GRAY LADY WHO WORKED WITH ME IN OCCUPATIONAL THERAPY TURNED OUT ONTO OUR WORK STATION A BUNCH OF WHITE CUBES, EACH ONE PAINTED GREEN IN PART. MY TASK WAS TO ARRANGE THE CUBES SO THAT THEIR GREEN PORTIONS FORMED A DIAMOND WITHIN A SQUARE ARRANGEMENT. IN SECONDS, SHE DEMONSTRATED HOW, THEN HANDED THE CANISTER TO ME.

I TOO MADE MY DIAMOND WITHIN A SQUARE, ONLY TO SLOW NEAR THE END. THE LAST COUPLE OF CUBES STUMPED ME. EVENTUALLY, JUST ONE CUBE REMAINED. BUT ITS RELATIONSHIP TO THE LARGER WHOLE ELUDED ME.

AFTER ALL THE SEMI-COMATOSE BEDROOM DRAMA, ALL THE HOSPITAL BOREDOM AND ITS ATTENDANT, SURREPTITIOUS WANKING OFF, IT DAWNED ON ME THAT THIS WAS NOT SOME MINOR INCONVENIENCE. I WAS, AS SENSATION NOTED SO CLEARLY THE FIRST DAY, FUCKED UP.

"I'M GONNA BE A RETARD FOR LIFE?"

I SET THE CUBE ON THE TABLE AND BEGAN GULPING FOR AIR. I CRIED HARD, WET AND LOUD WITH NOT A FEELING LIKE SHAME. THE THERAPIST CALLED FOR AN ORDERLY, AND HE STEERED ME TO MY ROOM. GRANDMA GENEVA WAS THERE. SHE ASKED ABOUT MY TEARS.

"I WISHED I'D JUST DIED INSTEAD OF ENDING UP LIKE THIS."

DOCTORS DIDN'T DIAGNOSE MY CONCUSSION, BUT LATER THAT WEEK I WALKED, WITH A CANE, OUT OF THE HOSPITAL. MY CORNROWS REMAINED WHITE-ISH FROM AN ELECTRONIC BRAIN SCANS RESIDUAL PASTE. TUFTS OF FRAYING BRAIDS SURROUNDED ONE CLOUDY MIND. CROSS COUNTRY WAS DONE FOR. SCHOOL FADED FROM THE FOREGROUND AND, EVEN AS MY SHARPNESS RE-EMERGED, SENIOR YEAR THREATENED TO SUCK IN WAYS UNIMAGINABLE. WITH NOTHING GOING ON BY MID-YEAR, I TOOK MY LAST HOPE AND PUT IT ALL ON THE AFRO-BALL, THE HIGH POINT OF THE SCHOOL YEAR FOR BLACK KIDS IN SANDUSKY. A TALENT SHOW DOMINATED THE BALL, BUT THE BALL'S APPEAL REALLY LAY IN THE RITE-OF-PASSAGE AFTER-PARTY. A BUNCH OF NICE-LOOKING TEENAGERS HANGING AROUND UNTIL SOMETHING HAPPENED.

I HADN'T BEEN, AND WAS STOKED. I INAUGURATED MY NERD FRIEND DON INTO THE WEED EXPERIENCE THAT NIGHT. WE SMOKED OUT IN HIS PINTO. DON WAS LIKE: "I DON'T FEEL ANYTHING." FINE. BUT ONCE INSIDE THE DARKENED S.H.S GYM, MY T.H.C. TOOK SERIOUS HOLD. IT WAS GREAT AT FIRST, SORT OF A HOMECOMING. THEN MY MELLOW FRIEND TURNED ON ME, RECALLING LAST SUMMERS CHAOS. MY HEAD GOT MUSHY AND IT SEEMED LIKE MY LEFT SIDE TWITCHED.

"RELAPSE!" I THOUGHT...

"MAN TAKE ME HOME! IT'S HAPPENING AGAIN. MAN I AM FUCKED UP. OH SHIT WHAT'S WRONG WITH ME I NEED TO SEE MOM WHY AM I SUCH A MAGNET FOR WEIRDNESS OH PLEASE GOD!"

DON DROPPED ME OFF AND RETURNED TO THE AFTER-PARTY, MAD BECAUSE I'D PUT A STAIN ON THE NEGRO EVENT OF THE SEASON.

I ENTERED THE APARTMENT TO FIND MY MOTHER WATCHING SATURDAY NIGHT LIVE. BUCKWHEAT HAD BEEN SHOT. "MOM, I HAVE TO TALK TO YOU. CAN I TURN THE T.V. DOWN?" I WAS AS EARNEST AS I WAS HIGH. MOM NARROWED HER EYES. IT WAS HER NIGHT OFF.

"I SMOKED WEED TONIGHT MAMA. I DON'T KNOW WHY I DID IT. THAT'S NOT THE POINT. THE POINT IS I FEEL WEIRD! LIKE IT'S A RELAPSE. I THINK I NEED TO GO TO THE HOSPITAL. WHAT DO YOU THINK?"

"I'D SUGGEST YOU GO IN YOUR ROOM, GET IN BED, AND PRAY REALLY REALLY HARD."

"OKAY MAMA, I'LL DO THAT..." AND THEN SHE TURNED UP THE T.V. TO EDDIE MURPHY AND THEN SHE WAS DONE LOOKING AT ME. I WENT TO BED AND PRAYED UNTIL SLEEP CAME. LIVED A LIFETIME THAT NIGHT.

MY MOTHER HAD SAID NOTHING ABOUT THE EMBARRASSMENT AND WORRY I'D PUT HER THROUGH. SHE LOOKED ON IMPASSIVELY AS THOUGH STUDYING ME THROUGH A MICROSCOPE.

That was the official swan song for me and that nigga Jehovah. The running obsession was done, too, in the traditional sense. Eastern Michigan handed out no free rides to limping, D-plus niggas from the class of '84, so northern California, the newest outpost of Graham migration, was the move. I'd do six months of dishes in the Good Samaritan Hospital kitchen to get a United flight out of Cleveland. Never made the 750-mile club, but I did get this: Coach Logue used to quote Vince Lombardi. He'd scoff at the idea that the will to win makes the victor. "Hell, Din-ell," he'd say in that soft, Pennsylvania accent, "everybody has that. It's the will to prepare to win that really counts."

Sophomore year, I'd been equipment manager for the basketball team, and the experience, strangely, prepped me for the distance game. Playing the rear and picking up after the ballplayers clamped down on my ego enough that I could hang back comfortably. Come spring, I'd linger in last until the final half-lap of the 800-meter race. The idea was to catch front-runners at the tape. Being ready for that lick was all. I was actually kinda good at this.

"You try to kick down that lead guy and you haven't paid dues on these back roads, Din-ell," Coach said while I breathed hard at daybreak, sleepless and hung over, "and you're gonna be in a world of hurt, bud. Right now is nothing."

My Ohio childhood was some kinda preparation. Donny Shell was a projectile out of Santown. Not even that concussion I'd suffered after touching teenage dreams could stop me. Maybe I'd come back—or not—but one lesson that didn't need teaching was how to run down first place at crunch time. I knew enough about being in the hole to never come up short.

The nub would be timing my outbursts so that the end saw nothing in the gas tank, even if that meant never getting to coast. It was now time to go all out.

4.

talk like sex

THERE HAD BEEN FOR DELBERT ANOTHER BRENDA, BOTH IN NAME AND reformer spirit.

A schoolteacher this one was, a queen he met before losing face at the ex-offender's program. This Brenda, who had gone to college, also witnessed the good in Delbert, saw the potential. She let him know when his scent got too ripe and corrected his language when it lacked adequate precision. Delbert got more clean than he'd been in years.

Brenda was the cream of Fremont, the biggest hamlet just west of town. This chick held degrees, yet still dug Delbert. Her kids enjoyed him. Three years into shacking up in her hood, Brenda married Delbert and moved to that lakeside town he now insisted was such comfort.

But she ain't much like it, didn't care for the superior airs of her husband's sister and mother. All of Sandusky struck Brenda as a self-satisfied joke. Yet there wasn't another Delbert among the locals. Oh, a lot of them were more handsome and taller, but you could tell they hadn't been past Toledo. *All* of them acted like their booties didn't stink. This arrogance unsettled her so that the couple foundered, even as the wife more deeply embraced the Islam her husband had introduced her to. Delbert legally turned his last name to Bilal, and Brenda gave her daughters Muslim names, Saa'na and Samira.

The lifestyle had Bilal losing his appetite for *her*-on. He rid himself of tunnel vision. Sometimes, he was being a father.

Only Delbert was not surprised when he started to let loose of the thing, the love that was saving him. In him a flight instinct emerged, like an internal memorandum. Delbert created conflict. He invited the flight. He liked the hype. He liked the pressure and, especially, long odds. Almost anyone he had ever come within an inch of he goaded into battle, so this was just another clash. Brenda had brought him to the brink of transition, and he picked fights and backslid on hygiene until she left.

With this second wife gone, the man felt his personal recidivism rate climb. An actual prison would have been superfluous.

Delbert again got heavy into *her*-on. He got more seriously into raising shepherds and pit bulls, these muscular beasts approaching one hundred pounds. Sometimes cops bought them. The dogs' papers were suspect, but good money still came. And the animals' temperament— fierce, yet loyal and focused—matched that of their master, Bilal the Dog Trainer. Delbert billed himself this way in the trades that took his goods out beyond Erie County. White men in white trucks made the foray deep into the South Side only because Delbert had found a new way to channel his dubious potential.

If someone trod on Bilal the Dog Trainer's turf without him present, the canines went ballistic. Delbert recalled how sometimes, from a glass hole in his boxed quadrant of the Alexander property, he had watched his son on the slim stone walkway framed by cages, before the boy split for California. The pit bulls banged against their pens, leaping, barking, drooling inches from Donnell, but the boy seemed aware that no harm would come. He walked and read: the *Register*, comics, baseball cards. Delbert would consider this image after slamming smack to the hilt, connected to the notion vaguely as a needle dangled in his arm.

SERIOUSLY, LOOK AT ME NOW. I'M EIGHTEEN. I GOT THAT MEGAFRESH Jheri curl—courtesy of Freeport Boulevard's King of Curls—you could enter it in a contest, it's so intricately wavy-slick. I'm six feet and 155, stained ebony by the California sun. Rock-hard from the gym (class). I'm pretty much a dork, going solo to see Merchant-Ivory productions and such at Tower Theater three times a week. Wearing glasses. Missing my mom in Ohio. But giving it the old junior college try.

I am alone in the backseat of Ricky's red, 1985 Cutlass Sierra, palming the brandy, craning my neck so that my face is almost flush against the rear window. Freddie Jackson's new tape is playing through a second program.

"You are mah lay-dayyy . . ."

Outside the AC'd environs are females unlike any I've ever seen. Even on TV, dude. Linda Faye, the girl I lost my cherry to just before breaking out the spot, she was fine. A 7.5 it seemed to me. Chocolate, outta Alabama. Pretty and stacked. Brick . . . Owse . . .

Actually, she was *foine*. Up her score.

But she ain't have that thing these Sacramento chicks got. Now it's Sunday afternoon at Land Park and I am twisted in my seat. Delicious treats fill the park as if the picnic basket of God exploded. Ricky and Herman up in front talk calmly above the smoothed-out beat. Every few minutes the E&J bottle comes around. We pass the brandy as we exit the greenery, and earlier, in a bended road deep among the confines of the sprawling park, we snorted a little crank. But only because we've not yet heard of crack.

Herman—aka Snake, a pimp friend of Ricky's—is riding shotgun. The two are talking about Pie, Herman's main 'ho. Then it's Ricky's turn: he references trouble with Laurie, the girl from Ohio he keeps up—she's much closer to my age than his—and Terry, baby's mama number two, out in Oak Park. I kinda wanna fuck Terry, but she's a cousin from Delbert's side, so, whatever.

It was so easy running away from me, being the me I was then.

The gist of the fella's conversating pertains to the notion that pimpin' ain't easy.

Turning to talk to Rick, but very nearly acknowledging my punk, buster, dead weight, Herman scrunches up his face and asks, "Why the bitch wanna *make* me beat her ass?"

This is about the Super Bowl Sunday smackdown over in Oak Park. Pie had a much, much worse day than Dan Marino.

But this kind of mackin' really doesn't seem so hard to me. It just seems to call for force of will. And I'm thinking I got that. It took force of will to psyche out Linda Faye when she told me she was having my baby. I told her, It's too bad you're with child or else I could move you out here.

She admitted there was never any pregnancy, and I dropped her. Didn't feel *nothin'*. And now I'm thinkin' I'm a pimp because I don't like love.

So yo, what about this? Like, what if I got Linda Faye out here and put her on the street, like the 'Ho Stroll over in Oakland that Herman put me onto? A couple of nights previous, after that downtown show with the World Class Wreckin' Cru, we drove to East Oakland, peepin' 'hos and snorting speed. Had a burger before heading back to Sactown. Hella educational. Like the ghetto Scouting program.

Makin' money off of Linda Faye. Turnin' her out. That would be some shit wouldn't it?

'Cuz I ain't got *no* money.

BUT AT THE END OF THE DAY I COULDN'T DO PIMPIN' AND HAD TO DROP out of mack school.

Mack withdrawal happened in the fall, a little after crack came to town. Ricky and I were on our way to becoming regulars at this northside rockhouse—'cuz rock cocaine ain't have no warning label when it debuted and the shit always tasted like more—and there was this girl, California unbelievable on the dimepiece scale. A physical 11, dark brown with Spanish influences. Babygirl Cracky was actually very nice, if quiet, and, after unk hooked it up, I went out with her.

Actually, we just chilled at her crib. Nobody home except me and her, but all I scored was the realization that there's nothing dignified about being on a blind date in a rock spot.

Now, an upscale crackhouse is most easily identified in its clutter-free sensibility, and at this crib, space was most barren, floorspace naked as the walls. My date asked if I wanted to listen to the radio and then turned on this tinny, big-dial-havin', thirdhand shit that would have looked antique in a documentary on World War II. When we ran out of things to say—which was straight from the giddyap—pop radio menaced in the fashion of diabolical audio torture.

Quiet, this chick was, but still fly. Alas, as a budding drug fiend, painting houses by day and taking night courses at City College, there were class issues. I was too upscale, couldn't relate to the rockhouse milieu. I said I'd call, but didn't, and then felt bad about it.

Babydoll Cracky was just sixteen, and just as it had been with Linda Faye, I couldn't play her. But only because I actually kinda liked her.

I gave up that whole scene because of a craving that went deeper than dope. Had a need bigger than addiction, a yearning more powerful even than that for stanky on my danky. Something other than the horror show emotion of falling underground and suffocating out of sight would be nice.

But I needed more and better game.

FORTY YEARS OLD, BIG, DULL, AND DOUGHY, PAT WAS A DISHWATER blonde from Huron, that cracker country just outside Sandusky. The South Side became more than just a place to visit when her twin trades, dick sucking and drug dealing, brought her path to Delbert.

Pat had been in the bathroom of his cousins' after-hours rumpus room, sucking off one of the boys, when her weed—a pound of it—sped off in a cloud of parking-lot dirt. She was broke and stranded, and sitting there, hunkered forward on the balls of his feet and cradling a gin and tonic, was Del, the one Pat had heard tell of so many times. Delco, Showdown Shorty, the legend.

She knew all about him, Pat confessed, hastily, strategically. And she wanted to offer her services. She could forge documents, work long hours, and had steady connections to money, via her parents. Pat had left her husband and six children for a fruit picker, back in upstate New York. Her exit made members of Pat's family change their minds about big-city life. They learned you couldn't pin trouble on a place.

What Pat didn't know was that Delbert's power supply of lore was now little more than starlight, a story that hadn't ended only because the conclusion was too mundane to come dying all at once.

Delbert, now forty, thought Pat was the best he could do in the wake of the Brendas, after so much lost time. She would work.

Looking up and down this plain and sturdy white girl, Showdown Shorty considered his renown: at the height of his game—now a decade past—he had never been more than a popcorn pimp. Delbert never truly got over. The locals who idolized him could hardly know. Now, about to take on a twisted trophy wife from a ghetto fantasy league, Delbert disdained those who once put him on a pedestal. And he had disdain for himself.

Yeah, Pat, you can roll with me. And then he whipped it out.

In this time of leaky hookup, Delbert did possess one tight and redemptive thing: the title of Durable Power of Attorney over the Alexander estate. His mother let him have it when the properties were in great disrepair. The title made Delbert feel he was in charge of the entire family inheritance, the legacy of sharecroppers who up and bought a small slice of a northern town. The title alone, Durable Power of Attorney, swelled Delbert with pride.

During the day he and Pat manned the kennels where the dogs got worked. Fighting the animals was the first niche of Bilal Productions. It was a gimme. Delbert would pick up a puppy from the humane society, then train it into ferocity. Pat drew up papers that increasingly appeared official. Only some dogs, pit bulls mostly, fought. Others, running round orange cones and stopping at whistle commands, prepared for a test that might not ever come.

Then nightfall. Then cooking. Then dissolve.

There was at this point no pleasure in using. That smack made him feel old beyond his years, as if he were being strangled slowly from the heart, outward. He could practically hear his veins collapsing. His blood sullied, his crotch enmeshed in the face of a female as low as he could want to imagine, Del would form the words in his head as a lasting point of pride: Durable Power of Attorney.

THE BURGEONING FLAMES OF ROCK COCAINE HAD LEFT MY ASS A BIT scorched, but when the scourge truly hit my hood of Freeport, Donny Shell had left the building.

The cats I had rode around with were taking it back East, to the home I thought of less and less, usually as a cautionary tale. They began to see the pawning of possessions as viable business. It seemed instantaneous, the way life was infested with new-jack hunger artists.

Trying to hide, I nearly wrapped myself in newspaper. There no one would recognize me.

When my gig in writing first started, it was a side hustle and did not pay. It was my first day class at Sacramento City College, Journalism 1A. Here's where my mother came in. Mom—with Gaye and my sister's infant, Robby, in tow—had followed me out to Sactown and gotten nursing work that doubled her income. Gaye's welfare was enormous, compared to what she got in Sandusky. Boldly, this trio started trying to live middle class. And they put me up, at no cost, in our first house since Arthur and Geneva's divorce. Mom bought me a $50 typewriter from Kmart and got all the pleasure you could imagine from our half hour together each morning at shift's end. This last glimpse of mother-son quality time fit a triad of overlap, joining the conclusion of my hard drug days and the start of the scribbling years.

MY FIRST ARTICLES WERE PUT TOGETHER IN LONGHAND THEN TYPED UP at SCC. That Kmart special ain't work. Doc Stephens gave me a D in Journalism 1A, but asked me to be the campus sports editor—mostly because no one else was interested, but a little because she thought I had talent. Then came the typewriter compositions, to be set for print in a campus office adjacent to the newsroom. As the rock and I were having a long good-bye, I'd still show up at the offices of the Sacramento City College *Express* coming down from a hit, irritable and internally chaotic, and because I was a junior staffer, no one was the wiser. I wasn't even seen. But I could freak words in print, so invisibility proved to be a phase. Doc, the craggy faculty adviser, ran the *Express* as a vocational program. Students aimed for the top: a job at one of the two city dailies. She allowed bylines on only the cleanest pieces. Some weeks "Donnell Alexander" was the only one in the student newspaper.

Even the most academically slack white kids at SCC regarded writing as a right and so dominated print studies, and suddenly, there were all of these Caucasians in my face. I had been on a Midwestern cross-country team and was known for bringing a honky or two to the Murschel House, but in my life overall, the melanin-deprived just didn't have the numbers. There were only one or two Caucasian friends I could actually crash with. Now, with music the only get-high I indulged on the regular, I was in the trenches with the journalism kids, slack ones and strivers, going all out for the *Express* newspaper. And they had game.

Like Brad, the art-school transfer. He was a jock type from a military family, but also a theater cat, good-looking and blue-eyed. He claimed his Cal Arts classmates didn't like him because he wasn't gay. At that elite creative factory, Brad insisted, a guy had to have at least episodes of homosexuality to get accepted into the upper echelon.

As editor in chief trying to build a crew, I took this theory like a skeptic.

"I don't know . . . You act, right? Maybe you should have acted like a fag."

"Believe me, I tried acting queer." Brad's eyes got misty as he said this. "I really tried."

Now *that's* a great failure. I knew this was someone who would go all out. Brad was the one to hip me to the fact that junior college reportage, of all the lower forms of amateur writing, was truly Butt

Wipe Journalism. You couldn't take it too serious. Literally, the most your work might matter would be if someone ran out of toilet paper in an administrative bathroom adjacent to our office.

And there was Suzanne.

The *Express* used a duo of critics to write movie reviews. Not alternating reviews, but shared-byline opinion writing. How ghetto is that? One writer was an archetypal NorCal art victim named Marjorie, a mod whose fiery personality would someday be medicated into submission. The other was Suzanne, who had a lot of flavor.

Suzanne and Marjorie would lie in the grass outside our office, writing under the auspices of golden Sacramento light. Pale Marjorie in boots, black mini, and white tee, sprawled flat backwards, eyes in shades and face bared to the sky; Suzanne, Cybill Shepherdy with alabaster skin and everything else opposite. Her hair, thick and bowl cut, dyed dark as can be.

Brad and I would stand outside the office and watch the critics while maintaining an insular patter.

" 'Everything I need and more?' There's no such thing as 'everything and more.' That's not good writing," Brad insists.

"Yeah, well, maybe. It's the spirit of the verse that you're supposed to go on. The feel of the thing."

"Kooky is what it is."

"Maybe," I say. "Now, that one's dope."

Suzanne removes her shades, brushes her hair behind her ears, and bends a page backward.

"How old do you think she is?" Brad asks.

"I don't know dude, old. I bet she's, like, thirty."

Suzanne was thirty-two and part of an insidious Sac City subculture: the self-conscious returning student. The bullies of experience. This woman knew the score.

When she and I talked, Suzanne leaned in close and spoke insistently, with a slow, vaguely Southern drawl, as if the world depended on the improvement of her writing, as if only I could show her the way. Not that she knew my work as intimately as Brad or Lisa, the managing editor, or Ginny, the faculty adviser.

She was seduced by my position. Now, how weird is that?

I smelled her perfume and cigarettes.

She asked if I would join her for a drink at her apartment so that we might talk about her writing.

I nodded with great seriousness and reserve. "Yes. I think that would be a very good idea."

So, I park my Schwinn and lock it into a fence downstairs from Suzanne's midtown address. She leans over the railing to say that her door is open.

Just past sunset.

And the door is open, as are windows. Curtains floating out on thin streams of autumn Sierra wind.

I dispose of my backpack and hover over Suzanne's shoulder as she pours a couple drinks. Only the browns in this house.

No, that's not a problem, I love Scotch. Oh, it's not Scotch? Well, whatever.

There's no performance exercise like playing down a bitter taste.

Near the end of our second drink, the let's-end-the-small-talk express revs its unsmogged engine. Suzanne stands and stretches, revealing her body's true contours. Whiskey in a glass balances high above her head, her navel above her waistband. I mention a record she just might have, and the posture collapses with epiphany.

Walks away, then returns and crouches down to me.

Suzanne drops her drink to the table so that just a bit of liquor and a sliver of ice spill out, propels herself forward to the cushion of my closed mouth, and the absolute otherness of white women becomes tangible as the fruity blend of smoke and liquor that I taste on her tongue. Her sharp nose is pushed up my nostril and she surges with torque, hitting me as much with bicuspid as she does trim lippage.

There has been one other, Jae from Black Lit, who last month invited me to see *She's Gotta Have It* and then, well, had to have it.

Before that, the north Sac blondes cruising Arden Fair made me lose my glasses and find some contact lenses. (I painted a house with Granddaddy to get those.) None of this seemed a bit less juvenile than my Linda Faye trip.

Suzanne brings something else to the table. It's the directness of her persuasion. There's a haughtiness. She wants what she'll get. Squeezing my butt and nuzzling my neck as we careen beneath the ceiling lights, she forces Sandusky to recede a couple of galaxies back. And, if asked, I couldn't find Freeport on the map. I'm *what?* From *who?* From *where?*

I had written in a journal assignment for last semester's psych class that I'd "fuck all these white girls." Dr. Dowdall scribbled back, "Why 'the white girls'?" And I thought, Why not?

You can have your small-town life, your marriage to preserve pigment levels. You can, for that matter, be a guy fucking guys till the cow comes home. Skinny chicks, young, poor, people with Jheri curls. Right now you can have them.

Other. I've unlocked her bra and in embrace am looking down the fleshy canyon of Suzanne's back. My hands burrow down and we're a hot fudge sundae.

She has steered me to where she sleeps, past the bathroom within it and onto the bed. I strip naked, lying backward. Suzanne tears her hair from the bunch of sweater she holds over and behind her head. The previously freed cups of bra sit back on breasts in the fashion of a CAT baseball cap on a country fuck. Her belly shows just this side of roundedness and she turns and tosses her top away. When Suzanne slides down and kicks off her denim, I see her shoulders from up high.

Big panties hiss off; sidelong fingerfuck, with tandem tongues swimming.

She reaches down and pumps me for information.

Just after the very first time Linda Faye and I did it, she told me she was surprised I had a big one.

"Why were you *surprised?*"

"I don't know," she said. "Just from the way you act, I thought you had a little one."

It upset me more than if she'd told me I was small.

"Oh God," Suzanne says, squeezing as hard as she grinds. Then she pulls me atop her.

I get between her legs, thrashing like a perch catching air. Like *I'll show her.*

They say it isn't what you have, but how you use it. But, if you're a fucking novice, it helps to have a big one. A lot will be forgiven. Suzanne is making a project of me.

She grinds her hips in a circle and, at the same time, forward. Her pussy is talking. We're going over her column. I get where she's coming from. Maybe for the first time ever, the physical world feels like it just might be my milieu and the give-and-take makes (exceptional) sense to me. With each uncorking and screw, a small gasp escapes her lips, grazes my ears. Suzanne grinds harder and faster. She grabs me, clutching my ass cheeks and shoulders with thighs, forearms, and nails. The flailing fish is caught.

Now as our swivels correspond, her breath is as though sobbing. Her body produces the surge, then the drone of heavy machinery. Overload and shutdown.

I unplug though still juiced. Her heart is what I want to hear.

I am lying facedown between Suzanne's breasts, smeared savagely with sweat and curl activator. Her hands come down across my back. She doesn't know that I've still got a boner. Which is fine, unresolved as I now am.

The talk washing over my underwater ears reveals the grain of Suzanne's voice. She uses nouns that are unfamiliar, takes a warped tone. She is other to the nth degree.

"... the bad name given witchcraft is something our society has absorbed totally, without questioning. But the secret survives because Wicca is an antecedent to all of that bad PR, Salem and *The Wizard of Oz*. White magic will be seen for what it is."

I turn my scrapy chin up onto her chest and try for eye contact.

"Wait. You sayin' you're a witch?"

"A white witch. I've suspected it from my earliest days."

"Come on now."

"—"

"I mean, come on. You can't believe that sort of thing can you?"

"It is conceivable that certain phenomena transcend mere human comprehension."

"Actually . . ."

"Yes?"

"Actually I think you're just a lonely little girl."

"—"

"You know, like that witch stuff's just in your mind?"

"—"

"Don't get mad. I mean, how would you know? This just doesn't strike me as being something a person could confirm, not on their own. It's not like I'm trying to insult you or anything."

"—"

My dick could cut diamonds.

"I think you should go home now."

"Maybe I didn't say that right, Suza—"

"Please. Put your pants on and leave."

Within minutes I am peddling down Twenty-first Street, crossing Broadway, a tent pitched in my sweats. I keep tilting across lanes. It's lucky that there's almost no traffic on a Sacramento Sunday evening.

SUZANNE STAYED WITH ME IN WAYS TYPICAL OF THE POSTADOLESCENT male. I savored the smell of her through six days without bathing; reimagined the backs of her knees against my shoulders; summoned up, first from the back of my throat and then memory, the taste of her mouth and the whiskey; all but harvested sex crust from my foreskin.

Weeks drained away, turning NorCal October coolness into undeniable fall, and while I hunched over a galley of typeset with the managing editor, Lisa, Suzanne walks into the office. Lisa notices her first and asks how this week's film review is coming.

This will be her last review, Suzanne announces. The work is too consuming for someone who sees newspaper journalism as mere avocation. But Donnell?

"Donnell?"

I look up from the copy I'm editing.

"Donnell, I'd like to have another drink with you, just as a means of thanking you for your support throughout the semester."

"For sure."

Suzanne turns on a dime and smiles at the managing editor, smiles at the faculty adviser, on her way out.

MY DATE WITH SUZANNE WAS ON THURSDAY, THE DAY BEFORE THE month's end. We'd meet late, as my gig helping out in the Sacramento daily's sports department would keep me until eleven. Suzanne's downtown apartment was a short ride away.

I had dreamed about the witch chick that week. Suzanne sucked my dick. And as this hadn't been something that had happened with any real sort of consistency in my life, in the dream I regarded the act with frozen surprise and awe. I didn't really let go. Rather, I fixated on her expert slurping.

Then Suzanne cast her vision up at me and bit down hard, bit through. The howl that I let out in my dream ripped me awake, and I did not sleep again that night.

I thought about this while lying in bed early a.m. on Thursday, October 30. Date night.

THE PRELIMINARIES MOVED THE SAME AS WTH THAT FIRST HOOKUP, ONLY accompanied by more artificial light and less breeze. The room was airtight, and by the time we were in liplock, there was no need to wrestle our way into the adjacent bedroom. We had acknowledged agendas.

Suzanne took a pee that echoed with hollow whoosh through the apartment's wooden confines, and then she came to me on her bed, pulling up her panties higher with each stride.

My writer friend did the most amazing thing: she lay down at my hips and provided my penis its first exploration of the human glottis. My only proof of its erect existence was tactile. My head sashayed in her throat. Both balls ballooned out and subsequently floated against her shoving kiss. Then out again.

At first I snatched the mattress, liberating its sheets. I tried to sit upright and see, and my torso felt a hand shove it back down supine. Then I covered my face as if in grief.

Suzanne was on an immensely slippery mission.

It was after midnight when I remembered the dream. All Soul's Eve. How could this be? Did I have premonition? And if I were indeed the recipient of such a gift, how much of a blessing could it possibly be, considering the circumstances?

Who could think about that? She opened her mouth's grasp, keeping it zen. I let my hips be.

Halloween comes and my hands are around her head, caressing the shoulders and absolutely surrendering to the pleasure that may well be demise. I am gifted and doomed. And resigned.

I pop free of Suzanne the slick chute, and instead of turning tail I guide myself back into her, because I have given myself over to the possibilities, to the fate of pleasure and finding out what will happen. I am a documentarian of the senses, completely given over to the blurring between her face and my crotch. Sentience turns effaced. Yet I retain a kind of control. Suzanne has turned me into a performer in a narrative, one whose subtext is more heavy with chance than I could previously have imagined. And when the inevitably protracted pitch of sustain extinguishes responsibility of who did what to whom, I'm already gone.

THE WOMEN OF THE *EXPRESS* SPOILED ME, MY MOTHER SAID, AND SHE didn't fucking know the half. Thrilling is the only way to describe the way they, the janitors, and the j-school invited me into the community of college. How I stiff-armed great bunches of open invitations called to mind that Groucho Marx adage, about not joining clubs that would have me as a member.

Check out Ana, Sac City's lit mag editor, exiting the *Express* so quickly she had to hold on to her beret. And me laughing through a smirk in a way that must have sounded as though I was giving the Bronx cheer. She published my poem about Jimi Hendrix in the *Literary Humanist,* then asked if I'd read my column aloud in some coffeehouse scene.

My column, "Just Naked," was whimsically named by Brad and me one day in the darkroom.

"What about 'Naked Truth'?" I asked.

Brad washed an emerging image in a chemical bath, waves of water yellow in the spooky light. "That's corny."

"What about just 'Naked'?"

"What about 'Just Naked'?" He never looked up. I never looked back. Just naked. Newly nude.

Solidifying on the photographic paper in Brad's hands is me, nude from the waist up, but implicitly buck-ass. It is the picture that will accompany my column.

The one Ana liked was about the time I had a beef with Aaron, the second of my sister Gaye's babies' daddies, while he was smoking that dust.

I wrote:

A couple of nights ago I had a run-in with an angel-dusted-out punk on the doorstep of my house. Homeboy's pupils were so dilated that passing birds considered making nests in his eye sockets. After about 20 minutes of arguing, it became clear I'd have more success talking to a bathroom fixture and called the cops.

Just before the fuzz took Mr. Felon away they told me they could only hold him for four hours on the charge of public drunkenness (public drunkenness?). As the cuffs were being slapped on the guy,

he turned around and mouthed something to me. I think it was, "I'll get you, Flintstone. I'll get you!" It was something like that.

A while later the fuss died down but I was worried—what was to happen four hours from now? It was at this moment that someone offered to let me borrow a gun.

Immediately I thought about my convictions. I thought about the editorials and Alex Rieger and how I'd always said I'd never sleep with a gun in my home. Then I thought about being beaten to death with a ball peen hammer, which, of course, would have been preceded by some forced sodomy. It took maybe 1.3 seconds for me to say, "Yeah, I'll drive by and pick up that gun."

The scariest part of this ordeal is how quickly I stopped feeling bad about having the weapon and how soon I began to enjoy it. Gunmakers make sure the weapon feels good in your hands. It's raw power. Liberal rhetoric ain't palpable and that's its major flaw.

That night, with a .38-caliber handgun an arm's reach away, I slept like a baby.

Ana thought the writing performance art, but I went "pfft" on that idea. What I dug about writing was how it let you stay shady. Say that stuff out loud? Nuh-unh. The request struck hard at my deepest internal contradictions about expression: On one hand was my deep ambivalence toward recognition. On the other was the Delbert in Me.

Regardless, even as I was white-outing my way to glory through sportswriting and Butt Wipe Journalism, I was plotting an escape route. The way reporters suffer unrepentant assholes—can you say "athletic department"?—and the disposable way in which readers regarded the work made it clear that newspapering was the busing tables of literature. On the low, I wanted to be a chef with words, like LL Cool J. I wanted to work with tangible facts, but for the show to be all about me.

I poured myself into "Just Naked," making it raw. Ain't no describin' the way that I was feelin' when I was vibin', 'cept I was feelin' like a deadly secret agent on assignment. The *Express* staff made buttons saying "I Read Naked," featuring my scrawny, black-ass self. And people paid to wear them. A great moment in Butt Wipe Journalism. I was writing myself into existence, but Ana was out the door.

FOR A NIGGA LIKE ME, JUNIOR COLLEGE PLAYED SOMETHING AKIN TO A dream come true. Ginny the adviser gave me an A in Journalism 101, even though I never sat through the class, because having me practice leads among half-wits and bored retirees was pretty damned absurd. During *Express* production deadlines, I'd disappear at lunch with Brad and Kristen, then reappear in three hours with pizza from Blondie's in Berkeley, ninety miles southwest on I-80. But if we caught any static, it only coated an appreciation for how cute and talented we were. This newspaper production stuff? We could do it in our sleep. I even kept up the city daily sports gig, but eventually could not deny that the time had come to ease my juco show on down the road.

We all thought we were so bad we visited NorCal deans and forced them to explain why we should continue our undergrad educations at their universities. I moved to Fresno because, at this town's daily, they said I was the one. On paper at least, I was the ideal minority journalism candidate, groomable, presentable, integrated, and skilled. Fresno was like a land-locked Santown. And the student mind in the mid-section of California had a quiet desperation that the Bay Area just couldn't match. I'd found a college just obscure enough to work.

Fresno State University was known for agribusiness, football, and a j-school past its prime. For my first day of classes at FSU, I wore a T-shirt from the Run-DMC/Beastie Boys show in Sactown that summer. The message on my back distilled my worldview:

Get Off My Dick!

The idea wasn't to have a whole bunch of fans or talk to a lot of extra people. Mike, a sportswriter crony from juco, was at Fresno State. Aesthetically, I was moving away from guys like him though, and my posture rankled the more humorless and anachronistic Bulldog faithful, and maybe I was the first j-school prodigy to see the honeymoon end before smudging my first syllabus ink. Which way to the margins, boss?

So there developed a clique of quasi-students and druggies who became my friends: Lloyd, that Jamaican employee of the city daily, slumming with college cats and eating mad acid; Tony, a Mexican photojournalist and the only homegrown member of our crew; T. James, the gonzo critic from LA; and Skip, a Fresno Oakie by way of Sactown. He once kiped a full tank of nitrous oxide.

We would light out for Vegas or Death Valley with sackfuls of hallucinogen. We had trench coats and bed hair and radio shows on the college station. We were fucking half the women at the *Collegian*, Fresno State's daily newspaper. But we weren't getting published so much.

That's mostly because we weren't students, really. I stuck around campus because of a job in the sports department of the city daily, work contingent upon university enrollment. And as much as I hated the business of newspapering, I loved the people: people like Lois, a bad writer trying to become good through total immersion, ignorant kids getting smarter by documenting the times. I became part of the college daily scene. We lived in a safe kind of seediness. A half dozen Mac computers on ten metal desks interspersed with bundles of dated *Collegians* was our office milieu. Its John Hughes ardor seemed to me final testament to the appeal of other grass's greenness.

Unlike Brad, Kristen, Lisa, and them back at Sac City, the Fresnans had never been to Freeport and had never met the fam. I dug that about them.

5.

holo my life

THE SCHOOL PAID YOU TO WORK ON THE *COLLEGIAN*, BUT IT WAS A party, too, for some of us.

Things rarely got crackin' until after dark, when deadline hit. Light like industrial glass before the newsroom would fill: Hanif, Kendall, and them typing, dialing, talking—some maniacal, some laconic. All racketing up a click-clack ring; JoAnn and Rob printing out stories they had rewritten, improvising headlines, ferrying copy and halftones between the edit desk and production. The tail end of the enterprise, where loud music—disquietingly new stuff: Ice-T's "Dog N Tha Wax," Meat Puppets' "Up on the Sun"—bounded out. Back there were hangers-on, drunk writers and photogs hoping to catch on, who spilled out of the production room into the area where people actually strived to put out a daily publication.

T. James didn't have much business in the office beyond some nebulous editorship, but he did have a guitar and an amp. Around midnight, JoAnn the Editor flashed the stat camera on photographs going to press. A greenhorn grad student bit his lip and struggled to bring his notebook full of facts into coherence.

And T. James and I rocked. We put electric sound rockets and verse on the far side of an office door. We hammered out an anthem.

Between sips of Old Milwaukee in a production room recliner, I wrote:

I toddled through the wasted years
Inhaled the lies, spat through the tears
Nearly wrapped myself in newspaper
But then I found my mind, and I couldn't rape her
A level head that would not mumble
A leveled building that would not crumble
Is where I found my ticket to: Some Mo'
(Pause)
Give me love and give me pain
Lance my ambition and watch it drain
Don't you know it won't be the same
'Cause now I got onboard a Guitar Train

In the black-walled production cavern, where I first finished the verse, I jumped up and ran out to the newsroom, to the editor's office, where T. James, hunkered down and hirsute, was working out an intro riff that sounded like the most phlegmatic version of "Sweet Jane" ever. Yet, captured in the chords were our mutual love of doing dirty nonfiction and our growing hatred of journalistic constraint. A good writing gig might have prevented the entire debacle. Then he came up with the chugging melody, all work-song-y and railroad-y.

Everyone we played "Guitar Train" for loved it. A band called Anemic Tony and the Pygmy People sprang up to support it. Street dreams aren't made of this. Mine was, though. I was the singer, T. James played guitar. Tony "played" bass.

My roommate, Skip, managed us, if managing means hyping and shit-talking. He lit momentum by altering a *Collegian* advertisement so that it appeared we would open for INXS downtown at Selland Arena. (Skip actually only changed a single issue, but the gesture generated buzz good enough for hick-town rock.) Almost immediately we got a gig at a spot called the Wild Blue, sandwiched between The Miss Alans and Walkabon, two of the biggest groups in town. We were to play a three-song set. Our only handicap was a near-total inability to play instruments.

We crash-trained at the crib Skip and I shared. Or at least we were supposed to. We talked about practicing incessantly, but mostly listened to records, drank, and smoked. School and work competed for our attention, too. Well, at least the other guys had that problem. I blew off Fresno State and remained mildly concerned with my sports gig at the Fresno daily, an awful job I was fucking up royally. Most of the sports editors there struck me as closet Klansmen, and I reciprocated irritation through showy incompetence and an unfettered disdain for athletics. Cael, a Republican friend from the j-school, whispered in my ear how Bulldog football might as well be horse racing, far as FSU boosters were concerned, and the whole thing got to looking like a white supremacy racket. I penned an opinion piece about how black athletes should strike until their ownership stake in sports improves. The paper published it, but lunch breaks got mad solo.

Maybe this was when I started exiting the stage.

At the height of Anemic Tony mania—well, *we* were crazy—high school hoops season hit the playoff run, and top-editor pressure to get my hyped words in print was offset by the jock department's instinctual sense that I might just not show up for games, leaving gaping coverage holes. Concurrently, I was deep into investigating a bar scandal for the campus rag. And Robin, my girlfriend from the apartment complex, thought I'd fertilized one of her eggs. Too, some sex thing, major and explosive, was about to happen with JoAnn, my *Collegian* editor.

Most importantly, the band was not practicing. At all.

Tony himself was the biggest problem. He was totally wilding out. Ostensibly our bass player, he was on one of those two-month, end-of-college benders responsible for so much prime-time newsmag wasted-youth death reportage. Tony's bad craziness pushed back practice for days on end.

The group had actually never practiced. And our gig at the Wild Blue was ten days away.

The whole of Anemic Tony and the Pygmy People finally got things going one Friday night. Two hours late, Tony and Mark, the drummer (who had no drums), strolled in loaded and Tim played some licks. I sang "Guitar Train," then Mark put on a Steely Dan record. Everybody except him howled a complaint.

"The only reason I'm managing this group," Skip said, "is to ensure that nothing like Steely Dan ever happens again!"

Then I went to take a dump.

Halfway through pinching a loaf, it occurred to me that the night marked the start of sectional basketball competition.

There sure oughta be a great bunch of playoff action tonight.

Tonight. Basketball. Tonight.

Aw fuck.

Wipe, up and out.

I grabbed my coat, hat, and notebook and sprinted through the door, saying nothing to anyone and mashed out in my LeBaron, the one from '81 with a bashed-in front driver's side. I ran the darkness to the town of Sanger, rocketing through South Valley raisin plantation short-cuts in the shadow of Highway 99. When the high school was in sight, I grabbed the first illegal parking space I could find and tore into the gym. Intermission was nearly upon all seven hundred of us.

I scratched down rebounds and points in a makeshift way:

#12: II
#5: IIIII I

Etc.

At intermission, I ambled over to the scorer's table and spotted the official scorebook. As one of the high school team's stat girls lingered above the numbers, the home squad's equipment manager offered me her squad's version. I thanked her, then got started copying the players' names. Like always, only later.

That stat girl finally finished. I checked the official tally of points and rebounds that I would need for the story to be written later that night, for the next day's paper.

Second-half action commenced. The visitors won. I drove to the Fresno daily newsroom and pounded out a piece, flawlessly told, in twenty-five minutes. The man, I was, I knew.

It was maybe 2 A.M.

When I drove through our apartment complex entryway, I steered past a truck doing donuts in the parking lot. It wasn't the funny, sophomoric yokel kind of donuts, but the manic, death-obsessed, and centrifugal sort. The truck resembled the stock image of clock hands spinning wildly that's often used in cinema to indicate time out of control.

Is that Tony? I thought.

I walked into the apartment and asked Skip, "Was that Tony driving like a maniac over by the rec room?"

Our apartment was trashed.

"Probably," Skip said. He was bent over the portable black-and-white, inserting an undone wire hanger into the spot where antennae ought to have been. "I've never seen anyone that out of control in my entire fucking life."

Skip knew skinheads and had run with speed freaks. I suspected we were in the middle of something that wasn't day-to-day zany shit.

I opened a beer, chugged it, then thought better of crashing for the night.

"I'm gonna go find that guy."

Shaw Avenue. Three A.M. in Fresno on a Friday night. Not a lot to see. Drunk cholos on Vespas, the occasional copper. Then, out of the predawn black, a projectile pickup truck. It speeds through a red light, past me, and tears up the down street, into a lot. The truck emerges from another business entrance and climbs over curb-level traffic dividers before disappearing again down Shaw. It's Tony, with our drummer in tow.

I give chase for a while, then park myself at Denny's. Awaiting my Grand Slam and the early edition of the paper, I watch the car fly back and forth from behind a picture window. My article reads well. Too short, but good.

On Tony's fourth 90 mph pass, I accepted that rehearsal, for tonight, was off.

Before dawn I knocked at Robin's Parkwood unit, then stalked past her and down the dark hall to her room. Robin, too, had side dreams of being a singer—actually sang, passably—and was resentful at being further from the stage of performance than her fuckup, white-folks-loving boyfriend. I dicked her down in silence, bringing her to orgasm from behind as she faced the blue, raised-letter label she'd marked my side of the bed with: The Don.

I slept deep into the afternoon, then walked across the complex to my place.

T. James called at about four to ask if I'd come with for his midnight KFSR show, and that seemed cool 'cuz Tony, Skip, and I had settled in around the living room bong, drinking coffee, perusing photo books, and talking about Pinochet. That would take me right up to show time.

"Bring *Metal Machine Music*," T. James said. When I got to the radio station, he was halfway through his show and I was halfway through a bottle of whiskey.

I had slowly gone insane. I knew this. What I didn't understand was that T. James, shambling grotesquely over the studio control panel, too, was slowly losing his mind, as were Skip, Mark, and to a more obvious extent, Anemic Tony.

HAPPILY ECCENTRIC, SANE, AND FUNCTIONAL, THAT'S WHAT WE ALL WERE one year before. Had any garage band, in the replicating history of garage bands, imploded so quickly? Before learning how to play?

A debut at the Wild Blue, something a thousand white kids up and down the Valley strived toward and dreamed of, was almost upon us, and the time between now and then would decide whether we were musical geniuses the world was waiting for or just excuse-seeking dilettantes, hell-bent on giving punk rock a bad name.

Through the glass bottom of my Old Grand-Dad bottle, it looked like we were making art from our randomly intersecting lines of craziness.

"Put the record on," I told T. James.

The Lou Reed album *Metal Machine Music* is one of the most famously antisocial and misanthropic recordings of all time. Some snuff films are less hateful. In 1975, outraged that fans had made *Sally Can't Dance*—a piffle that he'd made with only minimal effort—his biggest seller ever, Lou put out *MMM*. Composed entirely of feedback and random, shrill, and bleating beeps, the record was unlistenable.

I thought this wax was the most profound document ever and had combed the Valley from Sacramento to Bakersfield to find it. Paid $30 for my copy. Now, the crowning moment of this obsession: to batter the ears of late-night Fresno college radio listeners. That would show them. This I knew.

Metal Machine Music is a double album.

We were halfway through side two when an openly Greek reggae DJ called Aquaman came through begging to finish T. James's show. We were like, fuck you, pay me. But he said some stoned maniacal shit about the coming harmonic convergence and it sounded good enough that we let him off with promising to play the last half hour of Lou's horrible noise.

Back at Parkwood, I blasted the new Public Enemy.

Ladies and Gentlemen, the grand incredible Flavor Flav!:
Ay yo, Chuck they sayin' we too black man
Little do they know that they can get a smack for this

Leaning forward from the couch so that he could be heard, Skip said, "Do you think he's really playing that shit?"

Needle's off Flav. Tuner's on KFSR.

And we hear nothing but *irie* sounds.

Motherfucker!

"Motherfucker, I will kill you," I yelled into the receiver at Aquaman. "I gotta gun, and I'ma come over there with it. But I'm not gonna shoot you. I'm gonna beat you to death with it."

"Dude, chill out," the frat boy on the line said. "Just listen to the tunes, brother, and everything's gonna be alright."

Aquaman had to go down. Show the world what price, my muddled brain insisted, the unrepentant must pay.

I slammed down the phone, ran for the door. Skip and T. James stopped me with force, not reason. They either stomped me till I passed out, or I lost consciousness in the whirlwind of our struggle, but I woke up, after the night had passed, in that exact same spot.

SUNDAY, WHEN THE PHONE RANG, IT FELT LIKE MORNING, BUT DUSK WAS just a few hours away.

It was Cael, who worked weekends as a copyboy at the Fresno daily.

"Jeez, man. You made history. How does it feel?"

"I have no idea what you're talking about."

"History. Don't you read the paper? Man, the paper has never before run a story like this."

"Cael, just tell me what you're talking about."

I had taken the call in Skip's room. He stretched the length of the single mattress, wearing only his tight white briefs. He looked like shit.

Cael read a rewrite, a short retooled version of the basketball story I had penned late Friday. It seems the story I turned in had, among a half dozen other errors, implied that a leper came off the bench to lead Alpaugh's high school hoops team to victory. That equipment manager had a spelling problem. Lepke was not a leper. The sports department had to do more than run a correction, my piece was so deeply, deeply wrong. Alpaugh's leper had made the headline. The editors actually rewrote the story and put it in the paper again. A first, the copykid insisted.

"My God, man!" Cael said. "This sort of thing is unheard of. Can you believe it: 'Leper comes off the bench'! That's insane."

"Yeah, man, real crazy. Good-bye."

I was inclined to go buy the morning paper, but it was Sunday afternoon and I just didn't want to know. Couldn't stand to know. Skip asked what had happened. I repeated Cael's story, staring at the floor, intoning as though this shit happened every day. When I got to the part about the leper, I began laughing uncontrollably.

"A fucking leper. The leper of Alpaugh."

"Argh-hah!" laughed Skip.

"Haaaaaaaaaaaahhhhhh!" went I.

"I'm sure the defense was *not* all over him."

"Haaaahhhhhh!"

Skip's six-four frame was convulsing from the fulcrum of his tighty-whiteys. He looked like an albino bug on its back.

I was dying.

"Haaaaaaaaahhhhhhhh.

"Haahhh haaahh haaaahh.

"Haaaaaaaahhhhhhhhh!

"You realize," I said after gulping for air, "you do realize that I'm laughing because I'm completely hysterical. Ha ha haah hah haaah. Hahhh . . .

"Whoo!"

"Yeah, I know," said Skip, who had stopped laughing even before the shorter, truncated trio of *hah*s. In fact, he looked quite serious.

"Ha ha ha. Aghhh. I am totally flipping out. Totally. Haaaahhhh."

"Yeah, I know."

"I gotta get the fuck out of here.

"Haaaaaaaaaaahhhhhhhh." I staggered out the door in the clothes I'd passed out in.

I landed at the *Collegian* office, where only Kendall, the statuesque volleyball star/sportswriter, worked, typing silently. I moved directly to the editor's office and began making calls on that bar scandal piece.

No calls got answered. I thought about the leper. I thought about jerking off in Kendall's face, porno style. That would make it all right. I felt like a leper.

I called my mom.

"Mama, I need to come home. Right now Mama."

Never felt more like a wuss.

"Come home Donny."

Click. Head in hands for five fucked-up minutes.

I called Skip. "Dude, I am all fucked up. I'm in JoAnn's office. Can you drive me home? To Sacramento."

"Five minutes."

"Thanks. Oh yeah. One thing: Can you bring my sunglasses? I've been crying like a six-year-old lost at the county fair. And Kendall's outside . . . I've been thinking about jacking off in her face."

"And you think if she sees you crying that you'll ruin your prospects?"

"Exactly."

IT TOOK THREE WEEKS TO MAKE IT BACK FROM SACRAMENTO. THERE I LAY steeping in the cool spring darkness of the spare room at my mother's. Feeling dirty.

"Ah, the triumphant return," I'd said to Skip as he pulled up along the curb in front of my mother's house.

It was in fact a blessing to be alive. Only in hindsight was it clear just how out of control things had gotten. I found, scrawled on looseleaf, amongst my belongings, a note:

One thing's for sure. I now know that I will eventually commit suicide in a fit of emotion-filled thoughtlessness. But it's cool, 'cause that's a small price to pay for the honor of being the poster boy for flamboyance and spontaneity.

ALL HAD SEEMED RIGHTEOUS. I'D DEVELOPED MY PERSONALITY. LYING continued to be a struggle for me, even as I threw off clannishness and concentrated on forward motion and getting tougher. I understood that I'd largely written myself into existence. But managing the transition from ghetto anonymity had in it more struggle than I had wanted to admit. Riding the first rush of being out of context was much easier.

In an unfamiliar spare room at Mom and Gaye's new rental, a pad three times nicer than anything Mom could have afforded in Sandusky, my mind traveled back to insights penned on that South Side bedroom wall, to The Path, where I had run naked in the shadow of factory decay. The difference between now and then seemed simple, stark even. I had been nothing, and then I was something. It took deep digging to detect a difference between me and privileged white boy college stars like, say, Mark, the drummer. I had earned the right to act a fool. Now, as day turned to night and vice versa as one might turn lights off and on to simulate a storm, my literal livelihood, my writing life, felt in danger—more jeopardy than any one gig might present. Writing had become more than school or reportering. I felt as though I might die.

I HAD NO WORDS, WHERE ONCE THEY SEEMED ENDLESS. SINCE LETTING them out, since declining to keep them for my own, they had gained power. I fancied my hands on a typewriter to be like Walter Payton. In print I'd dip my shoulder into the onrushing opposition, bounce outside, then dance in to score, across the publication line. But the words had to be mine. Each time someone else's writing agenda ruled—when, say, sportswriting defined me—it broke my heart. I dropped the ball.

I CALLED MY OLD CITY COLLEGE HOMIES, BRAD AND KRISTEN. THERE wasn't need to even say my predicament. They just drove by and scooped me.

The three of us went to the zoo in Land Park, next to our old school. We hardly spoke. I didn't give my speech about how print was not the nigga medium and how teaching blacks to write had been punishable by death last century. Brad and Kristen had never bought me as a martyr. We simply watched the birds, the monkeys. Living creatures do what they do. All else is contrivance.

I considered my world of scribbling.

The words. Mine on a page suggested they might be able to turn noes into yeses. There was defiance in writing, my only form. I wasn't a hand-to-hand combatant and had no appetite for guns and stabbing and all the superficial wares of battle. *Griot* was a word I'd recently learned. It surged inside a bit.

It was a synthesis of drug and religion, not to be traded on. Equal parts cop-out and salvation. Ahead was a summer gig at the Boston broadsheet—likely more writing about stuff not close to my heart. I had to make that scene, but it was a means not an end. Recognition for writing that didn't speak to my life, no matter how much it got me over, was cheap. Disposable.

"Guitar Train" made me happy. So did "Just Naked." I even treasured the rap songs I freestyled when I first got to Cali. But that stuff was just kicks, nothing you could hang a life on.

EN ROUTE TO BOSTON, I STOPPED IN SANDUSKY TO PARTY WITH JED AND John, childhood friends just out of the Army. A couple of years before the nineties hit, we put our own stamp on the meaning of Hammer Time, getting ripped every night. John had installed a recording studio in his sister's basement. I hipped him to Anemic Tony, and he strapped on his guitar. Jeff played a furious drum part and we put down my little ditty called "Let's Fuck Until Our Loins Are Numb." It was beautiful, like "Say It Loud, I'm Black and I'm Proud (of Being Drunk)." My mental was like, man, fuck a newspaper. If Anemic Tony was falling apart as it appeared to be, I'd come back to Ohio and do this, The Butt Huskers. The only reason I kept Boston on the agenda was the weekly salary.

Then, with a quickness, I ran out of dough and found myself stranded, bouncing from couch to couch. I sobered up and got depressed.

Fucking Sandusky. Blue struck.

I stopped by my father's place after the Boston arrival date came and went. Delbert, who couldn't help my financial plight, smoked a joint with me instead. He lived in the same two-room spot between his mother's home and the building where he'd broke Mama's jaw. My father advised me, and I—clueless, considering the fix I was in—inhaled the speech without question, as if it were weed smoke itself. My father was little more than a stranger, but a stranger could know desperation.

Delbert told me, "Don't end up like these sorry niggas around here."

Bullied by mortgages and, if they were lucky, factory jobs, these people seemed like pained and luxuriantly trapped animals. People who had never tried cigarettes were now smoking rocks. My college thing impressed the Old Boy.

"All they ever talked about is 'I was supposed to do this' and 'That was gonna happen,' " he continued. "Don't nobody wanna hear that shit!"

Delbert cupped his hand to make like Air Force One and made it slowly take off.

"The story people want to hear is when this"—and his hand abruptly dropped halfway to the tabletop, as if shot down—"turns into this!" Here Delbert stretched his hand plane out until his arm was extended out past his head, recovered. "That's the story people want to hear."

I hurried the hell up in swallowing my pride and hitting Aunt Barb up for that traveling money. Maybe some synthesis of the Pygmy People and the Butt Huskers could indeed become the Midwestern, late-eighties answer to the Velvet Underground. On the other hand, I couldn't sing and maybe I was a second-rate James Brown Junior. So I played it safe and jetted from Sandusky like I was from out of town and it was the end of tourist season.

Drankin' all the way, Jeff and John drove me twelve hours to my summer home just south of Boston, where I split servants' quarters in a mansion in Milton, birthplace of Poppy Bush.

At the Boston daily I worked the night shift, covering cops, rarely getting bylines. In separate Harvard-adjacent nightclubs I saw Living Colour and Mutabaruka. Took a drive to Colby College in Maine with the girl of a brand-new buddy, a Catholic, conservative, hard-news prodigy from Northwestern. I kissed Beth without his knowledge. It seemed.

There was a lovely fling with Angela, who hailed from Manchester across the water—

"No," she said, the first time I tried to lay my lips on her. "Yer too O.T.T."

"Whassat?"

"Over the top."

"Oh," said I.

"No," she said, the last time I saw her. "I don't want to go home preggahs."

"Oh," I said, pulling back up my jeans—

And there was my slammin' Cambridge birthday party, cohosted by a queer named Jeffrey; I interviewed Mayor Flynn in a Dorchester park, and as Rakim's "Let the Rhythm Hit 'Em" premiered over an outdoor sound system, I blew the mayor off totally, just so I could say I heard the song right there, right then; and in Brookline, after staking out his house for six hours, in ninety-five-degree heat, I screamed out a question at Mike Dukakis, who was expected to name Lloyd Bentsen his running mate. He was pushing a manual mower, and at my screaming cue, the entire press corps began interrogating him.

The paper's intern program brotha overseer seriously, publicly suggested my insanity.

It was life fully pitched, but it couldn't go on, and one August Sunday afternoon, I drove through the sea-drenched humidity to Providence, with the Chicago prodigy, to meet a Brown girl named Tina and get a tattoo. The shop was closed and my girl ain't show, but dude thanked me in the end, on behalf of all the other good-school products who populated the Boston daily's program.

"I almost never have this much fun," Ricky told me.

No one does. I do have fun.

———

MY TIES WITH THE FRESNO NEWSPAPER HAD BEEN COMPLETELY SEVERED by the time my Greyhound pulled back into Cali. FSU evicted me. But I swore I'd be good and was back on campus when classes reopened. Rob, the new *Collegian* editor, reformed Anemic Tony as Jolly Carcass, then hired me as his second at the paper. The Carcass played exactly one lame house party, and I jetted—from the garage band, not school or work. I won my focus and some awards for writing. And almost a year after the breakdown, LA's big daily gave me an ace summer gig.

Delbert's recovering-airplane soliloquy during my extended San-town stay-over came to mind. I thought to reach out for my man, my seminally elusive man. Thanks was due.

It took a half dozen calls to catch Delco at home. When my father finally picked up, even the pause before his speech hissed with defeat and contagion. Before I could let him in on my LA recovery, he bitched me out over reports of my partying and running around with white women. Who did this nigga think he was, my daddy or somethin'?

I caught enough of a break in the litany of complaint to interject my brag. He gave me nothing. I kept on. Come on, this is LA, you're not impressed? The gig, I suggested, could do wonders for my career.

My father paused, then said, "You know, we all get these ideas that certain things are going to happen, but you know what? They ain't gonna happen."

I hung up. I cried. Then I swore I'd never speak to that mother-fucker again.

THE NEXT MONTH PEOPLE WERE BLAMING THE *DAILY COLLEGIAN* FOR starting the left-wing takeover that was in its second day of rage. In the midst of everything came news of Abbie Hoffman's suicide.

The Yippie shit was before our time, but Hoffman's death had T. James and me tripping. I was editing the FSU daily, but not enrolled in school. T. James was my right-hand man and sat at the Mac diagonally from me. Just us two toiled beneath the newsroom's cheap fluorescent lights, as everyone else was sleeping off the all-nighter that had been necessary to get full-on takeover coverage. We had no drinks on this day, the shitstorm was so fully on.

Student government was a sideshow of little consequence to *Collegiane*ers, but we had endorsed candidates. The FSU right lost races for the first time in recent years and responded by rewriting government bylaws so as to preserve its power. Lefties hit back by physically overwhelming the offices of student government. The rationale for blaming the unrest on us was that no previous regime of editors had endorsed any candidates at all. We had taken that lack of precedent as the best reason for endorsing.

"Hey, Tim," I said to T. James. "Can you write an editorial about Abbie?"

"Yeah, probably."

"Can you make it really long, because we don't have an editorial cartoon for tomorrow."

"Okay."

"Can you make it start 'Abbie Hoffman died for your sins'?"

"For sure."

"Can I one day co-opt and use ellipsis so that the dead parts are left out and you sound more developed as a writer than you really were?"

"Whatever."

T. JAMES, BURLY D. BOON/SST WANNA-BE THAT HE WAS, HUNKERED down over his keyboard for forty-five minutes. His stringy hair hung over his face so that I couldn't see his mouth twisted into a grimace. The keyboard clattered like horse hooves on plastic for ten minutes at a time. Then there was the whirred silence of the ceiling fan that preserved us in the Central Valley heat. I heard hard, single strokes, deletions, insertions, and changes that you knew not what. Big-ass sighs. His face in fingers that tried to pull out prose from his eyebrows, cheeks, and neck. Again riffs of typing that sounded as though the words were mere by-product. These keystrokes were the show.

A disc caromed into my desk basket like off the backboard and into the net.

Tim wipes off his glasses and raises his gloating chin. He shows only a sideways crack of his near-perpendicular front teeth.

"Done."

Under the headline "Death of the Last Honest Salesman," the next day's editorial read:

Abbie Hoffman died for your sins.

I like to experience pleasure, to have fun. I enjoy blowing people's minds. You know, walking up to somebody and saying, "Would you hold this dollar for me while I go in that store and steal something?" The crazier the better. . . .

There were few limits for Abbie, even fewer self-imposed. Life, as his own abstract construct, took on the dazedly whimsical feel of a round-the-clock carnival. . . .

Hoffman never allowed himself to be co-opted, an important distinction between him and the Tom Haydens and Jerry Rubins of his generation. *Co-opt* is a subjective term, in this excessively subjective era. *Sell-out* reeks of disuse, even as we say it. The polite thing to say is *compromise*, which we accept as a respectable fact of life, say, something we do when trying to close that leveraged buyout. "Respectability," in fact, has become one of the highest goals we can muster. Lawyers are respectable. Stockbrokers are respectable. . . .

Abbie Hoffman never gave a damn about being respectable. While noble ideas were being rounded up, hog-tied, and presented to consumers in living color in prime time, Hoffman went into hiding. A lot of people swore they would leave the country if faced with a continuing untenable political climate. Abbie Hoffman did.

The student takeover raged out of control for two more days. When I read these words from T. James Madison, I felt all again that night from more than a year before when I fed him the first lines of "Guitar Train." I heard the dissolve from the no-Vaseline roughness of his minor chord opening to the rail-yard rhythm of the song's major theme. I heard the vortex. And it all flooded in, the way people who'd only heard about how other people heard it wanted to give light to our creation. Intuitively, we took what was in our hearts and put together this thing that added to the hearts and minds of those in range of us. And those in range of them. Each one, teach one. We joined the mix of our world's emotions and got a glimpse of the power of change.

No lie: It was at this moment that I learned how a career in writing—the power of words, don't take it for granted—could be a life rich with music. With or without a pen, I might move the crowd. I learned that maybe I could love this game.

act 7

EMBRACE

6.

Chico, don't be discouraged

Up in Chico, they had Indians. Actual black people in little, remote Butte County—halfway between Sacramento and Mount Shasta—made for 1 percent of permanent residents. The rest was predominantly palefaces. In some parts of Chico, the local indigenous tribe seemed more prevalent than black niggas. Indians were more visible, in the papers, accused of crimes, and outside the liquor store, begging for dough. They had nigga jobs, and this fucked my head up.

I had come here with Johanna, the bad little mama I called my Cinnamon Girl. Johanna had so much flavor I forgot anything else counted. She had me dressing in Chess King sweaters and sporting a boxy, flattop 'fro. Without Johanna I might never have understood my capacity for shallowness.

We went together three years, and sex sustained us, as Johanna was tantalizingly sensuous. Ours was crapshoot lovin', all or nothing and either/or. The chick sold Mary Kay cosmetics, diligently. I insisted she watch Woody Allen movies and Johanna enjoyed only their elitism. But if we did the deed right after the tape rewound, all was forgiven by breakfast, at which point the pressure began building again. Everything there is to love about impending traffic accidents was right here, dripping. It was ill. We did hand-to-hand combat, topped it off humping. E'rybody ejaculated.

There was no setting this girl free, 'cuz Latin mommies don't let their niggas loose. Johanna's mother had to drive up from Visalia and take Cinnamon Girl home.

Which made me indebted to the Old Girl, because I was feeling this *poquito pueblo*. Downtown had a university that half the town's population was affiliated with, and late nights were wild in the streets. *Playboy* rated Chico State the country's top party school. MTV recognized it as a mecca for those who didn't wait for spring break to get loose. So carloads of kids from San Francisco and LA would park their shit downtown and just bug . . .

The fuck . . .

OUT . . .

I'm sayin': sorority chicks diped up in Depends for Thursday-night ragers, so as not to miss a minute of the alcoholic action! A cloud of intoxicants hung over the town, and even though I started off a homebody—for this context—I smoked out at Duffy's, a dark, dank Bukowskian dive, with officials from the local-government beat. Kind weed reached me via kids whose parents, too, ran the town. Contrary to what college had laid on me, this is how journalism got done.

Chico gave birth to an Ultimate Selfishness sequel, the Underwear or Watch Theory—the science behind this being that if you were ever wearing both drawers and a watch, you were moving through life overtight. It was fine to wear a timepiece, and some people really need underwear, but to sport both was to be way too wound.

Up here, a lot of us didn't need either.

I should mention that my high style was made possible because I was a contributing editor at the *Chico News & Review*, one of the original California alternative papers. Here the sixties weren't over.

After Fresno State and I agreed that I had to get the fuck off the premises, I spent the six months that came after the Gulf War in Sactown, bouncing between Mom's town house and Gaye's pad in the PJs, baby-sitting my sister's three kids and freelancing for the Sacramento altie. I was supposed to take a daily gig in Seattle, but

Boeing laid off a thousand people and that newspaper work dried up. The *News & Review* made me my best recession-era offer.

SHOWDOWN, PUSHING FIFTY, WAS BACK WHERE HE'D GONE WHEN HE first got into trouble, to the place where his mother was born.

On the way out of Santown he had a sit-down with Willie, his old rival. They drank and laughed about past squabbles; Willie stretched his legs out on a cracked coffee table. Delbert hunched forward in a chair so that his feet could be flat on the floor. He made light of how a pimp's oblique charm didn't mean shit to the new-school drug game. Crack had things open to every little kid who had access to weaponry and a sack of baking soda. Then Delbert finally let Willie in on how bullied the cat had always made him feel.

Willie rubbed his side, where scars from shot still remained, and he had just one question:

"But did you have to shoot me, Del?"

For *real?* Showdown couldn't even remember.

Looking across his life, it was hard to tell what was him, what was the *her*-on, where his nerves ended and the drug began. He wondered if he was ever really brave, or just reckless. Reckless and young, then hooked.

He had been bold before, when Hots was still alive. Back when he had that last dog named Tippie. (Delbert always named the little dogs Tippie, didn't know why.) He had the brawls that earned him the name Showdown before he'd had much stronger than beer. Blanche, that twenty-six-year-old diva of a ghostly quality, used to call him a mannish boy. She mussed his process, separating it one strand at a time. Blanche was the sort of woman who made Delbert's mother throw wads of cash into the collection plate every Sunday.

Please Lord, bring him home tonight.

Delbert dicked her down, and Blanche fixed him up, brought him to her world. *And I know you ain't gonna tell nobody, 'cuz this is gonna scare you to death.*

Going back to Carolina might make it all good, make it like before the law wanted him. Wanted him gone. Chased him away.

He had purchased the property in Anderson back in that last decade, before that first son, the one he claimed without condition, skipped town. A lot of women said they had his baby, but maybe four were his.

Back before disco, he used to get up onstage in Akron with the white boys, performing as Del Savage. They showed him the beauty of Neil Young, played the records while they got high, and they let him lead the band. The gigs were never very good, but leading the group was a hell of an experience.

Sometimes you can take more from failing in an effort to try something new than doing the same thing right time and again. This was something he couldn't say in Sandusky and expect anything but blank looks and silence as response. Shit, Neil Young has a lot of soul.

The sixties were long since over. Was he a brave man or was he just stoned?

A few years too late, that whole epoch ended for him, in Akron, walking up on the wrong dice game, being the wrong bagman. Delbert caught a .22 hollow point to the chest. It burned like hell, but didn't hurt his myth. Word carries just fine when the news is bad. He was getting older, but Delbert's legend wouldn't die.

The property wasn't quite an acre, and the house on it was about the same size as the sheltered postage stamp he dwelled in up in Ohio. But damn it was pretty down in the woods. Delbert brought down with him fifteen dogs, a miniature horse, and Pat. That's essentially how he regarded her, as high-end livestock.

All those Tippies were coon dogs. He loved 'em, but he killed some, too.

South Carolina might be geographic methadone. It wasn't as if he were looking to get high anymore. He just wanted to maintain.

———

AT CHICO, I REPLACED AN ALTERNATIVE PRESS LEGEND IN GEORGE THUR- low. Which was unusual, because I was only twenty-five and my skills were mad tartare. Bob the Editor hired me on potential, and stakes was high. I lived intensely, here in the land of weekend Mardi Gras, a scene just short of O.G. countercultural shit. A first cousin, at least.

In a new development, professional journalism didn't suck. For sure, I fought with some company people because my stories tended to make advertisers pull accounts. But to keep things bubbling between it and the Chico readership, this small-town paper let me stay on. The *News & Review* published stories under my byline about "the Malcolm X of Butte County" and local grocers who sprayed Raid on produce. My report on LSD's comeback in northern California spawned ten others, in big papers, magazines, and on TV.

This felt maybe a little kinda sorta like home.

IN CHICO, I FIRST HEARD SOMEONE TELL ME, "YOU'RE MY FAVORITE writer." It was a phone receptionist at the local AAA office, and I was like, That's great, but consider getting a library card. Writing was to me still too personal—I was still too introverted—to be anyone else's favorite anything.

Attention did have an upside. During downtown breakfast at Oy Vey Bagel, studying the facial expressions of students, profs, and downtown workers reading my *News & Review* stuff, I took the measure of every furrowed brow and exhaled at every chuckle. It was like the college daily all over, except that the blonde behind the counter thought it was, like, so awesome that I worked at the *News & Review*. You know, doing the right thing and all . . .

So, you're interested in journalism, sweetie?

Goddamn, some days it seemed they *all* were interested. I'd be guesting at a Chico State lectern, addressing the journalism students and scanning through the looks on those barely postpubescent faces. I'd nod, I'll take, um, you right there. Please step forward. Oh . . . *fuck buddies?* That's what you call it? Well, I'm with that. And on a beer-soaked Friday night, upstairs at the Mad Bear, I'd be kickin' it on the dance floor with two girls at the same time—O.P.P.-in' it with an ounce of Mendocino shake shoved down my drawers—trying to figure out which chick to get rid of. Or not.

Then, one day, as I stood behind a favorite partner, giving it to her as earnestly as she put it on me, I absently glimpsed the football game playing behind me. It was the Super Bowl. Dallas was up on Buffalo by a couple of touchdowns. I turned the volume down so that I could hear my girl's body talk better and then took a sip from the Foster's lager that sat atop the set. I slowed down for a second, perhaps to stem orgasm, and an awareness set in: This is the stuff we'll miss when carbon-based life turns to silicon, no doubt, but what does it mean? Is this as good as it gets?

That part within me that was unsatisfied sure needed to know.

MR. HOTS BEGAN GIVING THE SPEECH WHEN HIS BOY JUST STARTED GET-ting into trouble—little things, no police involved yet. He preferred giving this talk when he had a crowd around and a little liquor in him. Its gist was that the boy had to shape up or ship out. The details—always righteously accusatory—changed to fit the crime, but these lectures leaned toward ending on the same line:

"I want you to *be* somebody!"

It was this intended grace note that bugged Delbert the most.

The speech had gotten so redundant that Delbert could step to the beats in his head. Spin at the sigh of disappointment, kick on Hots' resignation ploy. Step, bend, twist.

Then, once, at the Prophets' house, when Hots got to the "be somebody" part, Delbert interjected, right on time:

"What is it that you want me to be?"

And his father was silent because he had no answer. Did Hots want his son to be like him? Obligatorily married and working three jobs at a time to live up to the people's idea of a successful colored man? It wasn't like Hots was never a boy. His own father, James, used the old standby about how he had walked off a Mecklenburg County, North Carolina, plantation with his brothers, wearing their best suits under work clothes. James Alexander would ask if he had put himself on the line so that Hots—Gospie—might just laze around. But disconnect came when Hots asked Delbert to regard the life he'd led as a worthy life standard.

The sight of his father speechless gave Delbert the opening for vengeance that grew into his reason for being.

"Go ahead, *tell* me what you want me to be."

But Mr. Hots ain't have no answer, so, without trying, he made Delbert's fire burn hotter and more out of control. He gave him money. Put a fifth of liquor in his hand if the boy was going out on the town. When his son started going to jail, the father would put the house up against a bail bond and hoped Delbert didn't skip town. His parents tried to give him the world as they knew it. Unfortunately, on the topic of what Delbert ought to be, Hots and Charlene had little applicable knowledge.

I'D LONG AGO LEARNED TO BE AMBIDEXTROUS WITH MY EXPRESSION. When I did my summer gigs at big dailies, the other nonwhite interns tripped off my ease among European-Americans. A few friends, like Fresno Lloyd, dug it, but they were exceptions. Ivy League buppie writer and brown-skinned immigrant photog alike, they thought I was hustling, and maybe they were right, to a degree. But the truth was, as I told them, if I could have white friends in Sandusky, Ohio, getting along with these Caucasians in Fresno and Boston and LA ain't no puzzle.

It was a goal of mine to make friends with one of the myriad Indians found in Chico. Just one would be fine. I didn't have any Indian friends and thought I'd have fully formed impenetrable game if I could call a Native American friend. It would all come clear.

Of course, that was foolishness. The depth of the Native American experience was beyond me. Most of the local tribe who ventured in from the reservation west of town were there for a reason. They were trying to get drunk or get paid and didn't have time for my ignorant ideas about unity.

Someday my Indian will come.

The riots in Los Angeles broke out my first April in Chico. I had a housewarming party planned with Joe, my new roommate, and I'd never in my life harbored more antiwhite feelings. It had occurred to me to make the eight-hour trek down South and help burn buildings. That never happened. I had committed to a backyard full of Chicoans— friends, I called them—fuckin' cracker-ass honkies that my heart had grown cold on. Our party's gimmick was for guests to dress in a style recalling their favorite concerts ever, so I slid a long, black wig onto my now close-cropped dome, put on tight shorts with sidelong piping— The Purple Rain Tour was in 1984—and got liquored up. Something told me that if it were at all possible to forget the existence of white people in Chico, blind drunkenness would be a prerequisite.

I chafed hard at the verdicts, sat making the screwface in Duffy's Tavern, watching TV helicopter coverage.

Before leaving Fresno State I'd concluded that my only valid expression was rebellion and thought even the closest of my friends defined me by my otherness. It was in my head that I could only be so close to white Americans, that they functioned merely as a conduit to my writing—the unacknowledged history between us formed too great a wall. Chico's relentless honkification seemed not only to confirm this notion, but also to go a step further: I wasn't feelin' niggas either: corny motherfuckers, circlin' the wagons and shit.

Until the riots. Feeling the chaotic uprising, but too far away to throw a brick or loot a store, I did what was my specialty: get tore-down drunk and write about the emotions I experienced at their most raw.

But first the party:

Joe and I had scored a two-bedroom house ($600 a month and a cat named Drexler) and used the vast backyard for our housewarming.

Of course almost none of the locals we invited bothered to follow the party's nostalgic theme. Either they sported a signifying set of earrings or combed their hair weird or maybe wore a faded concert tee. Everyone put on their drinking shoes.

I was hardly even lifted when this little green-eyed piece of sumpin' sumpin' chatted me up at the keg. This one, a crasher, didn't even bother with a lame gesture toward thematic righteousness. For this, I gave her shit. She tried to smooth things over.

"Your hair's really unusual. I mean, it's pretty."

"Yeah. I'm part Cherokee."

"It's a shame what's gone on down there in Los Angeles."

"Yeah. Right." I stiffened. Yet another guilty liberal could only harsh my buzz.

"I mean," she said, looking into her red plastic cup of Sierra Nevada, "so much coverage, and you never hear anyone talk about conditions."

Conditions. Years of listening to Public Enemy had imbued me with a Pavlovian response to the word. Praise be, 'cause I looked over and talking was this healthy, pretty thing, pretty in a hillbilly way— gussy, my mother would call it. She was a ripe creature, but she came at me without even the least bit of come-on, which counted a lot. Rare was the Caucasian honey in my life who, if she noticed me at all, didn't approach on the raw sex tip.

It didn't occur to me to think, Is she going to be one of *those?* Would I have on my hands one of those white chicks who were getting back at Daddy (or America), visiting Africa and getting mad when there turned out to be no return trip home. No, she had that glint. She gleamed with a transparency not of this earth.

I thought she was on acid.

"You stay right there," I said. "Don't move."

Amy was a photojournalist, two weeks out of the Midwest, and working at a paper in nearby Paradise. She had been set to work at a Native American publication farther east, but a college friend from Arkansas had convinced her to take this different job in northern

California. Paradise, with its conservative municipal government and surfeit of seniors, seemed a cruel joke, and Amy wanted to go home, to be in Indianapolis, with her social worker parents and beer-drinking high school pals.

If the volume is right, I can fall in love a dozen times a day. Then I fall out. Amy though had me wanting to marry her before my brew was through.

Late that night, after the party broke up, Joe and Alita—a colleague from junior college days—and Amy were in Duffy's. I was still sporting the wig. Otis Redding's version of "I've Been Loving You Too Long" poured from the jukebox. At this point, LA burning had reclaimed my mind. I ruminated quietly with my back to the wall. Amy was adjacent, leaning on me as if in a dream.

"Ooh. His sound is sooo . . . My father has all of his records."

"Yeah."

I shrugged her off. Phony displays of empathy are the enemy of life, and alcohol is a really bad drug—worse than making you clumsy and sick, it makes you dumb. And tonight this woman's expression didn't even have to prove fake.

"I bet your father's a real progressive cat."

Then I walked away.

This was my mean-ass drunk-skunk phase, and within minutes I had completely excused myself and walked the half mile home.

A nigga still wanted to get married though.

AFTER THAT NIGHT, AMY BLEW ME OFF. BUT WHEN SHE READ WHAT I WROTE on the riots for the *News & Review,* she agreed to go out with me.

I'd written:

My friend Don was on the phone from Houston the night the cops were acquitted and LA burned. We grew up together in Ohio, and nowadays we talk each other through confused times. The last occasion was when Mike Tyson was convicted of rape.

CNN's reactionary coverage could be heard on both sides of the phone line. We did nothing but vent our spleens. The suggested courses of action were rash and cruel. I'd never repeat them in print. Then the question came, the one I knew was coming, considering the context of the night. Usually, though, Don asks in an oblique way.

"So, how do you do it anyway," he wondered, "hang around all those white people?"

Always a tough question. One a lot of traveling residents of African America can't answer honestly.

White people, I explained to him, are not inherently evil, nor, for that matter, even inherently racist. They just do what they're told.

I told Don, a graphic designer whose friends include members of the Geto Boys and who doesn't follow politics in specifics, about the irony of *The Cosby Show*'s going off the air while the riots were peaking. No, we don't live in the Huxtable house anymore, but on the other hand who ever did?

Across the continent, Delbert, too, was negotiating his past and present, thinking to himself as if diagramming a manifesto:

As sure as Allah is the creator of all that is beneficent, I know one thing: If somebody shows you some kinda leeway, you milk it for all it's worth. I don't care who it is.

All these Rices, they accept Pat because she covers her head like a Muslim woman. That's what they say. But I know it's because she's from up North and because she's white.

Faith. Is it something you find or something you're born with and constantly finding a way to name? I believed, always. Believed I was a man apart, because Mama and, even Hots, they told me I was special and because life in that town always kinda seemed suspended.

Check out Cleveland sometime after you been in Santown. It will make you never want to go back. You should do it when you're still young. Even if you get lost. All that getting lost is part of me though. I don't deny that. A lot of it's the good part.

I was destined for something, and when that remarkable thing never came, I settled on infamy.

I think about things, cosmic thoughts. My will is weak though. I know this. It's why I pray.

Look at how I dress. It's been the same uniform for ten years maybe. The drab olive, the kufi. What is there to dress for? Where am I to go? I am the stillborn man. I am the Muslim suspended like a bee in honey from antiquity. Allah will provide.

We come from such a remarkable people. Do you know all it took to walk off that land up around Charlotte? Can you even get it into your mind, the risk? How many made that leap at a time like that? How many niggas could put it all on the line? I think of Pat sometimes, coming from so much advantage and throwing it all away for her urges, and I don't know whether to admire or spit on her. I've spit on her before. She is me, but ten times worse. She is decadence squared.

And we are paying every day.

It's almost ascetic, the way we live. The Spartan decor in this small, small home, the lack of conversation. There are half a dozen dogs outside. It smells canine in here and smells of smoke as well. But it's clean. Pat's a good partner. She harmonizes, finds her way around the middle, enhances, elevates, relieves. But there's air all around everything. And there's no true center to the living.

"I just don't like when people do things they say they aren't proud of and then blame it on alcohol," Amy told me the next time we met. She had to shout her comment so that it might reach me over the din of a third-rate Mudhoney knockoff pounding their instruments on the downstairs stage.

"Yeah, I hate that shit, too. I drink too much, especially for someone who doesn't even really like alcohol."

"My father's side has Indians—I don't know where exactly. I think that gives me a taste for alcohol, too. Anyway, Alita said I shouldn't mind you getting mad. She said that when you were in college, you were a radical. She called you 'Mr. Black Power.' "

I glimpsed Amy's imperfect profile as she watched over the rail, pretending to be interested in Mudhoney Lite. Just gazing blew me away.

"You want to be Mrs. Black Power?"

Amy shot me a look of complete confusion.

"Say that again. This group plays louder than they suck."

"I know. I said, 'Do you have any interest in being Mrs. Black Power?' "

She laughed.

"Do you?"

"Yeah, sure."

Then I laughed, relieved because I was gonna settle down and ask if she'd be my Sara Connor. Which would have sounded egotistical and obscure and she might have said no.

I felt like we had sealed the deal.

We finished our drinks, tripped down the stairs, then out through the advent of night to a sidewalk teeming with flannel and reeking of patchouli. In the park, across the street, I asked her to sit down on the bench. Without asking, I kissed her thin, soft lips. Amy pulled me so tight in a bear hug that I couldn't fondle the breasts that had, from the moment I saw her, competed with her eyes for my ocular attention.

That night we slept together, and we'd share a bed every night of the next month. Not having sex, just sleeping in the same space, splurging affection. And after we did finally do it, our meandering talk focused on having a child. Amy said that if she had a little boy, she would like to name him Forrest. The previous year, while crashing at my sister's, I'd been wowed by Forest Whitaker's performance in the Charlie Parker biopic *Bird*. So now I nod-nuzzled in affirmation.

We would make love for entire afternoons, coming six, seven times apiece. Sometimes we did it in the orchards out behind her house. We had burritos delivered, as leaving home would mean we'd have to stop being naked together for way too long.

Or we'd jump in Amy's white Nissan truck, reading to each other up the mountain ride past Paradise, where fresh, clear water cascades down and pools. Together on a boulder until the sun bakes her red. I want to shield this woman and absorb the rays, not only to protect her, but to insulate the love transaction.

AT THE *NEWS & REVIEW*, THERE IS MUCH FREEDOM. UNLIKE IN DAILY journalism, no one thinks I should be punished because I tend toward the marginal, and my reportage and discursive writing are treated with equal regard. The editor will retool my sentences at the drop of a dime, but almost any idea I come up with, Bob lets me take a crack at, whether it's about bungee jumping from a Feather River bridge, critiquing Disposable Heroes of Hiphoprisy, or appreciating Dolly Parton. They let me spearhead the election coverage. I send my old friends clips, and brothers can't believe how the skills have gotten. My journalist friend in San Francisco, Danyel, tells me I should come down, that I could make it.

In Butte County's funny little rural crucible, I have gone from college dropout to young writer on the rise. It feels unfathomable, like a wormhole or a wrinkle in space. Somehow it's become possible to make a legal living off the only thing I am exceptionally gifted at: consuming the stranger dimensions of popular culture and then talking about it. Now that I'm in a committed relationship, staying up late feels like work, but still, I could maybe ride this wave forever.

Chico being Chico, the writer groupies are out in full force. But I don't get down because they aren't there to me. All I can see is my purpose in print and the love of my life. Two fates, double helix intertwined. It feels as though I—bolder, tougher than I knew I could be—am finally in the game.

Some matters, though, I cannot shake. Bob the Editor asks me to hit Sacramento for a screening of *Malcolm X*, and my mind-set is so high up in the ether that I can't get past the derivative aspects of Spike Lee's work. Or maybe the issue was visiting my mother, whose health had taken a sudden, downward turn. Whatever it was, until the end of the film, when the tears come, my mind is stuck on my father, who once told me that while trying to transition out of his own Detroit Red phase, he heard Brother Shabazz speak. I can't stop thinking about Santown's Showdown Shorty and the bill of goods he's sold me.

Back in Chico, I write:

He was explaining the evils of swine. The problem with black people, he said, is that we ingest so much swine we can't think straight. His mother would not only fry up a batch of sausage in the morning, but she would also, for flavor, pour the grease from the pork into eggs and grits. I'd seen this done myself in the homes of friends and family.

That, he said, was why black kids couldn't sit still in school. All that swine was fuckin' with our systems and rendering us inattentive in the classrooms.

Now, I'd eaten a lot of pork in my life, and my high school transcripts reflect a definite trend of inattentiveness; but my favored hypothesis for the poor academic performance tends to indict my Muslim father. Mom, you see, worked from 11 P.M. to 7 A.M.—inadvertently allowing me to lead an unwholesome nightlife—because she had only one income and the night shift paid fifty cents an hour more. That fact of life gets my vote. Pork? Forget it.

You can claim Islam all you want, but if you're going to be a non-child-support-paying, absentee, chickenshit motherfucker, well, then, screw you.

Typed out on-screen, before sunrise, prior to the arrival of any of the other *News & Review* staffers, these words, their tone, surprised me. Since I wrote Delbert out, I didn't acknowledge a lot of anger toward him. His absence from my home life seemed a blessing, a fighting chance. I was twenty-six and becoming a pragmatic feminist, one who embraces the philosophy to keep his inadvertently gleaned misogyny at bay. The concept of single mothers made me angry; Delbert was just an unfortunate variable. We might have been friends. I thought about my father—never my "daddy"—in the same fashion I might Sensation or Jeff or Boo-Boo, the kids I grew up with.

Like, goddamn, whassat nigga doin' right now?

It had been nearly five years.

Nothing more comes of the reminiscence than a few moments of wonder. 'Cuz look: the fine print of my happiness license says that I don't really have to fuck with the past.

AND THEN THE BISHOP ASKS DELBERT, "COULD YOU BE DR. BILAL?"

He had just told Bishop Thomas that he'd like to be introduced as "Brother" when he addressed the African Methodist Episcopal tent revival. But the holy man had bigger plans for Delbert than such a common moniker would allow. He would be more than a brother, Thomas suggested. Delbert had a Northern accent, and the church's devotees would respond to the authority inherent to such a voice. Another layer of power would be transmitted if Delbert made use of that title he'd earned through correspondence with that—what was it called again, son?—yes, the Universal Life Church. It wasn't as though he were lying, as if he hadn't been bestowed a doctorate.

The assignment had immediacy and import and was potentially lucrative, so Delbert agreed.

Bishop Thomas had become a kind of mentor to Delbert. The two would talk theology in the rear offices of the Methodist's real estate offices in nearby Iva, and deep within the *talib* that rare feeling of admiration stirred. The bishop loaned him money, he called just to check up on Delbert's spiritual health. It was honor he felt when Thomas's luxury car ventured out to Delbert's shack on the forested edge of Anderson.

Here was a religious scholar who pulled off the marriage of religion and commerce he himself found so elusive. The AME movement had been around forever, in American black terms, and capitalized well on the race consciousness of the 1960s. (Black Jesus was the AME thing.) Now recruitment was down, as the eighties had seen a decline of young people who could be lifted to epiphany by the exhortations of a light-skinned, curly-haired minister and a tight gospel band. Still, there was ample fervor amidst the thousands who attended the tent revivals. And the congregation dropped major bank when the plate got passed. As proof, the bishop had the diverse business portfolio to go with his fifteen churches across three states.

But, yes, this younger generation was more intellectually rigorous. And diverse. They understood their options. Three streams of black spiritual consciousness are emerging in today's South, Bishop Thomas said. Soon we will have the Black Christian, the Black Muslim, and the Black Jew. What a blessing it would be to harness the power of this unbridled triad. After all, the three share the same final belief in the glory of God. Alas, it had been only marginally easier finding followers of Islam whose beliefs were malleable enough to share with the Christians than it had been to get Jews at his revivals. You, Delby, the minister said, you can be the one to forge this threefold ministerial alliance of the South. That would be a godsend.

And of course, you would be compensated for your appearances.

So Delbert was with it. He readily agreed to be called Dr. Bilal. For a former wanna-be Malcolm X with major show-off tendencies, the compromise didn't take a minute of thought.

Weeks later, Delbert shut his door behind him and stepped into the limo where he would rehearse the script he'd worked out the night before. It wasn't hard, just remembering the specific scripture he was supposed to dissect and putting just the right amount of Islam on it.

The tent revivals were *Showtime at the Apollo,* without the threat of booing. The Patricia Thomas singers did their patented set of gospel hymns, just as they had behind the late senior bishop Ward. None of the late Patricia's or her bishop brother's offspring had joined up to represent the Lord in the family fashion, so the musicians performed as though they were the end of the line.

They got the crowd ready for the bishop. Increasingly, the bishop got the crowd ready for Delbert.

And Delbert brought his best James Brown Junior show, moving the crowd with oratory verve, making sure that at the height of his show his rapidly fading Northern accent stayed intact, for it was his secret weapon. He brought just enough Muslim talk to the table, evoking Isa ibn Mayam, the Islamic name for Christ, depicting Jesus in his unique theology as Allah Jr.

Then Bishop Thomas would exhort the elevated crowd, "Isn't it wonderful that we got all of God's people here?"

And the mass of worshipers felt good about it, enriched. Here is when the plate got passed. And Bishop Thomas considered other business ventures.

And Delbert felt good. You knew that he would, now. It was a show.

The whole thing took twenty minutes, and the checks were for ten, fifteen thousand dollars. Delbert quit his factory job.

Of course, competitors quickly copied the hustle. The Georgia-side doc spit a little more bourgeie, the one upstate more Muslim. Checks dried up. The limo came less frequently, then stopped coming at all. And Dr. Bilal was left jobless, with a lot of mad local Muslims for company.

The bishop kept in touch in case Delbert ever decided to take his show on the road.

7.

european ball

HERE IS A FIFTH-DIMENSION REPOSITORY FOR ALL THE DONNY SHELL stuff you don't want to know about and has been left unexplored in the narrative thus far:

Okay now, close your eyes—you might want to meditate. Or smoke sumpin', drank sumpin', and . . . Look: There go one hundred hours of juco Shell fretting over his limitations as a typist, worried that a lack of keyboard agility will make or break his career. He'll never get hired at the Sacramento daily. Shell's really down, and . . . ahh, the worry floats away on a sea of forgotten sacrifices. . . . And, is this a case of aromatic deception or do you smell the musty newsroom of that job in the armpit of California, the one our hero took after leaving college? He's not been down that road in a long time, probably because no one's offered the requisite one *million* dollars.

Check it out, yo, Shell's listening to Prince on his Walkman, trudging in the dark down Hayes Avenue in Santown. His tears mix with the rain—right?—and he's dressed in the stained whites of a hospital porter. "Big Mama" Biechler, the kitchen-gig boss lady, tells him he's not good enough and will be fired if he can't unload the automated industrial dishwasher twice as fast. "Then it's to the Army whitcha, boy." Be glad that you are free, free to change your mind, free to go most anywhere, anytime.

Feel the presence of collegiate, anti-affirmative-action player haters alongside Grandma 'Neva's insistence that white people will never pay him for writing. Peep death's-door Granddaddy's self-satisfied smile after he tells an out-of-work Shell, "I'm proud of all my kids. You might not have turned out as well as I intended, but at least you aren't in jail." Thrill as he works the cops beat in Boston. Type sports page agate copy.

You smell that deadline?

Smaller . . . tighter . . . fading . . . distant . . . **gone.**

Well, thank the Lord Jesus for the liquidating nature of that repository device, because now we're back in the flow of our story and . . . I'm . . . I'm facing straight up into a San Francisco shower . . . and . . .

. . . and . . .

. . . *and* . . .

. . . my pants are around my ankles. Wetness rolls down my new baby dreadlocks, to my neck from the bare sides of my head and onto the hip and barren streets below. The young woman with her head in my hands is kissing me down there as though she thinks my name is Delicious Johnson. And she is not Amy. She is just a friend.

I am on the rooftop of my part-time job. I have shacked up with Amy, fled Chico, have it in mind that we can do bigger things. My fiancée has been coaxed-dragged, slave to my dream of making more the $25,000 a year (or should I say $19,000 and a shitload of coupons). Okay, relents Amy, maybe there *is* more. We have scored a pad downhill from USF, near the panhandle of Golden Gate Park, and are not poor—just broke in that middle-class bohemian way, which is to say getting by on entry-level media-job perks and the occasional loan from Indiana. We have Gaye's old microwave oven. Amy hostesses at the Houlihan's on Fisherman's Wharf and works part-time in the *Mother Jones* photo department.

I supplement the income from my popular *Bay Guardian* club column, "Scene-N-Herd," by half-assedly typing in nightlife listings. "Scene-N-Herd" gets me $100 a pop and guest-list recognition on both sides of the Bay, but doing listings bores me so much that people all over the Yey Area oughta be regularly showing up at the wrong clubs on the wrong nights. But I get into every event for free. And I get to know amazing women such as the one who is sliding her jeans down despite the wet weather.

She's a film chick. Bookish. Good schools, fluent in poststructuralism and all that mess. On the Mission District street where I first met her, she did what Cali city white women are prone to in our initial contact—she moves from shrinking back to heavy flirtation in the space of a storefront. It's fickle, feminine, fascinating. It pisses me off, but this one—let's call her Sophie—I forgive. She, too, is from the Midwest, twenty-seven, and a runner. Her face is round and pleasant, almost harmless. But she has a twinkle and heat about her that makes SF lesbians want to pass her around at parties like an *hors d'oeuvre*. She eats more pussy than *me*. And she's astride the kid, making the clapping sound with water droplets against my lap. I have my head thrown back so that the Bay Bridge is visible when I crack open my eyes. I let my contacts float. The skyline lights, glimmering like they do, make me wonder if anyone has seen San Francisco exactly like this.

Pounding in the rain.

It's not that I don't love Amy. No, I dig her more each day. In fact, the closer I get to Sophie the more I appreciate the singular wonder of the woman I want to have children with. She's my heartland, a remote secret territory, everything I ever loved about the Midwest—and a few things I hate—all of it familiar. She's not running away from her core. She's just trying to see the world.

San Francisco strikes my love as pretentious. Being wholly pretentious, I love it here. I love the battle. Amy and I have no money and our every aspiration shows twenty motherfuckers with trust funds queued up before us, trying to take their shot. Together Amy and I line up for our collective push. It may just be one more character quirk, but I feel like I'm with her even when I'm with someone else.

I feel I owe myself this indulgence. And it's not like we're married. I equivocate: If a car's tooling along—doing the limit, not speeding—and comes to a stop, there's going to have to be some braking. Stop too suddenly, and there's going to be skids. Just trying to be realistic yo.

And I'm getting fresher from the film dip, learning about things—Leni Riefenstahl and Henry Miller and Marlon Riggs, giving shape to my thoughts and refining my perspective. At breakfast, while Amy's working at Fisherman's Wharf, Sophie's luscious sapphic roommate makes us heavenly pancakes, bemused by my presence and showing skin. Here's a cooking program I would watch. We could do this on cable access. Get Brad involved. Let's put on a show.

I HATE THAT BRAD KNOWS. BUT HE'S MY DOG FROM WAY BACK. HE AND golden walking sunflower Kristen are the social center of my life with Amy, escape from our musty intellectual, social-conscious media gigs. On Wednesday nights my fiancée drives me over to the Sunset in her white truck so that we might have a suburban good time: Brad-Dog and I playing Ken Griffey Baseball on his Nintendo system, the ladies upstairs watching *Melrose Place* and *90210*. When I'm in this boho-proofed apartment, arguing the validity of the strikeout-to-power ratio assigned Manny Ramirez by the Ken Griffey cartridge makers, I'm not the "Scene-N-Herd" guy, no one wants me to listen to their demo. We narrate our play. I am Keith Olbermann and Brad's Dan Patrick, 'cuz we funnier than them. Young Sammy Cassell is the angry infant and Daughtery points are buckets scored from beyond the arc of predetermination—independent of player effort and ability—and no one in the house is certain that Michel Foucault isn't a Western Conference defenseman. We laugh, we shoot, we score.

Ain't a damn thing wrong with my life, nothing that I can see.

SOPHIE HAS MYRIAD ATTRACTIVE AND RESONATING CHARACTERISTICS. But nothing says more about her than this self-justifying thought from Henry Miller she put in my head:

> **I felt compelled, in all honesty, to take the disparate and dispersed**
> **elements of our life—the soul life, not the cultural life—and manipu-**

late them through my own personal mode, using my own shattered and dispersed ego as heartlessly and recklessly as I would the flotsam and jetsam of the surrounding and phenomenal world. I have never felt any antagonism for or anxiety over the anarchy represented by the prevailing forms of art; on the contrary, I have always welcomed the dissolving influences. In an age marked by dissolution, liquidation seems to me a virtue, nay a moral imperative. Not only have I never felt the least desire to conserve, bolster up or buttress anything, but I might say that I have always looked upon decay as being just as wonderful and rich an expression of life as growth.

No daring is fatal. Yeah me too dog.

I'm pontificating on the great pimps in journalism, and Sophie wants to know if I'm turning her out. Sophie and I have conversations like this, probably because the emotional distance central to how we gets down allows for brute honesty. We have been gifted with objectivity.

Turning you out . . . ? Let me think for a moment. . . . No, I'd have to say not. At least I don't feel like I am turning you out. It isn't conscious. And consciousness seems requisite.

She knows what's up—I showed her the piece I turned in to *Vibe* about how I love this one other white girl oh so much, the essay that the magazine's editors killed. She knows who I am. She cried, it was so real. We watch my favorite movie, *Chameleon Street,* in the jumble that is her bedroom. A film about a criminal master of disguise seems ample explanation. She knows who I am. But something is changing in the dynamic of our relationship. Our straining is bitter, almost violent, when we fuck—lights on, always—amid advance audiocassettes, postfeminist literature, and tapes of festival-circuit films that will never gain wide release. The women I pass in the hallway of the dark, Victorian apartment make light of my half-nakedness as I rush to the shower. I have to pick up Amy from the Wharf and not forget that, for all her exoticness, Sophie may only be an Ohio girl with a messy room. Amy is my love.

Casually, I tell Amy immaculate lies. Drop me off at the spot. You should go home. Because it's gonna be a late one at the Kennel Club. The Pharcyde, y'all. The future of music right now. So dope's the vibe that I'm not mad about no drink tickets. Chronic smoke hovers, and it's after midnight when an MC starts rhyming and close to two when another shouts, "Peace, out," and The Pharcyde is playing "Soul Flower" for its encore. No doubt, the joint is *slammin'*. All these rich dilettantes and the people who love them and the people who love their money are raising the roof. And Sophie the Other One is there, bouncing up and down to the hydraulic organ sample and having the hip-hop moment maybe she didn't know she needed. Bouncing and falling. There's no question what must happen when The Pharcyde walks offstage, when the DJ puts on music to exit the club to, because her crib is only three blocks away. Even as I slip backstage and penetrate The Pharcyde's postshow cipher, amazingly passing up the blunt to do this interview that will make my column hella tight, we know what must happen, because this Ohio girl is soaking wet. I'ma soak her up.

It's hardly sex. It's just dicking down. Getting off. Me. Me. Me. Shiver, no sleep. Tongue-kiss to a woman receding from consciousness. Skitter across the hall, as a roach might. Lights off, then on for seconds flat: soap to the crotch, pants turned outside-in, in the dark.

Then it's down the second-story stairway at nearly four in the muhfuckin' morning.

I run up the six blocks on Fulton, cut over to Grove at Masonic. Now realization gets set upon, a projectile in the mist that suggests dawn.

This is the most distant place. How much more out the Graham backyard could I be? Even if this were Indonesia . . . I could be standing on Pluto, but I could not get much further from Cedar Point's doorstep. I could not be less of a Jehovah's Witness. A line is getting crossed, erased, forgotten.

I WROTE FOR THE PRISON GUYS WHO RANG MY DESK, TELLING ME I WAS the man, and for the dial-up revolutionary who cryptically signed off,

"We want you to know, we're following you. Keep up the good work." And for the rappers who gave shout-outs, if only to curry favor. I was nothing to the Ivy League scribes who were slumming in The City, never would be. But, I ask, how ghetto do it be?

I was lovin' this life.

I wrote for a bedroom DJ who cornered me at the party and gushed, "It's just, I read you every week and, I dunno, I just wondered what it would be like to have a conversation with you, or something."

Stronger & faster, it was celebrity. Evidently, people out there were feeling me, a third-tier West Coast rap reviewer—and not from LA, at that. But again, the question is, how ghetto do it be?

At the California Music Conference, there was a rowdy argument with Golden State Warriors draftee Chris Webber. Billy Jam moderates a panel, and when I said rap music on the radio was getting precipitously wack, Webber, who was twenty, and maybe ten other audience members got highly upset, outraged. They did everything but boo me. Now, niggas is ig'nant, but that the former Michigan star was so naively engaged made Chris my favorite. Arguing about hip-hop went a long way with me.

Getting the time of day from the biggest rap stars was drama, so I focused on the local heroes. Oakland's Mystic Journeymen, who proudly announced that they were *Unsigned and Hella Broke;* JT Tha Bigga Figga, the majordomo straight out da Fillmoe, a teen hustler constantly cashing checks for tens of thousands, releasing from his crib albums that blew up at Mom and Pops in Houston and New Orleans. The rock bands I wrote about showed minimal aspirations. Sacramento's Cake, whom I caught playing in one of the worst clubs on Haight Street, wouldn't send me their demo. They went over to Brad's *Thrasher,* the skater mag Brad ran. Cake was worth chasing down, and when we all linked, readers thanked me for turning them onto their new favorite shit. They credited my sentences.

I was good, for sure, but the writing connected because everybody does it, putting their little pluses and minuses on the product. Siskel and Eberting. The time felt like hip-hop's very last heyday innocence, and I saw a gaping void in bold, smart nigga criticism. Let's do this, I thought, and get paid. The alternative press—hell, the entire record industry—needed me. Who else was going to give De La Soul's *Buhloone Mindstate,* the collected works of Crack Emcee—the best artist ever on the subject of rock cocaine—and, yes, even Fishbone the props they deserved? Me, DEA, the dopeness enforcement agent.

'Cuz at hand was music. Critical regulation about stylized notes in air was a rough gig, important & impossible, music being completely intangible. You had to totally lose yourself in the listening in order to add anything of significance to what the artist actually created. You had to dissolve to provide context. I'd get real high on whatever, write down what the music made me feel. Showing a private part of myself pimpishly, I'd then get straight, edit and add facts and subsequently stand facing the direction I thought the accolades might come from, ready to receive.

When *The Real World* started flirting with me, I blew them off. They couldn't do shit for me, except deny me the psychic closure of Amy's bed at the end of the day. And I wasn't having that.

I INCREASINGLY BEHAVED LIKE A GHETTO CELEBRITY, ARROGANT ON THE down-low until it got to be a lifestyle. Need a villain? Blame the *Guardian* and its famously bar-centric ethos of down-and-dirty journalism. Sometimes I'd be the only client in Jack's, examining notes or waiting to meet with an editor or a source, and the day-shift barkeep would invite me to the back room, for partying. Between complimentary drink tickets and musicians' surface-deep fawning, I stayed lifted in an ultravivid scene. Women not to be believed saying they loved me. Polite greeting kisses with tongues on the DL, the perfect counterbalance to Amyism at B&K's.

There were junkets, too, down for a Beverly Hills screening of Shaq's *Blue Chips* so as to research a piece about athletes' burgeoning multimedia presence. Junkets are part of Hollywood's marketing assembly line, but the whole deal seemed bigger than life: LA remained the mysterious center of the pop culture I'd been fascinated with since the days of Close-N-Play. To be a part of this at any level was a turn-on. I acted nonchalant on the Paramount lot. At the Four Seasons, I played cool on the elevator with Nick Nolte.

An Anna Nicole Smith–healthy brunette stood in the lobby, biting bits of lipstick off her grape-red lips as she poured over *Blue Chips* production notes. An idea came into my head, with childlike innocence: I know, tonight, I'll have sex with her.

I made this happen with ease and simplicity and never even bothered to learn her name. But said it back to her as I uncluttered her press kit, standing beneath the awning. She'd flown in from Orlando, and before the bus to Paramount parted, she patted the seat, empty next to them Florida thighs. As the bus turned onto Melrose, I said, hey, I know, we could have a drink in my room. Maybe Miramax will pay. Back up on my floor it was. Oh, let's see what's on TV. There's Spectravision, guess we don't want that.

I copped a Woody Allen line to get my tongue in her mouth, her bra on the floor. Brainside, I organized the article I would turn in up North. The lead was written long before anyone came, and the girl didn't care, as long as I scored another condom so that I could do her again. The next day at LAX, I kissed—god, what is it again, Elizabeth?—good-bye and walked through a tube and onto the plane. Forty-five minutes later I walked off the plane and through a tube and kissed Amy, the woman I loved.

SOPHIE WAS DEFINITELY CHANGING. WE TALKED SO WELL ABOUT CULTURE and art, I was satisfied not to screw. She started *taking* it. That wet scene on the roof started off as a discussion of *Triumph of the Will*. I was coming down with the flu and up there discovered you can come and seethe in a single, collapsing pout.

There would be no stress between me and Sophie were I not living with Amy. If I were smarter, I would have recognized the growing tension as a sign that trying to have it all is perilous work, for everyone. I didn't though, being young, dumb, and full of, you know.

Then, en route to a lunch, she made me erect as I shifted gears in the truck. I pulled into a parking lot and yanked her jeans until they hung off an ankle. Sometimes, in the whole of San Francisco, the sun only shines in the Mission, and the solitary streams screamed "enough" as I came bareback, pulling out in dubious fashion.

Did she know—did she really know—how much I wanted to hit her, just to smash her face against the passenger window glass she lay breathing hard against? Did she know I felt indentured and confused? Of course not. Neither of us recognized that what bound me—and her, by extension—lacked a Bay Area address. It went back further even than our Ohio roots.

AN ENDING, THAT'S WHAT I NEEDED. THE DAMN THING HAD FALLEN APART. This other woman could no longer stand to hear my heart's real name. Any mention of Amy elicited bitter observation, but as soon as we got our money right, Amy and I were going to get married. Our families, who each loved the new unofficial addition, were excited for that. They were waiting for that.

I ducked Sophie for a month, then, one night, called her from the phone next to Brad's Mac. He had loaned me his keys. The familiarity emboldened me. In my mind I'd gone to Sacramento.

I dialed intent on keeping the talk short. Amy was getting off from Houlihan's.

Sophie picked up; I started a prepared speech:

"You probably wonder why I've been so distant. I can't do this anymore. You should know that I've been fucking around. There was a girl in LA . . . And Amy, you know, she's the one . . . ."

"Donnell, I'm pregnant."

"—"

It's a late-twentieth-century phone call that must be made hundreds of times a day. Twenty-five times alone in the fuckfest known as San Francisco bohemian culture. The news found me however without the MacGyver-quick fix-it strategy with which I had sent Linda Faye Hinton into the back pages of my history. It fucked me up. I got monosyllabic, promised to split the abortion cost, and hung up quickly.

I rolled around the corner to my man Lloyd's apartment, where he dispensed that old saw about opportunity and crisis having shacked up. Lloyd let me hit the chronic, then I split for Houlihan's.

I couldn't look at Amy on our ride home from the Wharf. But I could avoid her until Saturday since her mother and little brother were driving in. Blame it on work so Matt and Marie can't miss me. This crisis showed no hint of opportunity.

AMY WILL HAVE TO KNOW, NO QUESTION. FAM WAS LOOKING FOR A MAR-
riage date, and even I couldn't let a pregnancy pass, g-celeb or not. I would tell her, just as soon as the Osburn fam pulled away for Indianapolis.

Perversely, not looking at Amy became impossible. *Mon amie.*

I didn't even have a checking account when I met her. Through that week my heart had fallen free, especially when I caught her and Marie chatting easily up in the front seat at intersections, stopping traffic, exchanging love. I hadn't experienced so much of that and had hardly witnessed it among other adult children and their parents. The family we planned was supposed to have this. *If it's a boy, he'll be Forrest.*

I watched her in the wide, scented aisles of Andronico's vegetable section, shopping for her mother and brother's so-long dinner.

Didn't even eat vegetables before her.

Amy did a pirouette at the Sunset basil bin, a spin especially for me. She tossed the bunch into our cart like a scoop shot, then kissed me on the lips, as though we were alone among the crowd.

We'd had spats about Amy's inability to navigate among fellow grocery hunters in The City's narrow food shops. "You have to be aware of your surroundings," I'd say. Now her obliviousness turned into another glowing hippie chick wonder.

I would take away things that I could never give back. When I met Amy, she had deep furrows of worry etched upon her brow even as she smiled. Within a week of our love—we seriously called it that, Our Love—they were gone. We were naming babies, making plans. How would life differ with what I was about to extinguish?

Another scoop of cauliflower, one more pirouette.

"Why do you look so . . . grave?" Amy asked while I zoned.

"It's a story," I alibied. "I'm all caught up in my story."

Early Friday afternoon, Brad and Kristen let me cry in their living room. I bawled through *SportsCenter* and lamented over Nintendo's Ken Griffey. Shame felt like a stage though, albeit protracted. I'd pass through without acknowledging the environs.

SATURDAY MORNING, NEAR SUNRISE, WHEELS UNDER THE CAR CONTAIN-ing Amy's mother and brother went into motion, pulling them away from the curb at the corner of Grove and Clayton. I wheeled on my victim as she waved on and on, Mayberry style. I needed one last look at her this way.

Sit down, there on the couch, I told her after we'd closed the door on the lobby. I had to pee, or something. My hands shook. Withdrawal. I jerked up the toilet seat and when I went to take my dick out, there was hardly anything there. My weiner had become a baby mushroom cap I was so scared.

I could *not* tell her. But no daring is fatal.

I was so not a pimp. It would have paid to be a pimp.

Face-to-face now. Fortified and fearful in a dark little living room, I let the whole story, all the extra fornication, come tumbling out. I again lead with the Orlando woman, as though revealing a volume of fucking might make the fact that I'd gotten another woman pregnant seem tacked on. Was Amy buying it? She watched blankly as I said I was doing it with Sophie.

And I said, "I swear I was trying to end it, but everything came unraveled. I lost control and now everything's all fucked—"

Amy opened her mouth before her expression changed.

"What are you saying to me!" she screamed. "What are you saying to me!"

And her face was no longer blank. It was in midcrumble, like a sand castle built too close to the shore. Walls washed away. And she exclaimed again and again, "What are you saying to me?"

There were tears, but more pronounced was this surprised ferocity, like that of someone ignorant of betrayal. I never knew her to scream so hard.

Her voice had razors when she told me it was either Sophie or her—forever. Pregnancy or not.

"YOU CALL HER. YOU CALL HER NOW."

The closest thing to leniency she gave was the opportunity to dial in private. I took the phone back to the bathroom and punched up numbers I knew by heart. I was about to destroy another woman. So I made a mental note:

Don't ever say no shit like that again. I told on my fucking for them bullshit ideals. Where them niggas now, while I'm tearing this chick apart, all offhand? How was my self, or anyone, served by this admission? Ultimate selfishness won't function so half-assed.

I thought, if Sophie didn't love me, I could do this.

Surprise. The conversation was a relative walk-through. Compared to Amy, Sophie was clinical. The sorrow I slobbed into the receiver while astride the toilet was merely part of the deal, the deal that the phone call with this woman would be my last. With Amy who-knows-how-close to the door's other side, we negotiated terms—I'd skip the abortion, but pay—and hung up.

Three-for-three and all at once, I anesthetized some hearts. It brought back that Orange County nigga in Thelonius Monster:

Ain't it funny how
history repeats itself?

She said she never knew
love could be so painful

There wasn't a story in my life aside from the one told in absentia, the one that hurt like history.

YOU SHOULD SEE SOME OF AMY'S TRANSPARENCY; BECAUSE HER FACE IS a constant platform for emotion pictures:

Those wrinkles, once dug in like a shar-pei's mug, remain unknotted. She danced, they turned to tracers. Now pain pours out, unmolested, from the face. The corners of her mouth drip downward, stubborn as stalagmites. Now, outside the Haight Street post office, across the Panhandle, she's an anguished pedestrian homeless men ask what's wrong. And Amy thanks them for asking but offers up nothing more than a sandwich.

Some nights I hear Amy crying—her back against me, legs entwined with mine—and turn up the volume on my snoring.

Back in grammar school, she had won an award for having the Most Christian Attitude. Amy's Hoosier Catholicism now plays out as fatalism. She admires my ability to forgive, but can't make the leap herself. Yet, when the answering machine by our bed plays Tommy from the *Guardian,* saying that Kurt Cobain has shot himself in the head, she sees my shoulders slump and rushes over in consolation. It's not quite forgiveness that brings Amy to me. It's not even me for whom she's there. It's Our Love, this admirable thing that's brought completion we hadn't known we needed.

Then there are no bedtime tears. New smiles from Amy filter through like daybreak in the Sunset, miraculous and true. And it seems that maybe gravity might be defied.

There is the couples counselor that I'm not at all interested in seeing because, let's face it, Donnell Alexander must work. I'm on deadline for a story that might get me hired at the *Guardian* for real. The fight between love and work is a first-round TKO.

Amy asks, "What's more important, your work or trying to make this better?"

"Right now I'd have to say—far and away—this story. Our crap will eventually get better."

She's a slow learner.

GARY, THAT FIRST BOYFRIEND FROM SEYMOUR, WAS STILL IN THE PIC-ture when I met Amy. She still believed in John Mellencamp songs. This was not something I had wanted to take away, but eventually I'd kill it. What Amy had gotten into by committing to me would take her years to fathom.

But I'm into optimism, that selfish thing that means you keep looking around the corner for an upside. Because of the Our Love thing with Amy, I finally understood the deep and multifaceted disparity between the ways common black and white people in America go about their lives. Running with a white girl was affecting my life at least as much as leaving the Midwest, in that it provided dope, intangible benefits beyond even the disarming knowledge of Caucasian frailty. I had middle-class white folks in the family. Furniture, clothing, vacations, and loans came my way simply because Amy's parents were not the least bit ghetto. Conversely, there was almost no chance that any of my in-laws would want to bond over, say, an 8 Ball and a session at OTB.

Amy threw an absolutely live twenty-eighth birthday party that summer. The whole of SF was in the house at the Panhandle, my friends with her friends and everybody glad they came. Kristen and Brad and the Crack Emcee, among the motley crew.

Objectivity had given me a bird's-eye view.

I finally knew what to write about, and it sure as shootin' wasn't so-called African Americans, that upwardly mobile class that had tried to write me off with long-lost Gaye. In their rush to mainstream embrace, these people let their predictable elitism be known. It hardly seemed we needed each other.

Why the fuck should I bring light to them when Fresno State was s'poseda be Harvard. No, my ongoing topic would be (drumroll please): Niggas!

If this calling had a name, that name would be hip-hop journalism. Musical Journalism About Contemporary Niggas. The first sample of it to put me on the national map documented the ongoing feud between rappers and the less rowdy writers who covered them. It wasn't Baldwin, but it rocked. Back East, weeks after the piece ran in the *Bay Guardian,* gangsters posing as MCs ran off *The Source* magazine's founding editors and transformed the seminal magazine into the media monopoly's prime vessel for denuding rap music. In Hollywood rap represented a blood-soaked replacement for its waning Schwarzenegger franchise. The last issue of *The Source* before the crossover—the one with Redman's first cover—referenced my *Guardian* piece to show how real it had gotten between rappers and my print fam. Dying happy now seemed a viable option. This was something for the time capsules, classic nigga shit. Matthew 5:37–type shit.

My hip-hop journalism was shot through with grace, and all, apparently, I'd ever be good at: creative nonfiction. KRS-ONE once described hip-hop as revenge on behalf of the black single mother, the ultimate unsung heroine of American history. How could I not be with that program, however ephemerally expressed? I sensed that a degree of the culture—something more pop than graffiti and looser than most reportage—could be brought to writing.

Besides, I was slicker than everyone else, anyway.

The beauty of these San Francisco days is that a bunch of other people were believing this.

SEVEN MONTHS INTO MY BECOMING A *GUARDIAN* REPORTER, *LA WEEKLY* called. The largest of U.S. alternatives, the *Weekly* had just lost Steve Erickson, Ruben Martinez, Michael Ventura, and most of the best stable of journalists ever assembled at a publication of its kind. Then a chain bought the paper. O.J. Simpson's case was about to go to trial, race was the story of the moment, and they needed a "street" secret weapon.

I worshiped the *Weekly*, but I thought LA was superficial. And I did need dough.

When word got out that I was splitting, my *Guardian* editors, ordinarily concerned with energy issues and New York noise bands, began treating me differently, like I counted, as if they'd always thought of me as more than a grunt.

"It's like when someone checks out your girl," Ron, my editor, told me late one night. He pulled another Pabst Blue Ribbon from under his desk and tossed it across the newsroom. I snatched the can from the air, popped the top, and drank it, warm. "And you think, 'Yeah, maybe she's not so bad after all.' It's like that." Always with the girls.

I was so out of there.

As Amy and I drove our loosely packed mini Ryder van down Highway 101 to our new Hollywood apartment, there remained hovering above the gearshift a big hunk of unresolved feeling, static not coming from the speakers. It faded in and out.

Just northeast of San Luis Obispo, a sports talk station quieted the dissonance: the Golden State Warriors had traded Chris Webber after a dispute between him and his coach.

At my *Weekly* office cubicle, I placed a magazine tear-out of Webber in his Michigan uniform, dunking, above my computer—next to Guru and Premier. Touchstones, heroes, talismen all.

8.

fountain and fairfax

TWO A.M. MY MAN P-FRANK AND I ROLLED THROUGH THE HOT, SHINY black streets of Hollywood, returning from Unity, a downtown club where Catastrophe from the Liks celebrated his birthday by moving the crowd, charging his mic with lyrics made up to the beat and on the spot. Tash freestyled like it was nothing, did a joint he introduced as the first single from his upcoming solo album, but never said the rhyme I'd waited all night to hear:

I rock loaded, I never get promoted
But through the bullshit my crew stays devoted

The way Tash rocked this one, you could hear East Columbus in his rhyme. I needed Ohio in my ears these days and was mad and said this to Playa Frank:

"Niggas be tryin' to freestyle *waaay* too much."

Frank called bullshit, then spit game about coming off the top of the head. I soaked it up.

Long before these languid August hours, before my first byline, I had my first rap rhyme. It went back to those primary Sacramento afternoons, bangin' on Sherry's table with Marlon. I was Donny D. I was on the mic. And I was droppin' all those styles I know that you like. I was rappin' big. (Ugh!) And rappin' em small. (Whut!) So that there ain't no way you could stand on the wall.

But I hadn't much freestyled. A rapper in The City called M.I.C. passed me a bunch of secrets on how to improvise endless rhymes. He and Cory and Tommy taught me how to work one rhyme ahead, developing lines two, three ahead of the one in my mouth.

But Frank had a new twist: when you were developing cadence, it didn't matter if what you said made sense. The sounds didn't even have to be words. Staying in your head—in the world beyond worlds, between thought and expression—you could brew verses in this fashion. Let them be and at least you had a chance at transcending the static. Invent, yes. Admit though that next up in the mix comes the fix. Here was a revelation as important as understanding the will to prepare to win.

That seemed deep to me. Like not being able to win unless you got into the game.

You could fix things in the mix. *Genius.*

When Frank dropped me off at Fountain and Alta Vista, I was bustin' my new rhyme style all through our apartment building's sylvan and turret entrance.

What I am is nuttin' like the average bastids be
Dadadda duhda dada religious ecstasy.
No standin' next to me
I'm bout to flex ya see
Daduhdada test the clout
Sumpin'
A route you know
I'm all about the destiny

Yeeaahhh! I was feelin' that. Damn. Opened the door. Started bangin' across the table, on the NordicTrack cushion. *Only suckas test the clout,* I rhyme for Kennichoa, our pet German shephard, *without a doubt.* Amy stumbles out and asks what the hell I'm doing making all that racket. Never mind, I tell her. Go to bed. See you in a minute.

There was two hours to sleep, as my man Heavy D was gonna be on our doorstep at five-thirty. D came with an extra ticket to the PGA championship at Riviera, O.J.'s country club.

On the Westside drive we talked about Jerry Garcia, who had died yesterday. Amy and I were flying to SF for the guitar player's memorial. Deadhead Dave talked about community, I mostly listened. The Dead struck me as a mirage, but the spell he cast over Dave and Amy and five million others made Jerry's legend undeniable.

I had never seen pro golf before. The tour's biggest stars—Colin Montgomerie, Greg Norman—were here, and the line into Riviera was a formal study of rich and Caucasian southern California. Security, conspicuous in their vinyl jackets with SECURITY stamped across them, could just have easily worn BURLY BLACK GUY icons. I was the only other one. They seemed the exact same cats who had harassed kids at Unity six hours earlier, only here they were docile and called everyone sir and ma'am. Buncha punk motherfuckers.

Punk muhfuckas, cannot stand 'em wanna burn 'em like toast
Duhda Duhda da da wet 'em
Turn around and get ghost

Dave and I approached the second tee. Almost everyone at this private affair had a drink in hand. It was seven fucking thirty, A.M. I grabbed a brew but was appalled. If I ever caught myself getting buzzed so far in front of noon, the *Daily Collegian* Internal Alarm System would have sounded and I'd have myself checked out. But this was golf, and no one seemed the least bit fazed at the libations. It seemed a key component in holding the crowd's attention, especially as the sun got hot and the day wore on. I saw this one Republican drink five gin and juices before 10. And wasn't *nobody* trippin'.

There's much subtlety to golf, like ballet with a gambling element thrown in. I was feeling it. *My deep desire is just to wet 'em.* Watching Ernie Els putt amid a singularly gentrified silence—*In my mind I fuckin' wet 'em*—I had the sense that here lay a refined aspect of sports culture that I had totally missed out on, that 95 percent of the population was missing out on. And the sense was that everyone here liked it that way.

I totally wanted in.

Regardless, D and I had to cut out early so that I could make my flight to San Francisco. Amy was waiting at the door with bags packed. I slept in the car. I slept on the plane. I've edited out the third person in our party. We crashed on Fell Street, at our friend Jennie's crib, but Bev, deep partner down from Chico for the memorial, had ventured out to Golden Gate Park, so I joined her crew just before midnight.

EASILY TEN THOUSAND PEOPLE HAD GATHERED AT THE POLO FIELDS. THE cops called hands-off on weed arrests and California love ruled. Girls doffed their tops and danced, some threw off their dresses and cared not that they wore no bottoms, spinning around and around. Cats cried openly, others banged percussion. Jerry did this. He summoned the drums, he and his drug music.

Amy and I slept together under the stars. When we woke up, five times as many people were there, taking communion, first to the tunes of a New Orleans funeral-style jazz procession, with horse-drawn carriages and swinging jazz bands and a tab of acid helping Bev transform into a cipher for all the pain and love being released.

Wavy Gravy took the stage, and Jerry Garcia's daughter thanked everyone for paying her college tuition.

Then jets strafed the Polo Fields.

Everyone's heads—those of the naked girls, the acidheads, the jazzmen, Bob Weir and Wavy Gravy—craned upward for a gander, and a thousand carnations swirled through the sky, making the planes silhouette gray. All around me, mourners were gently jostling for mementos. I looked at Amy and she was spinning, eyes closed, tie-dye a blur. My love held her hands outstretched, and a carnation landed in her grasp. She drew my attention, then smiled her most naughty and childlike grin. She knew.

At that moment, our son, Forrest Belle, left the abstract life we shared, taking human form.

For company, he brought along my father.

AND ISN'T IT FUNNY HOW COMPULSIVELY KEEPING TRACK OF YOUR LIFE can strain your credibility? The pink line showed up on the home pregnancy test the day the O.J. jury handed in its verdict.

My wife shocked me around this time. She and I were so cool, forgiving, due to the novelty of nice bank accounts and LA's nouvelle cuisine; amped that Our Love offered the prospect of human proof. Still, Amy fucked my head up as only someone way in love with you can.

She told me that it had taken roughly two years to confront her own racism, and she wasn't sure all the work was done. All her life there had been black people around, but she still found herself grappling with moments of chauvinism and bias. The more Amy was in my world, the more she understood the lack of simple fixes.

I was like, Wow. Amy always seemed the exception, the magically nonracist Caucasian American, that product of progressive, social-worker parents and friendship with classy Indiana Negroes. As much as her emerald eyes, feather-pillow voice, and earnest plans to start a Butte County chapter of NORML, Amy got me sprung on her ease with Gaye's kids and visceral understanding of Flavor Flav. I gave her a pass on all matters of race. Not once had I accused Amy.

The coming baby meant adding another level of commitment to our mutually cast-together lot, so Amy made her feelings known.

She told me easy, as if we were talking Flavor.

THAT SUMMER, JUST SOUTH OF COMPTON, A TEARFUL BLACK COP HAD told me that everything Mark Fuhrman said—the planting of evidence, the beatings—was commonplace. He had sometimes watched these things. It cemented in my mind the insidiousness of white supremacy.

The way certain Angelenos watched us as we walked down, say, the

Santa Monica Promenade changed as Amy's belly swelled. Black women now tended to smile on our union with new grace; white men affirmed Our Love with a nod, effortlessly adhering to stereotype. They maybe thought they had our number when they just had our area code.

So I wrote about race—about black and white, but for brown and yellow, too—sometimes snarling, sometimes with eyes wide. To do this, it seemed, was to write about humanity, to acknowledge how the citizenry surprises and how we see exactly what we want to.

Mine was a privileged point of view, enabled by proximity to whiteness and indifference to mainstream membership invites, and I wanted to put it out there for folks to handle as they might. When it flowed most freely, my perspective had a hip-hop flavor to it. I said "nigga" and that I didn't give a fuck, even when not literally using those words to connote.

MY TOP EDITORS WANTED CRIME STORIES FROM ME—WASN'T THAT WHAT hip-hop was about?—and if I couldn't come with that, pieces that posited niggas as pure victims would suffice. The *Weekly* was supposedly embracing diversity, but I was the only one who had to be diverse. The editorial mavens only deigned to see their favorite agendas in the vastness of my black mess: sexism, crime, poverty, whatever—when also all up in there were jokes and camaraderie, spirituality and innovation.

Stress at work turns to stress at home. There's a chasm of experience inherent to the American racial dichotomy that made my spouse wonder, even after years in the mix, how deep she was prepared to go. She had long ago leapt but wasn't close to landing.

What my bosses received well was writing about race that fell into the category my colleague Ernest Hardy named Water-Is-Wet Journalism. Water-Is-Wet material got praise and good placement within my host newsprint providers when it succeeded, foremost, at edifying white people. And I could dig that; that was they hustle. But when exploring racial issues relevant to LA's nonwhite majority (or some breathing subset thereof), I had to burn a ridiculous amount of space and energy explaining facts that were basic if you weren't white and/or middle class. In writing about the current lives of the 1965 graduates of Jordan High School in Watts, I first had to explain that Watts wasn't always a terrible place to live. Niggas knew that shit. Water is wet. And my flow suffered.

So, I thought about my next generation and stopped writing, except to engage aesthetic issues in rap music. DJs, mostly. No front page, like when O.J. was the lick.

I listened to twenty-five albums a week and stopped smoking pot. I dropped thirty pounds. I completely disengaged from the building on Sunset, holed up in nightclubs and the home office, and wondered what it meant that I was an outsider in even alternative culture.

The answer wasn't simple. The alternative press began seeming like another kind of ghetto, a clubby place where forward ideas get cordoned off. Like environmentalism, the basic idea that the natural world ought to be protected from its present episode of human infestation. Most people aren't ready for this notion, rural folk included, so environmentalism remains marginalized, put in a kind of public ghetto. The same goes for the labor, sex, and feminist talk that publications like the *Weekly* specialized in. To reward fresh reporting and thought with marginality seemed self-indulgent, almost suicidal. Shit, once you christen yourself alternative, you're married to being unpopular.

I had not even trace amounts of interest in being unpopular.

My kid needed to go to a Top Ten school, so this was no time for an identity crisis. The more my life improved upon the Santown days, the more those little ways it didn't worked to fuck my head up. The emerging crisis of my writing life crashed into prospects for family, into the life of this baby we would join.

I flew my mother down, had her talk to a tape recorder. What had only obliquely been acknowledged in the past I would suss out, rewind, and apply, all in the interest of not duplicating past pain and folly.

I had her outline briefly the Delbert in me.

9.

make my mama proud

IN MY LOS ANGELES INCARNATION I WOULD REGULARLY SPORT A T-SHIRT that insisted *Newt hates me*. Wore it at my wedding rehearsal, wore it on the job. My whole world was about how I felt abandoned in ways that could not be romanticized. There wasn't a white liberal alive who could make this better. For what I thought would be forever, my abandonment issues had been obscured by the nurturing dished out at First Street.

BRENDA GRAHAM CAN HARDLY STAND TO READ MY WRITING. TOO RAW, she calls it. I bet, I say, and yet I wrote myself into existence. My relationship with her was the first casualty in the battle to escape my birthright.

Of all the gifts my mother provided and that I blew off without a thought, the Jehovah's Witness upbringing ranks number one. This book might be called *Jay-Dub fo' Life* because, beyond the obvious attributes of a faith that requires more critical reading than some college-level coursework, the boldness born of door-to-door proselytizing, and an ongoing pass on the Pledge of Allegiance, rests an accidental bonus: comfort in renunciation.

Witnesses believe that only 144,000 ever go to heaven. The rest of the faithful get eternal life on an earthly paradise. Nonbelievers receive a second chance. Live out the span of a human life in a world without sin or temptation, and—ideology sez!—you, too, win perfect life forever. The only ones punished are little tongue-in-cheek mockers like me, the apostate. We are sentenced to sleep until the end of time. Since I don't sleep—and do in fact believe that sleep is the cousin of death—this assertion not only failed to scare me, it made me off the hook. An eternity of sleep is worth looking forward to.

I truly don't know where I'd be without the great myths underpinning *Watchtower* and *Awake* magazines.

Ma mandated that we grow up and follow our hearts, but the joke on her was that if we were to seek our freedom, we would have to leave her lonely, spirtually stranded.

My Old Girl always lived on a small patch of land, be she in West Virginia, the North Coast, or Sacramento.

SEE, I DON'T LIKE CHITLINS OR DOMINOES OR OL' TIME RELIGION. DON'T catch much TV either. My favorite show has a mutating plot that's hard to follow, and I'm the only star. And as much as I crave football and music and being embraced by plush women, I also need to talk about world politics and see foreign films and eat crème brûlée. Them shits weren't crackin' in the familiar, not when I was coming up. It was that impoverishment, even before the economic kind, that made me venture out the hood, in search of. Whenever I go home, I find that people are rarely taking in challenging art or eating properly. Instead, they're consuming bad TV (or downing BK specials).

Call me a sellout, but I ain't really fuckin' with Kool-Aid no more (unless you put some mild hallucinogen in it) (in which case I'd actually prefer a nice guava nectar, if that's not a problem). Mom couldn't have known she was engineering my exit.

In my twenties it was gut-wrenching, trying not to deal with other people's measure of what I was supposed to be consuming, supposed to be being. It took a minute to get to the good stuff. Truth is, the battle's ongoing. As a paid creative person, I have long bouts of incoherence and flat-out sucking, and the majority of funding sources I get down with take my variable humanity as an opportunity to pile on. That's alright though, 'cuz sometimes I see the occasions of my getting dissed and manipulated as—by virtue of being merely occasional—validation of my trip's overall success.

MOM'S HEART HAD BEEN FAILING FOR ABOUT TEN YEARS WHEN I PUT HER in front of that tape recorder. There was no guarantee I'd have another chance to learn about a legacy I'd in large part run from, but that, more accurately, the Old Girl kept hidden.

We did it at the kitchen table, and with my wife puttering about the edges of this conversation, our West Hollywood apartment grew brighter with each uncovered truth. The Graham family had taken great pains to keep me and Gaye from knowing that was I at the wedding, that Delbert used to pimp them 'hos. I felt disoriented, and, at once, more rooted. The wrong conclusion's an easy leap. Now my mother, unburdened by the successful life she understood her son to have, let revelations unspool so that her girly innocence melded easily into teenage motherhood. And my father's insinuating confidence games mirrored my own hustle of a career. Trip: We both regarded straight jobs and authority figures with an aversion like reverse magnetism. I used writing gigs like condoms.

Delbert's creepy ability to persuade a woman to put his interests over her own resonated in my own live-wired sex life. Within the first hour of three talk tapes, I was certain my appetite to get high was hereditary.

By the time the third cassette clicked through, I understood the matriarchal strategy of sealing out dissonance in my family history.

Ma's take on my birthright: it would sting everyone less if she never talked about it. *Psyche*. Sandusky's a small town, so I'd heard two hundred times about how my journalist cousin Mike Alexander had won a Pulitzer Prize in New York. Knowing next to nothing of my father only led to hopeless hoping that cousin writer cat would respond to the phone calls and letters I laid on him in the Chico days.

I was Showdown's son. Did a nigga like him toss my letters at the sight of the surname on the envelope's return address?

AMY AND I PREPARED TO GIVE FORREST THE MIDDLE NAME BELLE, AFTER Albert, the irascible home run king. This idea arose after an especially powerful session at Yoga West, as Guru Singh pounded the gong. Any son of ours would need to know his inner Albert Belle. Amy's nickname is Peace Frog, and my docile tendencies combined with hers to suggest the advent of another Brenda Graham. Who could have that, would wish that, upon their firstborn? Albert Belle was an unrepentant hard case who used the intensity of his hostility to put up Hall of Fame numbers. Forrest would need such a counterbalance, a constant reminder. He would have to go against the grain.

I was reading the Cleveland Indians box score, having just nodded in affirmation of Belle's hitting one of the fifty homers he'd smack that season, when Amy approached to say her water had broken. The slugger added another shot the day Forrest entered the world and bonked one more when my boy came home from the hospital. This was the stuff of Donny Shell's dreams. Forrest and I were walking, bopping, listening in the living room while the child's mother slept, with the graceful thump of Blackalicious's "Swan Lake" banging in place of the TV broadcast noise. And before Forrest's unfocused infant eyes, the Tribe's slugger hammered that third home run, completing a memorable tear that helped build one of the half dozen greatest hitting seasons of the twentieth century.

I DIGRESS, AS I OFTEN DO WHEN IT COMES TO MY MOTHER, BECAUSE THE meek shall inherit the earth, but nobody wants to hear about how their progeny often refuse the gift.

There's a different kind of abandonment story here. I've been mad at the idea of God since I was little; it never made sense to me that Mom's life had to be so hard. We separated for real when I was eighteen, and it was harder than I let on—maybe I'll get over all of that. When she finally leaves me for good—it seems she's been leaving me forever: to go to work, to get some sleep, ceding her girlish desires. The extended exit left me having beef with Jehovah Fucking God, even though I split on him first.

10.

the delbert in me

TWO WEEKS AFTER FORREST WAS BORN, ON THE FIRST FATHER'S DAY I ever paid attention to, Amy bought me a used turntable for $15. It was my son's first trip outside the home. We bought a cheap Gibson knock-off the next month, on my birthday, from Guitar Center. The bloodred axe went well with the new blond streaks in my nearly shoulder-length locks. Well, that's the mirror's story, and I'm sticking to it.

And I was now telling the *Weekly* to go fuck itself in new and imaginative ways. Marketplace competition had arrived in the form of a rival newsweekly—this one right-leaning—and the two companies battled for the middle. At stake were the suburban readers of the San Fernando Valley, LA basin expats and their daughters and sons. The old war, between *LA Magazine*'s Brentwood rich chick breast augmentation advertising and the *Weekly*'s Hollywood stripper-directed breast augmentation advertising, instantly paled. Whoa, these were different times. I couldn't buy a cover story. I had a beef with Tom, the new arts editor, a parasitic hustler done up in leftish journalism clothes, the sort who glommed on to progressive causes for pussy, money, and an easy way out. ("You write like a dream," Tom told me, "and like a dream, you need editing." No one who's real would say some shit like that.)

Then Tom deaded a piece in which I dissected by ear the eagerly anticipated second album by The Pharcyde. My friend Sara had passed me an advance cassette that was one of the most brilliant albums of the decade, but the final CD featured all sorts of rote pop-rap jigaboo gestures—clearly mandated by the group's clownish product managers.

I wrote about the truth in the chasm between what the group recorded and what went out to the public. Tom asked for a more traditional investigative approach—interviews, tangible documentation—which was, of course, completely untenable, as keepin'-it-real rappers always go down with the ship.

My article never ran, and The Pharcyde broke up right after the album tanked. Between me and the paper, it was all over but the shouting. A Donnell Alexander sighting in the Weekly, either its pages or its offices, entered the realm called spectacle. I still collected my 40K and benefits though.

VAGINAL DAVIS, THE FABULOUSLY OUTRAGEOUS ARTIST WHO FILLED IN for Ron Athey one day a week as editorial secretary, observed me walking through the newsroom—not doing anything tangibly egregious; just sauntering through the newsroom in camouflage baggies, garden-variety loaded at two in the afternoon—and said, in her inimitable buttery baritone:

"Ooooh, Donnell, you are gonna get it!"

It was like my attitude had become something people could smell.

I said, "No, Vag, that's just the point. I'm not ever going to get in trouble. Never nevah nevah nevah. Evah."

I felt bulletproof.

The Weekly killed my opus on the secret history of Los Angeles DJs. I responded with an article on porn king Ed Powers that I insisted could only run if it functioned as a piece of pornography, explicit and nonjudgmental in its narration, even though the editor in chief was a reserved Quaker and best friend of Susan Faludi. Confrontation was my morning coffee.

"I was the best hip-hop journalist in the country last year," I told the Quaker. "Too bad you missed it."

No question, Forrest, mocha brown and infant innocent, had altered me. Those tapes my mother had talked on, too, had fucked my head up. Not since Chico had it occurred to me even to ask about ol' ShowdownShortyDelcoDelbo. He had not been on any version of my and Amy's wedding invite list. Now I was doing a bad impression, as if mimicking an artist I'd only heard tell of. In truth, I had been writing about his imagined specter and associations from roughly the time I enmeshed myself with the Peace Frog. Now with Forrest in the mix my father became the only subject I ever gave passion.

I had begun seeing things, as that song by Xzibit put it, like I was living twice at the exact same time. But there were three of us using this life, and I needed to know more about the third. How had the patriarchal line evolved? My smooth and unformed little man is half-white, so our physical similarities struck me alternately as more easy and more difficult to ascertain. When he reached a half year in age, he began presenting mannerism and behaviors that mirrored my own. He cried loud, wiggled constantly, but smiled from his soul on out. At the same time, Forrest was shy. Didn't just give his goods away. I was mesmerized and withdrew from my world, falling into his.

I took parenting as an investigative assignment. Which part of this child's behavior is learned and which is innate? What of the son comes from the father?

Forrest Belle Osburn-Alexander would meet Delbert Alexander, I decided, so that he would grow up with a connection to his past more real than mine. I knew my mother loved me, but after thirty and - one-half years in the world, I still woke up most mornings wondering why I was born. My son would always know he was born for a purpose. Were he ever to assay his legacy in full, I'd first have to find my father.

LA IS SUCH A WEIRD, SELF-ABSORBED PLACE. NOBODY CARED ABOUT MY weird hair or my weird family ambling down Larchmont. Only a select few initiates cared about my weird writing. The ones actually open off what I put down seemed fanatically oblivious of—or absurdly invested in—the obscurity of my work. I put an ad in the *Weekly* classified section offering $75 a week for twenty hours of work—and fifty kids responded with résumés and letters of adoration. I interviewed six, sent the most groupiefied packing, and enlisted a poor little rich girl to help me buy my freedom. Freedom via freelance.

Tamara attended USC on her parents' dime. Her mother came from a long line of undertakers and daddy had ducats, so she knew not a thing about being broke. Tamara was not a fan. She was so hip to my weak grasp on respectability that, had our overcrowded Alta Vista pad harbored roaches, she would have walked.

But the distance of my new assistant—and the fact that I had one stunned my colleagues and bosses—helped to tighten up my hustle. (Finding a way to impress my spirit upon the world through the institutional avenues of advertising-driven print journalism had been nothing but a hustle.) I wrote with greater frequency, if not for the *Weekly*, to make a symbolic show of worth to the beyond-race rich girl from USC, and to get cash. Old fans got hyper off a Sactown DJ Shadow piece, and a groundswell of new readers gathered around my work in *Might*. I got to hot scenes early and reported them right, the idea being not to end up some newsprint Arvydas Sabonis, a phenom whose greatest days might survive purely as legend.

One night Heavy D and I smoked out in his 4 X 4 and drove to an advance film screening. Showing was the fight doc *When We Were Kings*, and when James Brown came on-screen during a concert sequence, the rest of the movie went by as if it had been canceled.

Delbert. Delibra. Lorain.

James Brown Junior.

Maybe it was the Godfather's mustache, but I couldn't get that nigga out of my mind. I ain't say shit the whole ride home, went directly to my computer. Janet, my new weekly editor, gave me the green light a few days later. There would be no turning back.

———

"WHY YOU GOING TO SEE HIM?" ROBBY ASKED. NOW TWELVE, GAYE'S oldest son lived in Sacramento with my mother and, whenever his grandma got sick, asked if I'd adopt him. Now he sounded betrayed. "You know he hit your mom."

I didn't know if contemporary twelve-year-old vernacular offered a polite way of saying, "I think I got the devil in me, and you do, too." (And wouldn't he want to see what the devil looked like if he had the chance?) At the outset it seemed Robby had as much chance of finding Delbert as I did. I didn't even know whether my father lived in Ohio anymore.

I called Barb, my father's sister, in Sandusky. She flatly declined to help me with the project.

"You'll just get your feelings hurt," she said. Barb was excessively polite.

My aunt and her brother hadn't spoken in years, and when they last connected, at a family reunion in Anderson, South Carolina, there was a nasty property dispute. My father threatened to shoot Barb, her off-spring, and her husband, together or apart. They could step outside and choose. Barb had held her little brother in infancy, but now Delbert maintained a grown man's grudge. He thought she had things that belonged to him.

Barb made my father sound crazy, but what I really seized on? Anderson, South Carolina. Now was the chance to pump Barb for info.

"Come on," I said. "It's not like I'm looking for him to start being my father."

"Oh *no*," Barb said, "it's not like you can do anything about him being your father. Just the other day I was going through some of Mother's things and I saw a picture of him. And I said, 'If that's not Donnell, that's not anybody.' "

MANY DAYS HAD PASSED WHEN MY COUSIN DELORES RICE CALLED FROM Sandusky with a bunch of telephone numbers she said would lead me to him. These belonged to relatives in Anderson, who surely knew where Delbert was. Last she had heard, my father was living in a building on his aunt Sara's property, but he'd not had running water, much less a phone. Delores suggested getting in touch with Sara's son, Duck. I'd need him, she said, "because there ain't nar' stoplight out there. Duck knows all those back roads as well as anybody."

AND WITH THAT, THE FLIGHT RESERVATIONS WERE MADE. FORREST, AMY, and I would stay in Georgia, then drive to Anderson, just across the state line. The South was another country, another strange presence to find fearsome and fascinating.

I did something unusual before booking our Super Shuttle to LAX. I phoned my sister, who had always worked harder to stay in touch with Delbert. ("Just to let him know his grandkids' names," she said from Sacramento.) Gaye was both pregnant with her fifth child and busy evicting T.J., her crack-selling babydaddyboyfriend, from her life.

Gaye and I got down so different that our lives at a glance seemed hardly of the same catalog. Still, we were ten months apart. It was Gaye I took to see the Liks back in SF, when I first heard their single, "Daamn!" We had the Close-N-Play, private jokes, and a full adolescence of sneaking between us.

Shit, my sister was proud of me, invested even, on some elusive plane. Gaye told me to follow my search through. She thought it would be less for me than for my father.

"I think that regardless of how Delbert screwed up, he probably wonders what's happened to his kids. And maybe he would like to have communication with us."

But that's the funny thing: Delbert wasn't communicating with me. In spite of the half dozen phone queries I'd made to various relatives in South Carolina—communiqués I'm told were relayed to where he lived—he'd not called once. Amy tried explaining Delbert's quiet as mix-up. But I knew, now.

It had been almost a decade. I thought my father would be happy to hear from me, at least to know that I'm not dead or in jail. How could he not be glad to hear from *me*?

I mentioned this apparent blow-off to Gaye, who in the time-honored fashion of little-sister tattletales quickly phoned my mom to tell of Delbert's latest rejection.

Mom rang. I had kept her vaguely briefed on how my search was going, and she'd been vaguely supportive. Now though she had talked with Gaye and learned something I wouldn't ever let on: the possibility of my hurt. As we spoke, her voice had the choked and fearful quality that freaks me out on the rare occasions when it's present.

"You don't have to do this," she said. She began extolling my virtues as a father, as a professional, as a human being in general. Brenda Graham knew me about as well as she had known my father. "You aren't anything like him."

I didn't tell her that the *Weekly* had purchased my airline ticket, and the assignment, with its rounding up of family and flailing, fanlike turn of notebook pages, had taken on the trappings of a desperate man's last act. Instead I explained the importance of understanding this story, and she backed off a bit.

"Just don't punch him out when you see him," she said.

Aha! "I thought you said I wasn't anything like him."

"Well, maybe just a little bit."

I GREW UP ADMIRING THE MOST INTERESTING PEOPLE AROUND ME, AND they certainly weren't doctors and lawyers or elders in our Jehovah's Witness congregation. Whether my attraction to the unseemly side of the community was innate, a fact of economic circumstance, or both is debatable, but I put direct and indirect responsibility for it on my father. In his absence I found him culpable for my patterning myself after people like Jimi Hendrix and Richard Pryor. These were my natural heroes. In a way, I was fashioning an aesthetic, a sense of cool, but there was something else. What I admired about these people was less their doomed qualities than their desire to go out with a fierce rejection of the lives they had inherited, even if—especially if—it meant trading the slow death of underclass life for a spectacular burnout of one's own design.

I thought that Delbert's behavior had helped me get hold of the savvy and imagination I needed to get this far. Raised on Mom's values and deeds alone, I might have become a sucker or a mark, trusting, earnest, and unfailingly striving to please. Didn't what I got from my father translate roughly as survival skills for a black man in America? Back when I stretched out my life and happened upon cooked cocaine that tasted so good it occurred to me to never leave it alone and everyone around me was bending to the will of the drug, I didn't need to be as gentle as my mom. It was my father's legacy that made me know I should take the sensation for what it was and get on with my life.

And bless his ass for leaving our family. Could you imagine the havoc that motherfucker might have wrought if he had tried to *stay*?

DOWN SOUTH WAS NO MORE REAL TO ME THAN BLACK-AND-WHITE CIVIL rights footage. Allman Brothers blues jams, and Alabama stories from Linda Faye and Boo-Boo. I didn't know what to expect of South Carolina. Would it be an alright place for me and Amy and the little boy who was still feeding from his mother's breast?

We took the red-eye to Atlanta the last Thursday in January and were on the road to Athens, our base of operations and the closest thing to a city adjacent to Anderson. By 9 A.M. Atlanta's eight-lane highways slashed across a pop-up book arrangement of fir trees and flatland, and the effect was that of gliding through my dissociative past. Framed by the brown death of Spanish moss on winter maple trees, busy business districts gave way to ubiquitous signpost Waffle Houses and plastic-flag car dealerships, and then a mind-numbing series of no-account farms.

After we unloaded our belongings at the Howard Johnson, I napped, then set out on the fifty-mile drive to the far side of the Georgia–South Carolina border, and Anderson. It was a good thing cousin Duck had been recommended, because no one else among the Rices of South Carolina was interested in hooking me up. The others were either too elderly, too busy, or too distanced from my father. Duck wasn't around, so that first night I merely scouted the town's outskirts on the eastern side of the Tugaloo River. For some odd reason, rural South Carolina, the first state to secede from the Union prior to the Civil War, offered a vast selection of fireworks stores the size of Cali grocery stores, elaborately lit even in January.

Back at the HoJo, where I finally reached Duck by phone, he sounded shocked to hear I'd actually made it to the area. Duck had had no luck in setting up a meeting.

"Your father's unusual," he said, deploying a distinct air of euphemism I'd not known until the past few weeks. At about the same time I'd tooled around the backwoods of Anderson County, Duck had knocked on my father's door and told him I was coming to town.

Cautiously, sparingly, Duck told me my father said he had to work. He never even opened the door. Duck and Delbert had once been close, back in the day when a trip to live with the Anderson Rices might have been enough to set my father straight. Four decades later, the two hardly spoke. Duck had used the South's black state college system and a love of the Lord to find a life that granted worldly comfort.

"But if Del doesn't want to see you," Duck said, "I'd sure like ya to come round."

That was nice. With Duck's words in mind, my family lit out for South Carolina the next afternoon, our last day before our scheduled flight back to LA.

AMY DROVE SO THAT I COULD TAKE NOTES. AS USUAL SHE WAS GOR- geous, without makeup. Forrest sat quietly in a lugged-along safety seat, a good boy here for the ride. He didn't talk yet, crawled the HoJo like a demon, and once we stopped on the Carolina side would have to attach himself to one of his mother's nipples. My wife asked few questions but offered up a dozen southern geographic details she had discovered on college road trips. I scribbled and asked follow-ups, forcing her to dig deeper and share.

Anderson—pop. 26,000—was desolate. Today was Super Bowl Sunday, and in small-town America, where the holiday's recognition was all but official, desertion was the day's order. We crept along in our rental Beretta, encroaching on a timeless nowhere. The rural South etched itself in our consciousness. Out past the old sprawling houses with widow's walks that city folks only see at the multiplex, beyond that home with cows in the backyard, we still hadn't reached my family's stomping grounds and were deeply lost. The sun set over a sign saying Pecans Crushed Here, and I let go of Duck's directions, becoming completely reliant on Amy's intuitive advice, the kindness of strangers, and ultimately, the Force.

Duck welcomed us just before night fell.

MY COUSIN TOOK AMY, FORREST, AND ME INTO HIS SENTIMENTALLY COM-fortable, ranch-style home having little knowledge of me and my brood. Duck's wife invited us to a dinner of roast beef, black-eyed peas, and collard greens, to be consumed after we motivated the rental by my father's house.

If a car rolls through an obscure Southern town while the Super Bowl airs, do its wheels make sound?

All was air. Driving our party through the countryside of Anderson County, I felt a calm that was at odds with, for example, the anger I'd felt in Fresno County over the other people's oppression of migrant farm workers and in Huron, Ohio's get-out-by-dark fear. This was a new sensation, my American Pastoral. Duck pointed out the home of cousin Jim Ed Rice, the Boston Red Sox's Hall of Fame–quality outfielder, who was a favorite before I ever knew he was kin. One of the outer Anderson streets was actually named Willie Rice Lane, after one of my forebears. Unbelievable. Here is where the black Rices in America come from, as far as can be told by reaching into our nameless past.

"I could live here," I thought for a fleeting moment.

———

DELBERT'S VAN SAT IN A GRAVEL DRIVEWAY OUTSIDE HIS GLORIFIED shanty. Adjacent to all this was a group of coops that occupied nearly as much space as the house, full of chickens, roosters, and pheasants as large and clean as the cages that held them. Duck said Delbert had been raising these creatures since he'd moved in at the turn of the decade.

My first nervous energy surfaced as Duck rapped on the screen door. Amy stood off to the side, as though there might be an explosion. But Duck's repeated knocks went unanswered. None of us said what the van in the driveway declared as fact: that Delbert was in there but would not come out.

Duck suggested we leave a note. I turned my pen over from end to end. What would be the proper salutation? No way was I calling him "Dad"—fuck that. Should it be "Delbert"? Or "Pops"? "Father"? No, now wait a second, what's really wrong with "Dad"?

"Man, I don't even know what I should call him," I said. "Duck, what should I call him?"

"Just write 'Del.'" Duck's patience sounded thin.

"Del"? It hadn't occurred to me that people might call my father that. Boy, I really didn't know this nigga at all.

FOR AN HOUR, AMY, FORREST, DUCK, AND I VISITED AMONG THE DOZENS of relatives on and around Willie Rice Lane. About these new family members was a similarity that touched me as meditations on a specific note, some more forceful in manner, some slower, softer. All essentially the same. Matriarch Sara, nearing eighty and legally blind, seemed a ringer for Delbert's mom.

We doubled back toward Duck's for dinner. Passing a familiar intersection, Duck blurted, "Hey, the light's on at Del's place!" And sure enough it was, now. Illumination from the front room reached halfway to the birdcages. He'd indeed been in there the whole time.

Duck went ahead to Delbert's door while the rest of us waited in the car. A few minutes later, Duck emerged, followed by a short, bald man with a big, brushy mustache.

Beat and hungry—but instantly wired—Amy and I spilled out of the car, with Forrest.

Delbert stepped off the porch, looked up, and said, "Hey!" We hugged as intimate as two shopping carts brushing in a grocery-store aisle. The big moment passed without distinction. My growling belly— or discomfort in hunger-pang's guise—told me to keep things short. "What's up?" I said, and introduced Amy and Forrest. Chilly, as the mild winter air nipped at his torn thermal undershirt, Delbert invited us to come inside.

Stubby white hairs dotted the high end of his forehead. It was the Michael Jordan balding-man's-camouflage thing going down, except wasn't nobody coming through to tend his crop on a daily basis. Along his jawline was the same. He seemed shorter and skinnier than I remembered; my nephew Robby would be this big by next summer. Delbert's eyes were small and slanted, as are mine, but time had crinkled them into double raisins, pricked bright at their centers. And beneath his long, hooked nose, that mustache hung over his toothless mouth like car-wash dry cloths across a salvaged Cadillac grill. I'd never seen him without his false teeth. The difference between the man before me and the Delbert of my memory was startling.

"Y'all came by while I was dyeing my mustache," he said.

"Dyeing your mustache?" I suppressed a laugh. "What's *that* all about?"

The front room the five of us occupied was smaller than an apartment foyer. At one end was a portable television, on which the Patriots were falling behind to the Packers. At the other sat a stereo, also portable, and a telephone. A woman's number was scribbled next to the phone. A fragile, sheetless cot bridged both ends of the room. My father said he had to rush off to work.

"Yeah, I always been a little cosmetic," he said, stroking the hair beneath his nose. Then he grabbed a fistful of my pencil-thin dread-locks and tossed them off playfully. "That's why you got all *this*."

Yeah, well, Amy did that. Still, I had not prepared to believe my father would go there. My deep-seated vanity? Right there's a subject that gets nearly no play.

He turned to Forrest. "C'mon. Boy, ah'll tear you apart! Your old granddad will tear you apart!" Right now, Showdown Shorty reminded me of nothing so much as Yosemite Sam. Slouched in a corner, I covered my face with my hands and snickered.

Delbert intended this as horseplay, but a look of horror came across Amy's face. She hopped up from the cot, tightening her hold on our son. "Uh, come on, Forrest," she said. "Let's go see the chickens."

My father took her place, and I sat next to him. Duck was in a corner. Delbert began updating me on past family entanglements—pathetic little Negro crumb-snatching squabbles that put the nigga in American blacks—and as he did, I noticed that he has that aural quality I've been accused of having: a voice with two notes in it. Chordal. It's that capacity to convey in one vibration both self-effacement and pomposity and shit. Our chords get difficult. The land battle with Barb came up, and Delbert just went on and on, rhyming, jiving, laying metaphor on top of metaphor—masterfully playing with words. For minutes at a time I ignored the narrative of internecine bickering and just tripped off the kick of listening to this nigga bullshit.

I mean, he hadn't seen me in nearly a decade, but he wasn't stopping to ask me a goddamn thing. It was cool, though, because the monologue was part sermon, part pimp talk, and part blues, and I was entertained silly. Beyond the language and the overlapping stories he told, there was a song in his voice, a song of someone who's more than once looked down the barrel of a gun and lived to crow about it.

HE TOLD ME ABOUT HOW HE MET JIMI HENDRIX.

"This was before Jimmy went to England and took some exotic drugs and met some exotic people, before Hendricks became Hendrix, with an *x*, basically. I met him in Milwaukee. He could never play a solo the same way twice. *Guess* that's like genius."

He told me how at eighteen he first started shooting "*her*-on" and about the prison boxing championships he'd won and how Buddy Miles had kicked him out of his revue while in Alabama.

"They told me, 'You're conceited, and you're never gonna succeed,' he said, "and then they fired me."

And about how he got all of his teeth knocked out in the seventies. All of this in, like, twenty minutes.

Delbert went on, beginning to float this idea that he had secretly been there for me. Like when his sister Barb's oldest boy insisted I was a punk, a faggot, and Delbert defended my honor. ("Donnell's just different. I want him to be different," he'd said.) And there was the time when he kept an Alexander faction from kicking us out of Grandma Charlene's rental apartment. We fell behind in payments, and talk turned to putting us off the property.

"I told 'em, 'If any uh y'all so much as move a tissue up there, I'mablowya motherfuckin' head off.' And I think yer mama pretty much moved out when she found the money and the right place. Y'all didn't know about that, now didja?"

I'd forgotten that my father talks about pulling out heat more than twenty-five gangsta rappers. And I wasn't sure whether I was supposed to thank him or just nod in acknowledgment. Did he need a show? I just nodded, and as I sat there on his cot at that moment, something like an epiphany registered: He's just an itty-bitty feller. I couldn't even fit into this bed, and I could kick his ass, provided he didn't go for his guns. *Ah'd tear him apart.* (This is not to say I had the urge to thump him, only that it was a surprise not to see in him the O.G. badass of lore.)

I studied my father's posture while keeping up eye contact and nodding and laughing at the appropriate times. He was leaned forward over the cot's side with his elbow on his knee, his head resting awkwardly in the palm of his hand. The other hand sat high on his thigh, as if its owner were about to jump up and do something. I checked myself and was seated just as he. Identical. It was as though mirroring me was that devilish energy I could never get a grip on no matter how many Grahams coddled me. Here was Donny Shell, only he was old and short, with a ridiculously black mustache.

It seemed now a kind of a nerdy way to sit. For sure if I had to be that Sandusky dork three decades ago, I'd have gotten a pompadour and covered up with a boxer's swagger—even bad boxers can swagger—and that awkward quality might have eluded everyone's notice. Here I could see that same guttersnipe intellectual affect I've spent years trying to justify but, unlike my father, never troubled with hiding. Now I could see my father as a punk, or at least semitender. I bet Hots sat like this. Maybe James Alexander got down similarly back in Mecklenburg County.

WHEN I THINK ABOUT ALL THE SHIT DELBERT'S PULLED, AND WHAT HE'S become—and what I've become—it's easy to see who's lucky. Yes, as had he, I ingested my first opiate at the age of eighteen, but I hadn't the popularity to ensure that the next hit was just around the corner. It turned out to be my last. I hadn't been the half-pint J.D. son of a small-town patriarch. The woman who had raised me didn't want me to be anything but good. I can as much realistically go to what his formative years must have been like as I can imagine being part of Scandinavian royalty.

My eyes lingered too long on how he held his hands to his face, and he noticed I hadn't been listening to him. A panic flashed into Delbert's eyes. This sense that I'm ignoring my father changes him remarkably: he gets real. I think that if he'd been a little more effective at boring motherfuckers when he was younger, he might have gone further in life.

He turned the subject to my mother.

Before, when Mom first hipped me to my father's pimping, a story had accompanied: One night, while Uncle Rick baby-sat me and Gaye, my mother and a friend experienced that thought-to-be-extinct night out in Santown. Mom ran into her babies' daddy. The two talked for a few minutes, then Delbert walked away, returning minutes later with a run-down young chick.

"See, bitch," he told his date, "that's what a real woman looks like."

"Your mother," Delbert said, elevating from his aged-out-nerd pose, "was nice, very nice, but I always had a thousand replacements out there." My father pursed the lips of his toothless mouth. "Look around me now—they're gone. Now my kids are the only family I've got."

AMY AND FORREST WERE BACK FROM THE PORCH, AND DUCK SHIFTED IN his seat with an uneasy politeness. It was dinnertime at our ride's crib. It was breakup time.

Our flight left at dawn, so staying in Anderson overnight was not an option. Delbert's sadness at the news seemed discernible, and at this time I felt the only emotion of the journey that almost overtook me. Delbert had burned the hours I had set aside into less than one, and again, I kept my thoughts in my head: Now who the fuck's fault is it that there isn't more time?

He hugged Amy, who hugged back, then Forrest, who did not. And then me. Call Gaye, I said. She would appreciate it. I updated him on Gaye's life: her children, the boys she'd gone with who had been no better for her than he had been for Mom, and how she'd pulled herself from the welfare rolls. Delbert smiled. A toothless grin never looked so good.

"Gaye's a slow learner," my father said, "like me."

AS A KIND OF TALISMAN FOR THE TRIP, I'D CARRIED A PLASTER SCULP-ture of Abraham Lincoln that Delbert had made in youth reformatory. I think Grandma Charlene had given it to me, and it's actually pretty good. This Lincoln in profile has the classic hirsute visage, as well as a broad chest and shoulders that give The Man Who Freed the Slaves a naively heroic bearing; I can only assume that Delbert completed the project before being reached by the NOI. The crude genius that shows in the lines and impressions of the piece gives away its maker's limited understanding of how he fits into the world.

My father's humanity always seemed more possible when I looked at that sculpture. When I was young, it made me wonder about visitation days and the old story fragments of him. Did he charm his mother like he did everyone else? My father was a singer, and by most accounts a performer who got over on the same personality he used to turn girls out. He wasn't good. Maybe that music stuff was not his calling. Maybe he was a writer. ("I'll send you my prison writings from 1973–1975," he wrote me soon after our visit.) But newspapers weren't hiring his kind around his time. No Nathan McCalls in 1965, so if you were possessed by your own creative energy, you had to hustle in the street. There was no such thing as getting paid for saying rhymes, so you hustled. My father would have been a dope rapper, but he was born ahead of his time. Instead he mainlined.

Delbert's primary gig these days was the yarn factory, with that janitor gig on the side. On weekends he sold afghans, T-shirts, and such at a giant flea market. Competing vendors, Delbert said on the phone, resented him because he hawked his wares like a carnival barker. He was now praying to Allah five times a day and fasting for Ramadan— that's why he was so skinny—and suggested to me that he stepped more lively than the competition at his third place of work. I couldn't help but find something admirable in that.

I finally got my father caught up on my life, on a long-distance call. He was pleased. "See," he said, "hustlin's been up in this family for about a hundred years now."

Getting to know Delbert shined a new light on the distances I put between myself and my people. All my folks, not just the family I was born into. And the only thing harsher than acknowledging the habit is the fact that distancing almost invariably proves to be an act of self-preservation. My people have no idea where they're going. Like those Alexanders on the plantation in North Carolina, they flee their captivity with no preplanned destination, with little more than the means of transportation they're born with. We tend to contribute to our marginalization or leap into chaos.

Sometimes it works. All I knew about coming to California was that the plan entailed getting the fuck out of Sandusky, and it got me living kinda cool. That will to do something—anything—is in all of us, no matter how poorly prepared my folks are to make moves. And even though this gift will get a nigga locked up as easy as it will earn one reward, there is hope. I know this; I saw it in the smile of a toothless child.

act 3

REPUDIATION

11.

totally nude

AT THE END OF THAT YEAR, JUST BEFORE CHRISTMAS, LATRELL SPREWELL of the Golden State Warriors grabbed his hectoring coach by the neck— during a practice in the East Bay—and, according to most subpoenaed observers, squeezed. The welts on P. J. Carlesimo's neck ignited a passionate moment that transcended sport, one whose symbolic meaning split many a room. (A 70/30 division is a split nonetheless.) Sprewell and Allen Iverson had begun wearing cornrows, basketball shorts were getting thug-life baggy, and demands from the NBA workforce had experts predicting a lockout. The story looked like the last great racial flashpoint of the twentieth century. I observed all of this from the common voyeur's perspective: I watched it on cable. Didn't talk much about it, certainly not in print. The antijock left was my employer and they could not easily see the news value in spectacle of this sort.

Not that Sprewell was the biggest deal around. I was still getting over that last ugly West Coast moment, the springtime shooting of Biggie Smalls, which happened about a mile from our new crib on Dockweiler. I felt hip-hop die a little bit the day it lost its Kurt Cobain. He went from ashy to classy.

Donny Shell felt sick about Big, empathized with Spree, but experienced the stuff strictly as the guts of a news junkie's dream fix.

I never knew these niggas.

I was knowing fewer and fewer people, actually. Amy left *LA Magazine* and started cooking and inviting friends over. I was cool with the scene, 'cuz, day-gig drama aside, I'd become even less a scenemaker on Hollywood's periphery, withdrawing more into watching Forrest feast on fistfuls of rice and beans that Amy or Lorena, the nanny, would cook up. You didn't catch me at rappers' birthday joints so much, as predawn mornings were for rides down Crenshaw and over to Western and back with little man, Lee's donuts in tow. *I'm Bout It* bangin' in the tape deck.

My tender toddler terror was straight southern California, communicating with Lorena in Spanish as much as English. The nanny loved the boy enough that on her off nights she'd drive from East Hollywood to our second-story niche northeast of Pico and La Brea, seeking out his energy. Geovany, Lorena's four-year-old, would come, too.

We had a darn good show at over on Dockweiler. Gig beef up on Sunset escalated as the seasons wound down, but LA life was otherwise sweet. Amy and I figured a new way to do the town. She didn't smoke pot, but did as much yoga as possible.

Then, days before the annual Osburn-Alexander holiday trek to Indianapolis, mail from my father came through. Delco and I had been talking on the regular, usually by phone, as I'd wanted to turn my writing about him into a book. My father was written back into my life.

Now he was writing me . . .

. . . when the nigga usually calls.

This shady Negro had my Spidey senses tingling.

So I tossed the letter into my suitcase. The Laker game was on that night. I coughed and hoped I could fight off this cold. I packed *The Duke of Deception* and my stash in such a ways as to wedge my father's envelope against my spare high-tops' backsides.

It wasn't until we settled in the Osburns' perfect brick house in Butler-Tarkington that I read my father's words. Delbert's words, so foolish, so educational. You don't know how apt? Ponder this: it takes a fool to learn that fame don't love nobody.

NEITHER THE SUPERVISORS NOR THE DRONES AT THE CAROLINA MILL called Abney had ever seen a union handbook. The textile factory was not that sort of workplace. Come the December rush, you did your twelve-hour shift without question and were glad the $7.50 wage jumped to time and a half after forty hours. These eighty-hour weeks, mandatory, made you look on the bright side. That, or drop out.

Nativity was audible in the grain of their voices, the loud ones just above the machines. A few of the Anderson people who put in work alongside Delbert were older than his fifty-year-old ass and had been on the job since sophomore year of high school. Almost to a person, they owed Abney's credit union and were paying back loans over time. No, they hadn't read no union manual, and them niggas couldn't quit if they wanted to, unless them that tried their luck on the other side of the Georgia line.

The bosses were third- and fourth-generation Strom Thurmonds. They didn't play no sick days. But Delbert wasn't about to make a run for the border or go anywhere, actually.

Delbert paid in poor circulation for decades of vein abuse. He reported to the mill with a cane by each week's end. He was tired and resigned, but presented himself unfazed. In fact Del was grinning, quite frequently, during the act of bearing. Abney was the gig now. He had grown too old for the quick con, and Bishop Thomas sure wasn't calling. There was also, arguably, no one left in Anderson for the man to jive.

YEP, AT ABNEY, THEY DID NOT PLAY NO MISSED DAYS. ESPECIALLY DUR-ing speedups. You had the summer speedup around when specialists came in and cleaned up the machines. This was winter, the push pre-ceding holiday layover. Weeks before the mill closed down, bosses accelerated productions to meet goals.

Delbert's job description was "duffer." A duffer tends to a cotton spinner, which is constantly weaving yarn. In the spinner, rough soft stuff goes, out comes streamline product. When the machine cycles down, it begins dumping out big spools of fabric that the duffer empties into a cart and ferries to be weighed. From there the spools of yarn go to shipping for an order's fulfillment.

The duffer pushes and empties her or his cart, then brings it back and starts again.

At eight that night, the start of his shift, Delbert planned to follow his usual schedule, with a break at ten and another at midnight. Ordinarily, the bosses let you rest your feet at intervals. But this speedup hadn't gone well, and all of the night crew was behind in production. Delbert missed his ten-o'clock blow and the next break, too. A couple of minutes past one, he turned off his machine, grabbed his cane, and humped to the snack room.

The straw boss, the pusher, hit him with a dirty look. Delbert stirred cream into his coffee. He glanced back cautiously down the coffee counter at the pusher, who was not in charge. It was unstated, but true. His gig was goading in a style that Abney's credentialed managers had no appetite for.

Maybe those supervisors had said to make up time tonight. Maybe something in Del's makeup just drew the ire of certain kinds of men.

The straw boss's stare called into question Delbert's expectation of shooting the breeze with the boys over a cup of mud.

The duffer slid into a seat at a table alone and in the corner.

"Del, what are you doing in here!"

"I missed my ten-o'clock break," Del said, thinking he'd not have to mention the actual a.m. hour. "I thought I'd take advantage of my break."

"You take a break when I tell you to take a damn break." The pusher turned around, pointing. "And that goes for everybody in here!"

All snapped to attention. A few shuffled out.

Delbert reached down to his best Ohio stuff, his junior Martin

Luther King bag, and took a careful sip of his coffee. He stared straight ahead.

"Dael! Do you hear me?"

Millworkers on their way back to spinners and looms stopped and watched. Delbert tore his creamer open and poured the powder into his styrofoam and Folgers.

"I said, get back on your machine," the straw boss went. He turned around and pointed. "That means everybody!"

Here was Delbert's Abney fifteen minutes.

At the risk of this pay.

And the last time he phoned Bishop Thomas, there had been no return call.

He broke down his focus on the styrofoam and Folgers.

"Yes, sir," Delbert mumbled. He tossed his coffee down the sink and then joined the line.

Then there were no more stragglers. Delbert joined the crush of machinists who crowded out the door. And he thought about his son in California. He could almost reach out and touch him.

CHRISTMAS MORNING HAD BEEN A HELLAFIED WINNER, INDIANAPOLIS coolness with wood paneling and a mountain of shiny things under the tree. Joe and Marie, Amy's parents, wrapped up a camcorder and attached a card with my name on it. Killer, dude!

I waited for my wife's parents to go do their social work. Then, up the carpeted staircase, I told Amy what was in my father's letter. I told her that the day after we got back to LA, he and his luggage would be at our doorstep.

BRIEFLY AND EVER SO SLIGHTLY, AMY'S EYES BULGED. THEY NARROWED right thereafter. She stood intent, hands on her belly, which was round from the baby weight that still clung, but she offered up no expression.

My wife looked down the stairs and pursed her lips in silence. Her mouth was a horizontal bar. Then it was an orb collapsing, backward.

"No Donnell. We are not doing that."

Forrest was relentless in his quest to get down the stairs. So I picked him up. Then I handed the boy to Amy because gesturing would make me less likely to shout.

Amy was not trying to hear this. She acted cool toward Delbert, but only because she found him beneath reproach. My father had lost her at Brenda Graham's smashed jaw, and I understood her, if just because arguably only Ma and Grandma Charlene had suffered more Delbert than my wife. To her, the man was the worst-case scenario, incarnate.

On the other hand, Amy now knew my father had boarded a Greyhound headed toward our pad on Dockweiler. She probably pictured him in little-ass clothes, in Main Street, Anderson, looking like the black Charlie Chaplin.

Did I ever tell you Cathedral High School named my wife winner of the Most Christian Attitude Award? Class of '86? Shit, next thing you know we were unpacking in LA and decking out Forrest's room for the new houseguest.

IN THE IMPOSSIBLY SUNNY LA BREAKFAST NOOK ARRIVED A PIECE OF voice mail that sounded completely bizarre. Disney was starting a magazine. "Call me back," said the recorded editor.

Pacific Bell's computers insisted our missed phone calls had piled up to double digits while we were in Indy. I scribbled and waited for Amy to finish scooping eggs onto Forrest's suction-cup plate. Summarizing messages in the morning's natural hue, I cursed RJ, then Nyesha and Drea and Ben and Lisa and the rest for not taking into account basic rules of brevity. Kim was curt.

The boy ate while in this clamp-on child seat that jutted sideways out of the table. It didn't matter if the Janet Jackson record-release party was the night prior, we had breakfast in this room, as a trio. Forrest sported the precious overalls his maternal grandmother had laid on him, us, and I sighed relief upon noticing the extra length of material cuffed at his ankles. This winter Amy had worked only sporadically.

First impulse said to ignore the message. Underneath its notepad top spot lay a sea of creditors, editors, and friends to deal with. Who needed the drama? Fucking Disney. But something, probably the bulging fabric of my son's sized-to-be-loose T-shirt, suggested taking note.

I cued up the message again, grunt-gestured toward the ceiling with my chin. Jamiroquai on "Baby's First Mixtape" vibrated across the apartment. Talk around town was of a coming, protracted storm called El Niño, so we savored bright warm mornings like this. Amy took the phone.

As she listened, she made faces as though hearing Esperanto. Amy shrugged.

"Whatdya think baby," I said, "should I even return this call?"

THIS PIECE OF VOICE MAIL WAS AN INCOMPREHENSIBLE INVITATION TO write for something called *ESPN The Magazine*. I'd actually heard about the venture from a commercial that was airing daily during *SportsCenter*. Underage Minnesota hoop sensations Stephon Marbury and Kevin Garnett were featured in a great, transgressive advertisement. Marbury and Garnett suggested the mag go nude. *Totally nude.* You know I loved that shit. Sometimes I timed my morning writing ritual so that I could peep it in the stream of a.m. *SportsCenter* reruns.

Now, me and ESPN went way back, to the days of old Sensation, when we'd pretended to be Larry Micheaux and Clyde Drexler on the playground. The cable trailed on through coach-potato scenes with Brad in SF to where Forrest found me most mornings when he wandered out from his mother. I had probably taken in more ESPN programming than I had dope.

The voice on the far side of my return call said, "In our greatest moments of hubris, we say we're going to revolutionize the whole magazine game."

The mag had been hipped by a consultant who knew me.

Shit sounded cool, but Disney owned ESPN. I was not really trying to fuck with that company. No other giant media company had tipped its hand so purely in imposing its hopes for an ahistorical, sepia society. Not able any longer to do *Song of the South,* Disney seemed on some postracial *Pocahontas* bullcrap in which to be of color meant having a nice tan. This new guy Stuart Scott aside, Mickey Mouse seemed to see self-contained cultures as mere blender fodder, puree waiting to happen and enhance the corporation's place in the market. Pretending to be down with that program would do me in worse than wasting away at the *Weekly.*

On the other hand, I thought about Miramax, the Disney-owned company that had produced *Pulp Fiction.* Hollywood Basic, their old hip-hop label, put out great material by Fusions Raw and Organized Konfuz.

And I thought about how great it had been, over the years, exposing a potential quarter million SoCal readers each week to below-the-radar data. The Coup, *All Power to the People, The Hemp Conspiracy.* Yet, at a point, the work felt like a gimmick, a lazy thing, preaching to the converted. Maybe this sports deal would let me take my hustle to the malls.

Shit dog, I dunno.

My yearly income had gotten up around forty grand, mostly through the after-hours slangin' of record reviews to magazines and Web sites. Amy's work editing pictures brought home decent dough, but making rent was getting harder and harder. The boy's overalls wouldn't stay cuffed forever.

Besides, that Garnett-Marbury commercial was really, really fresh. Freshness begets freshness, always, no?

I played it safe, figured I'd angle for e-mailing them articles from the coast, another way of augmenting my *Weekly* take. Just one little dance with the man wouldn't hurt nobody. Then, after my father's taxi arrived, I booked a flight on Tower Air's Backache Express.

Delco's West Coast debut lacked portent and was newsworthy mostly because of our airy, open home's newly tangible funk quotient.

He shuffled around a lot and slept on the couch despite having been assigned (and reassigned, emphatically) a room, Forrest's room. Turner Movie Classics blared when I came to set up for my predawn *Sports-Center* fixes. Delbert crowded suitcases around the empty crib in the room where Forrest had slept. The boy slept with us now.

Amy stayed smiling from a distance, seething in a way so private only I could know. (If asked, she'd not admit it.) But Amy instantly picked up Delbert's patterns of speech. My father walked down the hill to La Brea, tapped at the sidewalks of Pico with his cane. He couldn't hold his aura and gently marked the apartment as his before hitting the streets.

Bouncing a fussy Forrest on her lap, Amy would echo Delbert's calming incantation "You doin' good!" with the remainder of her Indiana drawl. This impressed, as at first Amy's strategy seemed to be to experience Delbert always from at least one room away. Her father-in-law could be overheard, but my wife allowed no further insinuation.

WHETHER I CALLED IT SELLING OUT OR BUYING IN, THE IDEA OF GETTING in bed with the mouse was hard on my head. What an ending, I thought, for the only hip-hop journalist who mattered. Would hip-hop even go on? At the height of media East-West hype, I'd written in the *Weekly:*

> Even if it turns out that the person who shot Biggie Smalls was a gun-toting emissary of Suge Knight himself, don't call it an East Coast–West Coast thing. If the gunman was singing "California Love" as he squeezed off shots, had on a Shaq jersey and a Jheri curl, don't call the killing a result of "the East Coast–West Coast rivalry."
>
> Biggie had beef with a couple of people representing the Death Row record label, which is not the same as beef with Los Angeles or California or the whole West Coast. And relations between artists on both coasts have been strained because of various economic and historic issues. Primarily New York's unassailable position as the

seat of hip-hop has been challenged by the commercial viability of gangsta rap, which is all but a West Coast invention. West Coast innovators in turn have become resentful of the East Coast media establishment's distorted representation of both the West's creative gifts and moral culpability. In the wake of these conflicts (which, predictably, provided hip-hop with its only occasions for mainstream news attention), minor examples of group mentality's most base inclinations—the symbolic and spectacular Westside Connection and the specter of secret East Coast dis tapes—have taken on lives of their own. From far away, hip-hop must look like a house divided rather than a culture grappling with a diverse set of internal conflicts.

No one was saying this stuff to an audience like mine. I was *sick*. I was the one.

But who the fuck was I kidding? Everyone on top of the *Weekly* masthead thought I was a lazy malcontent, and providing capsule summaries of adult film classics was the best assignment I'd recently received. All my prose got turned in at the last possible minute, subvertin' the editorial system. And while my immediate editors showed me love, putting them shits through, the bosses wouldn't even speak my name. I'd been convinced everyone from Ice Cube to RZA was biting my lines, and Ras Kass showed me love every time we met up. Medusa or Mark Luv might come at me like, "You're killin' it. Off the heezy, fo' sheezy." But my cover stories got killed like a blind kid playing Tomb Raider.

So fucking with Disney couldn't really be considered selling out, could it?

ESPN PUT ME UP AT MADISON AVENUE'S SLEEK AND ULTRAMODERN Roger Williams Hotel, and for someone who had never been to Manhattan, I played off being overwhelmed quite slick. I had borrowed a winter coat from my man Clarence, but walked, for the interview, up

Madison Avenue with just a dress jacket. My hair was pulled back in a ponytail. East on Thirty-third, I looped over, pretending not to gawk at the Empire State Building. Livin' just enough for the city. Two European seniors asked if they could take my picture. I capitulated, just like in West Hollywood when people started conversations with me under the assumption that I was Vernon Reid from Living Colour. I was into it.

A block backtracking on Thirty-fourth and seven elevator stops up, the future world came alive.

The nerve center of *The Magazine*'s broad, metallic office was a life-size scoreboard. In its middle lay a digital clock. Each foot-high numeral glittered a JumboTron gravitas. You could all but hear the music from "Final Jeopardy" being piped in. A neatly pressed, button-down brand of folks I only recognized from investment ads rushed with obscure purpose through the airport-airless environment. They were six weeks away from debuting their company's first major print product.

I found *The Magazine*'s fluorescent, antiseptic environs sexy, nostalgically so. In mind was the Boston internship, *Lou Grant* episodes, and "signs, signs, everywhere signs." About me gleamed the suggestion of stardom. The players here acted like I was the one.

Across a grid of cubicles, in the corner office, was Max, the editor in chief. His real name was John, but he asked to be called Max, so as to separate him from the swelling mass of editors here who were also named John.

Max slid shut his orange rolling door, glided across black plastic to his big Mac, and urged me to recline. Then he hunched toward my person and intimated, "We think you're the real deal."

In some ways, the whole thing seemed too much. I quelled the urge to ask if my first story could be sports editors on crack. The next editor on *The Magazine* tour got grilled:

"You people have done your homework?" I asked. "You do know I'm kind of an asshole, right?"

Doesn't matter at this level, I was assured. The deal sounded real to me, and before a nigga skipped town, John had me calling him Max.

"Thing is," I told him, "I always had this idea in my head that I could do one great thing in my life. Maybe this job has something to do with that."

A day before the sojourn's expected ending with western get-back on Tower, a dozen urban media people—friends and fans from *The Source,* New Line Cinema's new black film cadre, and such—met me in lower Broadway's Bubble Lounge. We toasted with a Hennessy-champagne combo.

"The cream always rises," intoned my man Dimitry.

No question. Bring on the Hype Williams establishing shot. (I got a suit on for the occasion.) 'Cuz, ladies and gentlemen, da survey sez:

Donny Sheezy is off the heezy!

(Fo' sheezy.)

BACK AT THE ROGER WILLIAMS, I CALLED AMY.

"They say I'm the real deal, can you believe that? They want me for me, baby! I think I gotta do this."

"That's great, baby." She sounded much more cautious than optimistic. "So you'll just send your articles by e-mail, right?"

"That's a little issue right there. . . . They want us to move here. Like, right now."

"Now? That's insane."

"Not now. Six weeks. What do you care? You hate your job. What exactly is your job anyway? Anyway, they'll double my salary. We ain't got no money, let's go!"

"No Donnell, we are not doing that."

We had already had three scenes like this.

"What about our friends?" Amy demanded.

"I know. That sucks. But this will be an adventure. We'll try it, and if it doesn't work, we can always go back. . . . Amy? C'mon, we'll make new friends."

"No Donnell. This is not something I think I can do."

I reached into my nigga bag and changed tactics. "Look now, Amy,

I'm not asking. I can do this with you or without you. But I'ma do this. I'm not wasting away at the *Weekly*."

"___"

"Okay. You know I wouldn't leave without my family."

"___"

"Aw, Amy. Come on. We don't have to decide this now."

She would come on.

MY WIFE DESPISED MY FATHER, BUT DID SO POLITELY. I'D DRIVE DELBERT up north for slapdash visits with Gaye and her kids, just to keep up the loyalty thing. My mother avoided seeing her ex.

After my last day of ESPN interviewing, I scooped up the Old Boy in Sactown and got to know him on the way to LA. My energy flagged, but his talk kept the car on the road for the last three hundred miles. Delbert's constant passenger-side pontification provided the first scopes of insight into him.

"Most people don't know that the salutations in Hebrew and Islam are nearly identical," Delbert said, his voice rough and Southern, hardly at all like mine. It was news to me that Delbert was a comparative religions autodidact. Past Fresno, he explained his journey from the Nation of Islam to the Sunni Muslim camp. Delbert grew features.

When we were again at Dockweiler, he was simply an awkward grandpa.

Helluva thing it is, getting your first unfiltered sense of your father by seeing him play with your son.

Sleeping in the next day was my reward for finding a possible alternative to the job I had and hated. Killing a roach as I picked out bass lines in the office signaled my routine's reemergence. I stumbled into the living room to find my boy, chubby and mostly toothless, on Delbert's lap, bouncing. Forrest had infancy's wildly patchy curls—tall on top, bushy on the sides—like the accidental 'tweener punk-rock style my friend Josh termed a Grohawk.

As distant from Delbert as possible, Amy cradled the phone to her shoulder, setting up a model casting call.

My son and my father watched *Barney*. The Old Boy had tears running down his face.

I love you
You love me . . .

"Bye Barney!" cried Forrest. The video was his inspiration, his first TV. He clapped the only way he knew, wildly.

Delbert wiped his face dry.

Well. Alright then. That's some shit I never thought I'd see.

My father turned to watch me watching him. He made no attempt to hide emotion as he said, "If anyone had told me a year ago I'd be sitting here in California with my half-white grandson, watching *Barney*, I'd have told 'em they were out of their mind."

If ever there was a doubt that a man earns the booby prize by walking out on his family, here was confirmation.

I WAS TEN DAYS INTO THE NEW DEAL, SCRAMBLING TO QUIT MY OLD JOB, pack up my life, and move to New York. Then ESPN surprised me with an early assignment. Young and West Coast, Latrell Sprewell was a total mystery to the sporting press. Throughout his career, no one had written a profile on him. Not out of malevolence. Sprewell's Golden State Warriors had imploded following the defection to D.C. of Chris Webber, his best friend. CWebb split before he ended up choking the next old cracker. Sprewell pouted, writing his buddy's number on his sneakers, three inches high. The Warriors tanked. Then he put his hands on the man hired to right his team.

The media were going on Sprewell's silence, his shocking ghetto cornrows, and one article from a Frisco daily. In the thin career recap, a practice fight was recounted. The participants were Sprewell and a burly, truly thuggish Byron Houston. Sprewell reportedly stalked out of the gym afterward, shouting back, "I'ma go get my piece!" He had actually said that he was going to get his "peeps," meaning people. After the publication of this article, the shooting guard's image became more notorious and provocative than enigmatic. Latrell Sprewell crossed over to the point where 60 *Minutes* wanted to put him on.

Now the whole world wanted to know about this ballplayer. Spree hailed from Milwaukee, and my job was to mine the entirety of his Midwestern backstory in time for *The Magazine*'s launch, but this would be difficult, as an NBA investigation had put a gag on him.

Disney Corporate Travel hooked everything up. I had quit the *Weekly* literally minutes before I could get canned. Once more, I hit the road.

I catch Donnell acting surprised. My first hours in California, I found the numbers runner. He said it hadn't even occurred to him that the neighborhood had one, said he was glad to be getting into a more square line of work. Now, what's that supposed to mean? I love my son. I'm proud of him. Just look at his friends—nice, clean, intellectual, that Frank and Clarence. He doesn't need to know anyone who plays the numbers anymore. I'm just saying, why does the boy act surprised? What did he think he would see?

Then he was hunting down his contact lenses while I was at the bathroom sink. Donnell coughed, wiped at his runny nose with some tissue paper, and then, as I recall, he caught sight of my open toiletry kit. He saw a set of dentures. I had lifted another pair from a different bag.

"Why on earth do you have two of these for?"

"Well, son," I said, "one set's my teeth for working in, and the other's my going-out teeth."

I caught his reaction while bending over to wash out my mouth. Directly to my rear, Donnell shuddered, perfectly quiet. The boy must think my ghetto's false bottom has a false bottom.

A rage peaked in me that was probably more about me than our houseguest. I allowed my father to store his gun on the top shelf of the closet in his room. Forrest's room. The apartment was becoming boxed up, and the nerves were starting to go.

A lifetime away and I could not outrun his gangsta. My M.O. was to keep my dirt in the street, but Delbert had it in the house. The day before catching a flight to Milwaukee, I had to again deposit my father with Gaye.

Before heading off on the I-5 ride, Amy and I strategized and dried dishes. She considered her New York photo contacts. Forrest was in bed. Delbert entered the kitchen, shaken.

I asked him what the deal.

"I'm jonesin', just havin' a bad cravin', Son. You got anything I can use? Some weed or somethin'?"

Right about now I was too focused to score, never mind smoke. To my father's crushing disappointment, I had to tell him no.

But I did pour him a vodka triple, filled up a tall glass. Delbert's Adam's apple teeter-tottered as he made the drink gone. Then I emptied the bottle for him.

Amy kissed me good-night and, while my father finished, winked goofily. I walked Delbert over to the seats in the living room. For the next two hours I affirmed recollections of an Ohio I never knew, pinching myself awake in response to each woozy "I jus' love you to death, Son."

Precisely here is where the amusement factor in my father thing completely drained. As a premature cummer might recall baseball stats, I dissected deflated delusions. Any bond shared between me and this man had to be chalked up to chance or quirk of geography. He was hopeless, and in the middle of his delineating another anti-Delbert conspiracy, I faded out of my chair. Another Turner Movie Classic played.

He was asleep on the couch, sitting up.

NEXT MORNING ON THE FREEWAY, HE HAD MY CONFIDENCE AGAIN. MY father had a gift for fealty. He sussed out a means of obtaining it, then made allegiance materialize.

Delbert told me more than I'd planned to know about prison sex. (What non-ex-felon could ignore the sweet portent of an inmate with "legs like a ballerina"?) Few questions were asked of me. He let me in on his aboveboard life after Mom. He had remarried, then divorced. There was Pat and the tenets of Islam. Good stuff, but I was exhausted. It had been an intense two weeks, as I was also doing Ice Cube for *The Source,* and one at a time, I was telling the crew so long. Already missed them. My mind drifted.

The radio faded on the Grapevine. New stations rose in Bakersfield to die out in south Fresno County.

Then details turned compelling: There's Delbert the barker, with flea-market inventory that's the same as everybody else's. There's recession-era tensions at the Anderson swap meet. There's a white man from Calhoun, Georgia, with two truckloads of flags from the Confederacy.

And up pops a proposal. Delbert has the Georgia voice down.

" 'I'm talkin' about business; can we talk?'

" 'I've got two semi-truck loads of rebel flags. These people love the rebel flag here, but I cannot get out here and sell them. I am tired of keeping a warehouse full of them. They are tying up my trailers and my trucks.' "

"I said, 'Nah, man, they'll kill me.' "

" 'They're not gonna do anything to you. If you stay with those flags, you can sell every one of them. Just don't pay any attention to black people and you'll sell them flags.' "

To me, doing ninety-five a few miles outside Stockton, the cracker's pitch doesn't sound like the sort of thing that even Clarence Thomas, with a severe head injury and rent due, would support.

Please, Showdown Shorty, tell me you didn't . . .

"And, as a matter of fact, I came to tell the man no . . ."

He told the man yes. For a piece of the action, my father loaded up his truck and brought the bounty to South Carolina.

I look at my father as if he's human feces. Not mine. And I really, really need a joint.

There is, finally—belatedly, admittedly—the urge to ask Delbert, "Why are you here?"

"I seen them lining up to buy that flag, and after I checked my cashbox, it was fuller in two or three hours than it had been ever. My reservations started to subside."

"So, alright. Um, why did you stop doing it?"

"I ran out of flags to sell."

IT'S A LONG STORY—NOT EVEN A STORY, BECAUSE STORIES FEATURE REA-son—but I need his company on these last LA days. Amy is confounded, almost wounded, by the allegiance, but if I'd bothered to ask, she would almost certainly tell me that my addiction to this bad drug who is my forebear is entirely about knowing the edge. It's about the edge and everything investigation makes you leave behind. My wife might even smile in the telling.

Sprewell's coming into focus, the move is coalescing, and Delbert's back in town. Just downhill from the crib, he and I catch the Big Blue Bus to Santa Monica at Pico. We watch LA transform from ghetto to fabulous. It's shocking, the rise I get from watching him watch the ocean. Back at our end of the boulevard, we lunch at Roscoe's Chicken and Waffles, my treat.

THERE'S NO TIME FOR THIS, BUT I DRAG MY FATHER TO SUNSET 5 TO SEE a *Jackie Brown* matinee, and while we are downstairs in line for coffee, flossy Laker point guard Nick Van Exel circles the interior's modish architecture. Nick is LA's last ghetto celebrity of the millennium. On the brink of playoff extinction, he'll end a "One-two-three break!" team cheer with "Cancún!" where the "break!" should be. Nick Van Exel will be sent packing. The tide is right now building toward this, and Van Exel has his head down, sweatpants unzipped along the side to the billowing point. I can't say why it feels good to be with Delbert.

I will finally deposit my father up north. The Sunset art house is almost full and this is a movie I've already seen. Emboldened by the rustling darkness, I home in on the expressions flashing across Delbert's profile as Pam Grier's dope deal sours, even before she knows it.

And Bobby Womack is singing.

"Across 110th Street / I did what I had I had to do." Yeah yeah. He. She. We.

Delbert sings out, as if we're in a packed Cleveland nightclub and the year is 1973:

"Bobbay Wo-mack!"

I jump back while seated, like looking around the theater to see if that muhfucka's in the house.

Perhaps it's a clique thing, this call of recognition, and this brand of celeb just does wild shit dutifully. No questions asked.

No more outbursts. No announcements, not even critique, until we burst out of the cinema and into the light.

Down the elevator to underground parking, Shortness and Son standing side by side. Delbert doesn't have to tell me how much he enjoyed the flick. But he does. Then he's quiet.

I pull the Accord, which a great big company is about to ship East, out of the garage and up San Vincente to Sunset. Nick Van Exel. Bobby Womack, circa '73. Pam Grier stripped clean of her diva. I can't shake the attraction to this phase of nigga, its sublime and ephemeral purity.

Exactly what do I have in common with them? If I'm in the ghetto—doing errands around Crenshaw or cutting loose in the a.m. at Unity—I am not considered especially street. Yet I am, if I allow it, a kind of celebrity in the midst. But when I'm around my well-heeled famous friends, I'm regarded as particularly ghetto.

Heading home I wonder why, after all these years, do I think "Donny Shell" when I conceive of myself? No one's called me that in more than a decade, but somewhere there's a permanent reminder.

Who is calling me this? Who sees me in such terms?

Okay, let's say I am a ghetto celebrity. We still haven't figured what it's going to do to me while I'm down with a corporate media entity averse to blackness beyond a skin condition. Could the infusion of Donnell Alexander into The Mouse's worldview cause anything other than internal damage? Will I come out alive?

El Niño's kicking up dust. Rain and sunshine intersperse. My feet could not get colder.

I pull off Sunset just after La Cienega to buy a six-pack of St. Pauli Girl. Unfamiliar beers thrill my father like mulattoes do hicks. We push on to La Brea, go right. There's this Westside album cover in my mind. *The Ghetto Celebrities*. Their CD cover showed the group straight up, without the aid of airbrush, makeup, or probably even a comb, and while the music was typical gangsta hustle, they did do that one perfect thing. They gave the g-celeb a contemporary face.

For once, silence in the ride with Delbert. There's just The Beat's Top Five countdown filling up air between us. Delbert's head bobs at "To Live and Die in LA." Tupac won't ever die.

Maybe my father knows. Stranger options had brought about answers. We're nearly down to the strip mall on the north side of Olympic, almost home among the boxes.

"I just wonder, how is this going to turn out? I don't want to sell out. I got this good thing going, you know? It feels all homey and people seem to appreciate what I do. They tell me all the time in the clubs. At the Rakim show, fuckin' my favorite bass player, this cat Norwood from Fishbone, told me he loved my shit. The way I came into the game, that means I'm s'posed to die happy, right?"

My father smiled absently and I knew he didn't have a clue.

But I'm my father's son, so I keep talking. We pull up to the curb. He undoes his seat belt and I tap hard, two fingers on the steering wheel, so he pauses.

"They told me in letters. Man, you ain't even knowin'. Violet Brown, David Mills, all them niggas. It seems like I fuck around a lot, getting high all day, having lunch. Writing every once in a while. But all I ever wanted to do is the right thing.

"So? What do you think? Do you think it's possible to do this

Disney thing in a way that's *good?* Can I work this thing and not sell out? Should I even care?"

Delbert clicks his tongue across his false teeth. The sound is portent at its most hollow.

"Son," he says, "sometimes it's just like what my man says in the song: Ain't no map from here."

Ain't no map from here? I raise our power windows.

Delbert says it once again: "Ain't no map from here."

We both get out, then wend up the spiral stairs, Delbert first. *What song?*

Wait, I don't want to know. It's too perfect in the dark.

SO THAT'S HOW PIMPS GET STARTED, BY NOT HAVING DIRECTIONS. IT'S funny, but if you were a soothsayer and I believed in you, thought you had the stars and voodoo and all that shit on your side— if you had proof of a personal past-life experience with Nostradamus his own self—and you told me that at this late stage of the game I'd start that pimp shit, I wouldn't have believed you.

The only way you would have surprised me more would be by telling me my writing would be the 'ho.

I LET MY FATHER SLIDE, DISAPPEAR, AS HE HAD DONE SO MANY TIMES, more often that I probably knew. How he could be a tangible presence in my life, something other than an occasional source for folksy axioms, was now academic, this much I had concluded. My life was on a continent away. In all the ways that really counted, Delbert was just a bit player, the scenery chewer who got away.

But who the fuck *is* that calling me Shell?

Donnell's gone and El Niño is in Sacramento with me. It rains e'ry damn day, water up over the sidewalks.

I settled into my oldest girl's life. She's thirty. But my daughter's Oak

Park household—Gaye, her boyfriend Pops, Gaye's four youngest, and now me—is coming undone. Conditions in this fixed-up crackhouse are going downhill.

Her brood plans to relocate.

I get along real well with my daughter and, I'd say, pretty well with the oldest two kids in the house, Destiny and Ryan. Torrie and Tiaree, the little ones, are four and almost one. And they love Grandpa. But that might be the problem: Pops wants to marry Gaye and doesn't want her long-lost father movin' with them. She's my daughter, and if she wanted me gone, that'd be one thing. But Pops is just a gangster asshole and the two of them don't really have a relationship.

Maybe I'm a little crass, but I told 'er that.

My oldest daughter, too, is a writer—albeit unpublished, huh! She leaves a note on my bed tellin' me she hopes I'll put a cap on the length of the visit, because the dynamics of her marriage're bein' affected. Gaye's relationship with Pops is, at best, unstable. They fight somethin' hellacious. But, hell, her telling me this is more direct speech than Mista Dah-nale ever offered.

The storm keeps its momentum, for weeks at a time. Water's coming out the sky like some kinda celestial bailout. I didn't see it coming and am not prepared. If I'm gettin' the boot, I want it clear. And I tell Gaye that. I say, "I done lived under a lot of circumstances in a lot of states, a lotta cities. I don't have no reservations about goin' out there in that rain, I'll tell you that now. If the point is that I gotta make it on my own, I can."

Just let me know, and I'll get good to go.

Gaye says I'll have a couple of weeks to wait out the weather before the landlord tells me to leave.

Ryan acts all sad, but doesn't protest. Not in my presence, anyway.

"The little ones are gonna miss you," Destiny said. She just turned twelve. A month before, I was just a buncha words to her. But she's this beautiful girl, 'bout to look like a queen. Looks like Mama's people, a Rice if she's anything.

I tell Des, "It's not like you're leaving town. Yer only moving a few blocks away. I'll come visit you." Hearing her say she'll miss me just touches my heart.

Pops' boys do the moving. I stay behind, hiding from the rain. All I ask Gaye is that she leave behind that collection of pennies and some reefer I came across. I have a roll of money no one knows about. Gaye's left behind a mattress, but I sleep on the floor, as a means of preparing for the rugged days ahead. I been homeless before.

12.

if you don't know me by now . . .

GO BACK FOR A MINUTE.

There are about forty in our party at Hamburger Mary's in San Francisco, a day before the wedding in Golden Gate Park. Amy's parents are talking with one of my groomsfolk, Maryanne, a naturist from Ventura County. Nephew Robby, one of The Better Men, is playing pinball with Nona, Amy's best SF friend. In the middle of the restaurant, where Lloyd holds court before my mother, Jamaican blood ever so subtly seduces West Virginia soul.

Amy chose to have the rehearsal dinner at Hamburger Mary's because, number one, if anyone's had a bad time there, we've never seen it, and number two, we don't have enough money to pay for a rehearsal dinner. It's the only good place in SF we know that all wedding party members can certainly afford.

We forgot that the off-the-cuff and graphic queer art on the wall might blow any detail of the day, major or minor, out of each family member's head.

Everyone is at least mildly uncomfortable, and I'm sitting with Geneva Graham, catching up on whatever—pretending not to notice her sidelong looks at the penis parade. She's got me waging bets against myself over the chances of her seeing humor in anything right now, on any level. Grandma 'Neva interrupts me, asking about the ring on my left hand.

The accessory's dynamic facade is the steely symbol of the Bauhaus movement, a sharp-featured profile rendered with clean, succinct lines. Amy and I call it The Power Ring, and what I love most about The Power Ring we share is that neither of us had any idea of its meaning, any idea about Bauhaus when we bought it. At my most pretentious, the ring reminds me that I'm common.

And Grandma asks, "Is that supposed to be something demonic?" Because vigilance against demonic onslaught is like a part-time job for Jehovah's Witness.

"Naw, Grannmaw. It's a symbol for Bauhaus."

"Baw-what?"

"Bauhaus. It was a movement in architecture and design that came out of Germany in the twenties. Bauhaus influenced a lot of post-war art and is actually, like, really prevalent in typefaces you see in advertising. It's like, print that has serifs on it? Those little flourishes like this here"—point to a stairwell rest-room sign—"as opposed to this one"—now wave at a Pop Art poster by the gaming machines. "You almost never see serifs in an ad. Some people consider that to be the biggest triumph of the Bauhaus movement.

"You know what I'm sayin'?"

Grandma looks at me without expression.

"I didn't understand one word you said."

And I laugh, because Grandma may not understand, but at least the ring isn't demonized. All this fag art is one thing, but if I was bringing demons into the equation, we might have to call it a night. It's all good, and she laughs, too.

I GOT PAID FOR BEING DOPE. IS THAT LEGAL, IN THE WORLD OF FAST LIT-erature, I mean? Doubt it. And with a handful of exceptions, I thought of my entire Cali crew, at one time or another, of being feds: P-Frank,

Heavy D, Jennifer, Mina, Ernest, and Philippe, all were suspected of compiling dossiers on Donnell Alexander at one time or another. Coming from where I did, my life felt so outrageously contraband that I couldn't believe I was getting away with it. So all of my confidants had to be narcs. Except the Crack Emcee. I couldn't see how even the CIA was advanced enough to hide someone like him among their minions. Add Amy in there as well. Her pain and joy was all too real.

I may have been paranoid but I'm actually a pretty mild-tempered fellow. That's at the core of me and, most days, on my face. It's in the middle where things get hectic. Between the me I've cultivated and the soul who came through Brenda Graham's womb in 1966, there are all these layers of vengeance and will that can make life hellish for the roadkill wife or random editor who has the raw misfortune of having their mission and mine not mesh. I have not a bit of guilt about the explosive collateral damage that these in-between layers inflict on the world. My momma told me not to put my truth on a leash.

This matter often puts me in mind of Michael Jordan. At the height of his powers as an advertising pitchman, he was practically a comic book icon. Don't misunderstand me. I admire Jordan as much as anyone, but *Space Jam*'s cartoon antics were perversely redundant. His selling point was a lack of features beyond smiling ebony vigor. Mike was a black cartoon. Powerfully out of time, from a different universe than Tupac. At the heart of his image was an information void as selling point. His aura hinted at vacancy and the republic's wish list.

It's a good thing that entering the millennium wasn't contingent upon the whole of Western culture coming to terms handling the detailed black man, or else 12–31–99 would have been *Groundhog Day* like a motherfucker.

'Cuz, yo, athletic ability didn't keep us from being like Mike. Humanity did. Fitting then that O. J. Simpson paved the pitchman way for Jordan. When he turned to be the opposite of what Americans projected onto his vacancy, one athlete's apparent crime broke the collective perception template.

Resolved: Nicole Simpson died for your sins.

Okay, yeah, I admit it. I am in bed with criminals. But I'm not malevolent, though maybe reckless. Definitely reckless, 'cuz rational thinking is crazy overrated. If I knew the dimensions, if I'd used my better judgment, I'd have devotedly watched *Family Feud*. By all reason, it should have been damned affirming to get my choices ratified by the almighty "Survey says!"

Sheeeeeit . . . I was *not* trying to consume fabricated culture in that way. Sure, I wanted the rush of football games and to be carried away by light-play miracles on the big screen and popular music to make me shake my ass, but I needed to be able to sift through its entrails, dust for prints, when I came down from the high. Pop residue told the most, like the drugs I've taken, the spaces where I've touched down and all my friends and enemies. Only broader.

My artist friend Josh from Pasadena used to accuse me of being a closet sports guy, which was the boho inversion of having your man-hood questioned by a jock. ("No I'm *not*," I simpered.) Sports are cool though because they are formalized competition, stylized fighting. Real fighting always struck me as being extra, redundant. With all due respect, Mr. Ishmael is wrong: writing is not fighting. It's better than fighting. Writing's a fixed match that at its best convinces all involved parties—writer, subject, audience—that the scrapping in print is actual battle. Even at its most virtuoso, writing never gets more like actual bat-tle than good WWF. Art beats sport every time because the artist main-tains more control over the outcome than the quarterback, even while preserving gray areas.

(No actual battles were fought in the making of this book.)

AN AMORPHOUS BEIGE DRAG IN A STAMPEDE'S RUSH, OUR FAM OF THREE wobble, stroller first, from Kennedy International Airport and into the February rain. We are debuting in New York. The line against the curb for cabs that haven't yet come runs thirty yards, so we are happy that the small West Indian man offers up a limo. Our first. And $35 seems a good price for this kind of thing. *Hey boo, we're ridin' in style!* Then a dozen other commuters cram into the less-big-than-you-would-think backseat. The glee subsides.

Almost two hours later and we still haven't gotten to our temporary Financial District digs.

Max and them told me they'd hold my hand.

Your life can change from day to night.

THE EXCHANGE IS IN THE HEART OF WALL STREET. NARY A HIPPIE IN sight. Come morning, when we transport our stroller and wills from the lobby to outside, my wife and I recognize the Indy 500 of capitalism, stiff fucks in suits knocking over their own mothers whenever she's blocking the way to, say, a good cup of joe. Amy's traumatized. Forrest isn't much for talking, but clearly finds the chaos fascinating.

And I am Tony Robbins, spitting cheers of blank uplift—"It wouldn't be an adventure if it were easy out the gate!"—even though I only survived LA because traffic tension was never mine. Lived life safe indoors from seven to nine, in the morning. And be the cause work or play, I was straight up like eleven between five and seven, in the p.m. Now, a quivering in my jawline undermines my preaching positivity.

Immediately I know this is wrong, wrong, wrong . . . am confounded by the subway map and don't know where all the hamburger stands have gone . . . it's bananas here, the most expensive whirlwind ever to blow through Earth. Like Hebrew slaves in Egypt, we shoulder the stroller down and up MTA station stairs. Then night falls and the Financial District is a ghost town.

Our prefab digs lack diapers, food, and contact-lens solution. Where do they keep the Ralphs? Okay, Kroger's? Great Scott, I'll take Fred Meyer! Forrest's wheels clunk into narrow side streets, along sky-high walk-overs, and across taxi-heavy thoroughfares while a downpour drapes Manhattan. I point out landmarks as if they heal on sight.

Back at the Exchange, somewhere amongst the boxes and stranger furniture, a telephone bleats. It's ESPN. They need me in their face yesterday. Overlapping editors talking on speakerphone. Two, three, four voices haphazardly braided into one.

Get here, shoulda been here. Now. Now. Now. We got a guy to write with you, Shaun. Hop a plane, find Sprewell's long-lost teammates, dump your notes. Then kiss your wife good-bye.

I'm at Wall Street, they're in Midtown. Do I take the subway up or down?

It's not possible to overstate my level of disorientation. Corporate Travel puts me on a plane to D.C., and at Washington's palatial MCI Center—where CWebb, Sprewell's best baller friend, toils for the Wizards—a bewigged Negress with government midmanagement written all over her gives me the evil eye as I slip toward the standard forty winks I gather during the national anthem. That bourgeois death-stare makes me rise.

CURSES, HOLY JOURNALISM GODS! SPREWELL'S HOMEY DON'T REMEMBER me. I need for him to, but am not mad because CWebb is otherwise no joke, and in that he's an exceptional athlete. He has opinions, a voice, and a large collection of art from blacks in America. I used to talk a lot of shit in print about rappers—the way Tupac never had a record until he made a record, how he let the ghetto define him. But compared to jocks, they are thoughtful revolutionaries. There's never been a No Limit of sports, no community-based, self-sufficient empire. Not one. That's because, after all the discipline is weighed and tossed, a pair of athletes aren't half as vivid as one rapper, even a wack MC.

A lifetime of buying into The System goes into being a professional athlete. Yet the supply of jocks sacrificing their bodies never runs low, regardless of niggas witnessing daily that The System cares not about their interests.

If you want to figure how big a business sport is, you can't just tally attendance figures and merchandise. Once you've factored in the billions of dollars television contracts pay—which spill over and boost pay for actors across the TV landscape—and ad revenues that exceed $1 million a minute per major event, you still aren't done. It's necessary to account for the revenue made by the runoff media enterprises—by ESPN, local newspapers, and talk radio. The chain links on to the billboard owner and the guy who cleans it and the next man who fills his gas tank. The trickle down is reminiscent of human-cargo-boosting lifestyles in Mid-Atlantic seaports three centuries past.

Athletes, despite having boosted these games from playground phenomenon to entertainment cash cow in less than half a century, hold no equity in the major leagues. The blacks on whose backs the empire of sports is built have minimal management presence. Ownership is effectively zero. And at the end of the twentieth century they are only just beginning to get a foothold in the media world that markets and delivers the fruit of their labor to the masses.

You doubt my claim that black Americans get less than their fair share of the trillion-dollar sports pie? If power were commensurate to contribution, would AIDS be raging in Africa as it is? How fucked up do you think niggas is?

I'm out of my little Cali alternative-paper haven and starting to learn just how much muhfuckas aren't knowin'—starting with me. It actually seems valid to document, through the writing for *The Magazine*, this part of show biz. Minus all the cussing, first-person, and discursive writing, of course.

Something draws me to the men who run the show at Thirty-fourth and Madison. I am enamored of their polish. It's the opposite of the alternative papers. The prevailing style of management reminds me of the Fresno State Sports Info Guys, the athletic department's clean-cut cheerleaders. The *New York Times* NBA guy, Mike, was one. We *Collegian*eers condescended to Mike and guys like him only because S.I.'s rah-rah PR looked disconcertingly like journalism. They had direct lines to coaches and the athletic director.

I now think maybe we were jealous.

13.

my writes

THE *MAGAZINE* IS WEEKS FROM BEING BORN, AND ESPN HAS ME BACK in Milwaukee. National Rental Car, the official auto provider of the Walt Disney Co., has me looking outside a lunchroom window, at the snow piling up about Washington High, with the solid race man who is Latrell Sprewell's first basketball coach. But it's Rick James who's got this black boomer talking. Coach Gordon forgets to regard me as an emissary of the media lynch mob. He can't help himself.

"Yeah," I say. "I was up in his crib! He lives in the Valley—and he's still rich."

"Really? I figured he smoked all that money."

"Man, there ain't enough cocaine in America for Rick James to go broke. He wrote all them songs—Mary Jane Girls, Teena Marie, Temptations, even that Eddie Murphy mess. Every rapper sample. He owns the publishing rights. 'Can't Touch This' alone made that fool millions."

Coach Gordon purses his lips, absently flips the papers in his folder. He's stunned.

"Wow." He signs a hall pass, wowed.

"He's got a new record, you know."

"You're *lyin'*. Is it good?"

"It's ridiculous. Better than anything since *Street Songs*. He's grown. And, he did a lot of fucked-up stuff when he was way out there, but he ain't do *all* that mess everybody thinks he went to prison for either. I wrote about it out in LA."

"I didn't even know."

"Yeah, man, it's underground. Cat messed around and got lost in Hollywood. That's a cardinal sin right there. He's tryin' to get right though."

"That's all he can do."

"That's all any of us could do."

I slide my tape recorder onto the table and flick it on.

"His real name's James Johnson. And he still fills up arenas. . . . Look, I just want to tell the real story about Spree, that's all. Did everybody call him Spree when he played for Washington?"

"Nah, his teammates mostly called him Latrell. His mother used to call him 'Trell, though. He's a sweet kid, not at all like y'all media people are making him out to be."

Most of Sprewell's Washington teammates got to know him about as well as my sportswriter peers while Gordon developed him, which is to say hardly at all. The coach had seen him around, heard the six-four, skinny kid with a high-top fade could play. But the boy only really was into gymnastics and hanging out in the basement, fiddling with stereo equipment. And he moved around a lot, lived in Michigan for a minute with his drug dealer daddy. Coach heard Latrell was a good boy.

After everybody graduated from Washington High's league champion team in 1988, Gordon recruited the kid, the only time he ever did that with a boy who was headed into his senior year. Latrell had split time between parents, between Milwaukee and Flint, but Coach Gordon saw right off he had character. The kid couldn't shoot a lick but scored 28 points a game by struggling near the basket, and Washington was good again.

James Gordon's exception went further than any other player he nurtured. Sprewell still had no jumper, but hard defense got him through junior college, then to the University of Alabama. The summer before his senior year Sprewell shot twenty-five-footers until he didn't suck at it anymore and got drafted by the Golden State Warriors. Nobody back home saw it coming.

They didn't see the Carlesimo thing coming either. Some understood in hindsight though. Latrell Sprewell's daddy wished his boy had done the coach worse.

It's a crazy story.

Coach Gordon stops to banter with another little girl, signs her hall pass, then leans forward conspiratorially.

"They're always talking about who's gonna be the next Michael Jordan, but if you ask me who has the kind of story that's inspirational as Jordan's?"—hard, sideways two-finger tap on the table right here— "I'd say it's Latrell."

It takes even me a while to digest this one, the notion that the replacement O.J. could switch with the most honored. The problem's not that I don't believe it should happen, it's that I don't know how you tell something like that. Where's the context for this story? How do you make the average reader see what it's like from the bottom? This calls for more skills than I've got right now, but this is the story I want to tell.

'Cuz, if he'd have *presumed* to scream on me, I'da ripped P. J. Carlesimo's nuts off.

THE ONE PERK OF MY NEW LIFE UNQUALIFIEDLY WORTHY OF ADMIRATION is how I frequent hotels I could never before, not on my own. On the eve of *The Magazine*'s launch, I catch up with Sprewell at the Marriott in Marina Del Rey. He's bone-thin, cornrowed, and hiding behind costly shades. We go down in the elevator, joined by David Aldridge and two kinda hot assistants from the office of agent Arn Tellum. Until yesterday's interview with Lesley Stahl, Sprewell had been silent, out of basketball all winter. I lean in close and murmur the name of his closest Milwaukee friend. Sprewell peers over the top of his sunglasses.

"Yeah, ya potna Chris Powell told me to tell you whassup." Barb,

Delbert's sister, hooked me up with this connect. Spree cocks his head, then baritone giggles in the lobby.

The driver out front carries us five across the way to the Ritz-Carlton, Aldridge up front with the driver, Spree and I in back, with Tellum's assistants on our laps. Space limitations, you see. And here, in the same SoCal where I dwelled for three years, I have a revision: *this* is as far as I'll get from Sandusky, Ohio.

BUT, SURPRISE, WRITING FOR *ESPN THE MAGAZINE* BITES THE BIG ONE! Who knew when the hiring editors said their product would be on the edge that they were talking about its pioneering graphics and network synergy? No one is better than the parent company at turning scribes into pitchmen. My literary aspirations? Time to put those shits in my pocket, for later. Here it's all about the product, and the product will never be about me. My byline will never, ever matter half as much as Dick Vitale's. Or Stuart Scott's.

When the editorial staff isn't meeting, there is much TV watching, rearguard ESPN channels on our state-of-the-art Macs, financial fare on the screen bunches dangling high from columns at our desk aisle's end. Seven floors from the street up on Thirty-fourth and Madison, cablecast cathode rays and type flicker and jet across the faux-hoops backdrop. The scoreboard that drew me, it's despicable. Fucking cable.

Among the Boys of Sports Info, *Jerry Maguire* is the touchstone cultural text, but they live for *Seinfeld*. Knowledge of George and Jerry's madcap doings function as the lingua franca of *The Magazine*'s meetings. Alluding to *The Simpsons* is a dicey social gesture, suggestive of probably a junior staffer. S.I. mavericks watch *Friends*. Assisting reporter Anne-Marie is a fellow *Mystery Science Theater* nut—she's impressed that I've met Joel Hodgson—and I suggest she keep her affinity on the down-low. This is the land of "Must-See TV," and even a too slow or obviously forced guffaw at the newest and most ingenious reflection on Kramer's hilarity could be read for not owning a television at all. Then where would ya be?

To blame the overarching air of wackness totally on ESPN would be wrong. No one in the entire J. Crew–clad Sports Info set really wants to know what's going on. Sports journalism is the most anti-intellectual of all nonfiction writing because organized sport itself is all about cut-and-dried conclusions. Winning's not the main thing, it's the only thing. A tie is like kissing your sister. Meanwhile, the creatine of my writing is gray areas and unusual contradictions. When Max and the S.I. set drafted me, they brought into its fold someone who spends his screen life waiting for something that tops Jim Marshall's wrong-way run. And they're seemingly unnerved by this.

Yet there is no quibble with the quality of my work. The assignment is street cred—I'm penciled in as designated hipster—and the Sprewell piece gives the mag that. So does this thing on tattoos I whipped up in forty-five minutes and turned in as a first draft. On the road, young columnists and beat reporters show my style love. A radio guy in Miami tells his audience I will revolutionize sportswriting. But in *The Magazine* proper, my stuff is like cayenne pepper—just a little is desired and it's to be watered down as much as possible.

Editorial meetings take place in a long room beneath and to the rear of the scoreboard. I am not mad at Jerry Seinfeld's little program, but for shits and grins I posit that the show peaked six seasons ago. At this, eye contact fades away, à la Allen Iverson automatically taking a J. In time it becomes clear that the solution to unwanted ancillary chatter is for me to say, "Oh, I dunno, *Taxi* was a superior show." If I go for *WKRP in Cincinnati*, the Barons of Sports Info may even prematurely end a meeting.

MAY DAY. AN EARLY MAY DAY.

I am so fucking late, and the press entrance of the Charlotte Coliseum is so far. This first-round NBA playoff action oughta be into the second quarter now, but not only am I outside the arena, I'm just stepping onto the Coliseum parking lot. One rare midsize space available was beyond the greenery rimming said area. This saved seven bucks, but Jordan's inside, probably working his last playoff magic, while I'm ducking between cars and getting outta breath and sweaty. It's a good thing I scarfed half a pan of *good* brownies on the ride down from O'Hare, or else I'd be really upset.

For once the tardiness is not my fault. I was practically out my room at the Ambassador and only moderately weeded when the phone rang. It was Nancy, the contact for this NFL kid I'd been chasing down. I couldn't put her off, because she was officially talking to no one in the press, and her boy 'Zo is sportswriting's Moby Dick, the Out of Control Athlete of the Moment.

Alonzo Spellman is twenty-six, a gigantic defensive end from a small-town hood near Camden, and he has a $12-million deal with the Chicago Bears. Around about when spring workouts happened, 'Zo went on a rampage. First this big nigga is dancing nekkid in gay clubs and lecturing late-nights on project housing blocks wearing only his drawers. Then he broke down in Nancy's place in the burbs. 'Zo ended up fending off a dozen cops with a belt, going to a mental hospital, and having an exorcism performed on him by Mike Singletary. Dude escaped and went on something like a five-state crime spree. The Bears are about to cut homeboy, and not just because he's almost literally a fugitive from the law. Somewhere Latrell Sprewell is exhaling deeply, because this motherfucker makes him look like Kirk Cameron.

Paradoxically, Spellman is also a real cool cat, a thoughtful jock who gives excessive amounts of time and money to poor kids. This story's an enigma, and I'll go all-out chasing it. It took ninety minutes of game, but I got Nancy's confidence. I agree to write 'Zo out of the margins. Then I'm ghost.

BECAUSE MJ WAS WAITING. I CAUGHT THE NEXT THING DISCHARGING dangerous toxins to Charlotte.

Now, funky and disoriented, I'm inside the arena. I'm askin' that the action be *fan*-tastic.

All that runnin' for nothin'. Jordan schooled Glen Rice and them, and the actual highlight was schmoozing in the tunnel with Antawn Jamison and his UNC second banana, Vince Carter. One of Jordan's lieutenants makes this happen, and he promised more of the same at this one sports bar where Ron Harper was set to be on display.

The bar is not your average Hooters. Thick and miniclad strobe-light honeys swish their hips standing atop pool tables as them 8-ball games drain on. The DJ might blasts the hottest No Limit records, but "The Choice Is Yours" is coming next. A winding walkway connects the sports bar to a pitch-black, humid dance club, and party people flow freely between both venues. One cover, two nights. By two-thirty, I'm in the back room of the sports part, drinking with dude from the Jordan crew. He's trying to tell me how I be like Mike.

"I ain't lyin' dog. Remember those gold chains from the 1988 All-Star game? You seen the pictures. The NBA ain't tryin' to bring that shit back up. But Mike made sacrifices, made choices. Dig it: his grandchildren are going to be millionaires. Guaranteed. How deep is that?"

It's deeper than Atlantis. I let the brotha talk.

"Yeah, he's up in his hotel room playing cards and unwinding, but, fo' sho', he wants to be right here. Nigga, he played at UNC! He just another street nigga, just like you and me. But he can't come up in here. It would be a panic."

Dude's cellie blurts, and he picks up. Uh-huh. Cool. Peace. Then he excuses himself and leaves me alone with my greyhound to ponder the possibility that Superman and Clark Kent are one and the same. Neither of us pays for our drinks.

I actually kinda met Mike a couple of years before, back in LA. It was at the *Space Jam* premiere, and I didn't know the venue was Mann's Chinese Theater. I thought it would be some studio-lot, small-screening-room shit. Dipped in cutoff sweats, Tevas, and wire-rimmed glasses held together by tape, I wandered onto Hollywood Boulevard with my nose all up in the pages of *Shadow and Act,* distracted. The scene is out of what Amy used to label *The Li'l Donnell Show.*

I ain't show the red carpet gatekeeper the business end of my critics-only pass, which I had turned into a bookmarker. He let me up the walk.

Children in bleachers surrounding the gate screamed and waved. I scanned pages to figure where I'd left off. I nodded to Coolio, then some UPN bumpkins. Having scampered down from her seat, a seventh-grader on the other side screamed in my ear. So I raised my hand for her. Her part of the crowd clapped louder.

I'd pulled my nose out of Ellison, at least until I got sheltered from this ridiculous din, but I came up on Mike and his wife Juanita in tuxedo and gown. I said whattup, they both smiled benignly.

Finally I figured out what was wrong. Come on, now. This is Michael *Jordan*.

It was too late to get off the red carpet. At the theater entrance Mann's doorman, a balding Armenian cat in a suit, asked for my full pass and saw that I only had a serf's credential. Dude fully fucking flipped, wasn't even trying to hear my explanation about how compelling Ellison can be.

"What the fuck are you trying to pull!" he sputtered. "Gedt ottav here!

"And use the side door!"

Based on this memory, any resemblance between Michael Jordan and me seemed too far-fetched even for APBs in the burbs.

Recalling our meeting, I've exited the sports bar's back and stand against a main-room wall. 'Zo Spellman would be feeling this space, that's a bet.

It's 3 A.M., and the room I share with two hundred other high people is still more alive with greasy vibrancy than any club I've yet experienced in Manhattan. Wholly mesmerizing is the casual undulation of Southern women, even as I'm thinking about getting old and square and the need to pack it in. Ron Harper has bellied up for a drink. There is, barely perceptibly, a small stir by the back room.

Towering above the scrum is the bald head that launched a thousand shavers, the one that renders cornrows suspect. MJ. He's spotted his teammate. Jordan reverse nods, Harper raises his chin in recognition.

The superstar starts wading through the fifteen feet of party that separates them.

Easily 95 percent of them that's in da house aren't aware of the special one in their midst. But one by one they start catching on. It's the domino effect and Mike can't delay it. A woman, then a man, then another, acknowledge him with pointing and waving, then handshaking and elbow grabbing. It's a dangerous swirl of gut-felt admiration, but MJ won't admit it. He forges on. His dress jacket becomes a fluctuating fabric of hands, his minuscule progress stalls, and suddenly Michael Jordan jerks backward. His smile remains, Harper's acknowledgment turns to a gawddammit-seen-it-all headshake, and when I look back, MJ's coasting out the door in the clutches of security—the only white man I've seen here all night.

Just like that, Michael Jordan is gone, and I pay homage to the gods of ghetto celebrity.

BACK IN BROOKLYN, I KEEP ASKING AMY IF SHE'S FREAKING OUT, AND she says, as we settle into all-outdoors-smells-like-garbage season, that she's not freaking out. That first Manhattan week, back on Wall Street in February—before we unpacked our lives in a luxurious Brooklyn basement—I accidentally trashed her contact lenses and then jumped the LA flight. She hasn't stopped bitching since. So I have to ask. Ask, you know, if she's freaking out.

Amy thinks I'm a bastard for this—accuses me of accusing her of something—but the truth is that I am wholly out of context and unashamed to admit that I'm freaking out and am completely stunned that she could not be freaking out. If I was her, I'd be freaking out.

'Cuz, in case I must restate it, I am freaking out.

But Amy cannot relate. She's too mad at me. Me who demanded we move and is now spectacularly unhappy. I'm hardly ever even in Brooklyn. When I'm around, I'm tired and stoned and depressed about my writing life. She is here with Forrest most of the time. Occasionally she's out doing work that's temporary and demeaning. All of the picture-editing jobs she had in California count for next to nil because they happened outside Manhattan publishing. Amy might as well have been on the dole.

Her hostility manifests itself in her face: her outer mouth is in slow recession. Our relationship is hardly recognizable. She's about to mope off to another job interview.

I sometimes think about before, when I could put the headphones on Amy, output from my CD player something truly odd, and in a few minutes be like "Wasn't that amazing?" And she'd be glad I did it. Or when, during our preparental lives, I'd aw-shucks admit, yeah, I took a bunch of acid, and the only appeasement necessary was painting her toenails.

Play like that belongs in the Museum of Our Love. These days I make a simple preseason observation about the playoff prospects of the Tennessee Titans, and she says:

"I can honestly say I'd be more interested in hearing about your bowel movements than anything you'd have to say about football."

She sometimes says things like this, not looking up from her *Harper's*, ignoring my trenchant insights about the AFC Central, even the NFC East. She's become more Catholic, more staunch and prosaic. Her feelings are stacked in opposition to me.

There is almost no fucking going on in the basement apartment at 6 Strong Place.

And there is absolutely no kissing going on in the basement apartment at 6 Strong Place.

And I am, essentially, but not exactly, like: It's a shame we have to go through this. We don't even talk. Girl, we don't even kiss.

Forrest, nearly two, is for months at a time the sole reason for even maintaining the facade. He's Lisa Bonet beautiful, smiles as naturally as a dog wags its tail. Near the door, he dawdles silently with a plastic wagon containing shoes where blocks should be. His mother sorts through boots.

His not speaking is poetic. Weeks ago, he began protesting the long road trips by hiding my suitcase in the midst of packing. He recognizes that Amy and I are breaking new ground in the realm of protracted unhappiness. Here in the hallway of our $1,800-per-month basement, he tries to bridge the gap by standing between his parents and grabbing hold of us both.

"Mommy and Daddy together?"

He pulls with both hands as he says this.

THAT LAST TIME I WAS IN CHICAGO, FOR GAME 3 OF CHICAGO VERSUS Utah, I introduced myself to Isiah Thomas on the United Center floor. *The Magazine* had me gathering quotes for one of the senior writer's stories. Isiah was in full makeup and about to go on camera.

"Excuse me, Zeke. Um, I'm Donnell Alexander, *ESPN The Magazine.* I was wondering if—"

"Ah," Zeke said. "So you're the one."

There had been a flash of pub about the network's hiring me. Max the editor talked me and Steve Roderick up in *GQ* after the premier issue. Then a newspaper article revealing that *The Magazine* had only one black staff writer originated in Philly and went out to all of Knight-Ridder. Among those who follow such stuff, it was a big deal that some unknown was among the half dozen Negroes in America with a staff writer gig at a major glossy.

A mystique could be cultivated by being nonflossy, the last incog-negro in the land.

"Yeah, that's me, dog. The One. If you have a sec, can you give me something on what makes Jordan such a powerful competitor . . ."

But this Chi-Town occasion now, a quick fall jaunt, lacks even that conflicted sort of glamour.

I'd been all over the Spellman story, darting from New Jersey to Chicago, scouring party places, project housing, training camps, and Manhattan public records archives to find out what the deal is with this guy, 'cuz it seems he can't help himself and I'm fascinated. Spellman's parents aren't too different from mine. However, he's a millionaire in torment, with all his money frozen by the courts. The NFL has all but blackballed him. Chicago familiar with 'Zo, however, insists dude is bipolar.

When the story breaks, Amy and I are dead broke, about ten grand in the hole from when Forrest was born and the move East. American Express is suing me on the grounds of knowing how to act, and Amy's obviously about to be out of work because she's a feminist photo editor and *Gear,* the men's mag she signed up with, is gradually becoming a half-assed stroke rag.

This is when Spellman's angel, Nancy, calls. She's got this weird notion that I can save his life, that he'll play ball with me—of all the sportswriters in the country—because I'm ghetto. I've got this one sure shot to catch my subject live. Eight A.M. Monday at a Chicago court date.

It's Sunday night when the call comes. I have exactly five bucks to my name, no credit, no money in the bank, and am feeling cool with no prospective lenders on this coast. So I get Disney to book a plane and I race to Chicago with my five-spot and meet this guy in court. I take the subway downtown from O'Hare. Three dollars and fifty cents left.

In the muni courthouse hall, 'Zo pounds his enormous fist to mine. Around us is his crew, raw enough to make Allen Iverson's entourage resemble the Huxtables. A crack-'ho-thin girl with tatts on her face rails at me over 'Zo's right to wild out. "They let Dennis Rodman do it!" she says. Her eyes are wild. Babydoll keeps on. The bailiff makes a beeline. All seven of us get the boot from court. Both of my tape recorders are confiscated, but dude and his "family" let me ride all afternoon.

I land at the airport with enough dough to take the A train downtown from Kennedy and hit a Smith Street bodega for a bag of Skittles on the walk home.

The drama's result: Not only does ESPN run what some call one of the best football articles in ten years, but maybe the guy gets saved. (Definitely his career.) After the human-interest angle comes out—and

Deion Sanders speaks up for him—buck-ass 'Zo finds himself starting for the Dallas Cowboys.

And the motherfucker never even tells me thank you!

FORREST HAS ESSENTIALLY STOPPED TALKING, BEFORE HE GOT STARTED really. Back in Cali with his stay-at-home dad, he'd grown used to long interludes of music and silence on early-morning rides with me around Hollywood and up and down Crenshaw. Interspersed were days with Lorena, relating in Spanish, eating rice and beans and running amok at Chuck E. Cheese, all loose and free. After dark, with Mama so lavish with love, there was no need for words.

At twenty months, Forrest was saying the requisite Mama/Daddy stuff, but he otherwise spoke in jargon—like "udelish" for "go to this." Little man did a lot of pointing, a ton of pulling, and after becoming a New Yorker, his talking flatlined. I secretly blame my weeks on the road. Still, the boy is so expressive. When he does talk, his minimal language skills are overstuffed, fuzzy with intent. It's total punk rock, very *Zen Arcade*. What gets me most is the pantomime. It is perfectly elaborate and sharp. Time could only dull its brilliance.

Once, in faint bedroom summer light that fiends for nightfall, while I struggle with the chords to a song I want to call "Who Dat Is? (Not Just My Baby's Mama)," Forrest hears through the back-porch window and runs to join me. He picks up the harmonica I put down three corny vamps ago, and when I let go of my guitar so as to assist, Forrest wordlessly urges me to keep strumming. He wants to jam.

For sure, at first I make romance of Forrest's speech issues. He's mashing the faces of playground peers who don't respond to his incomprehensible talk. Terrible Twos, I say. Then, one brisk Brooklyn morning on the front stoop—right in front of my fucking face—he undoes my DJ Rectangle mixtape, and in an instant Little Man is desperately needy. I call down to the basement apartment:

"Goddammit, Amy, get the boy some help!"

"I BET IT'S AUTISM." THAT'S MY MOM, ALMOST OFFHANDEDLY, SITTING IN our kitchen. Her trip from Sacramento couldn't have been timed worse if she had consulted Satan. Her heart condition sometimes deprives her brain of oxygen. She says ridiculous shit. I try taking it in stride. But this is still My Mother the Nurse, and when she utters *autism*, the blitzing blind-side linebacker of new-parent fears, I suffer something barely less potent than a petit mal seizure, excuse myself, and walk around the block, blazing some garbage stress weed. It is not yet breakfast.

October's air bite puts me in mind of oppression, and I wonder if my boy's problem is something he got from his father? Is it all the drugs I took? Perhaps I played one Invizible Scratch Picklz record too many. Or maybe it was that sunrise ride to Beverly Hills and back with Mystikal's *I'm Bout It* turn on repeat. I know these things fucked *my* head up.

Maybe I've been disabled all my life, carrying some shit Delbert's crazy ass gave me and Forrest has inherited.

IN THIS FOURTH QUARTER, AMY'S NOW WORKING STEADILY. SHE IS LESS visibly pained and cloying with Manhattan around to distract her. I squire Forrest around to the hearing specialist in Carroll Gardens, then the play therapist's office over in Brooklyn Heights. I am not aware until this moment that there is such a thing as play therapy. Our doctor's eyebrows rise because Little Man doesn't narrate his block stacking and plastic car racing. She's scribbling in her dossier that Forrest's play doesn't go anywhere. He is getting bad reviews.

We will get our son into a good program, a special program at the Montessori school. And I will drop him off, the walk home conspicuously against Court's heavy pedestrian traffic. Back at 6 Strong Place I will smoke dope and make pause tapes all day. Sometimes I struggle to wrangle together a book about the Delbert in me.

Or I'll *not* roll back against the lemmings and cut through an alley between the Montessori school and the Bergen Street F-train stop. I'll burn a funker in the alley, then suffer the office, headphones on. If the implications of living like this become too much to take, I'll contrive a reason for Disney Corporate Travel to send me to LA or the Bay.

I am of two minds about the Forrest quandary. If it's Monday, Wednesday, or Friday, the episode ain't nothin' but hype. My son is Whitey-Me, the privileged version of Donnell Alexander. ("He don't talk 'cuz he ain't got shit to say.") On Tuesday, Thursday, and Saturday, I'm wrenched because Little Man might never be able to speak his truth.

On Sunday, he's just my boy.

"PUT MORE OF YOU INTO THE PIECE."

It's a strange little article. Someone in photo unearthed a book about a prison ministry that featured photography of a teenage Jordan having a watermelon chopped off his belly. Because Jordan had been NCAA-champ North Carolina's sophomore grunt, he was volunteered to take part in a prison evangelical showcase. Next thing he knew, a religious fanatic was halving a big green melon over his belly while Jordan lay on a weight-lifting bench. The sword went too far. Like Mike ended up stitched together at the prison infirmary. But all's well that ends well, and all that mess.

The writing was a bit restrained, and Max said to put more of myself into the piece. I'm offended by the very notion. He no more wants the real me than the NBA wants to see Sprewell become more popular than Grant Hill. You got a bunch of cats praying for all those Eastern European players taking up NBA benches to mature and overcome. And I am supposed to think they want more of Donny Shell?

So I throw on my drab olive field jacket, go home, make the story streamline and neat. And I add the following passage:

Huge chunks of watermelon flew across the stage and into the crowd. Niggas thought it was a fuckin' barbecue.

I resend the story, via modem, and take the F back to *The Magazine*'s Herald Square stop. Just for shits 'n grins.

When I stroll by his office, Max has just read the latest version. He is pacing, hard copy in hand. When I poke my head past the corner office's sliding door, the editor looks up.

" 'Niggas thought it was a fuckin' barbecue'?" Max says.

"Hey, yo, you said to put more of myself in it."

" *'Niggas thought it was a fuckin' barbecue.'* "

Then my editor looked away, frozen in a goofy smirk. He repeats the line and walks toward the copy desk. The secretaries are nonplussed.

" 'Niggas thought it was a fuckin' barbecue.' "

Such amusements are about all that get me through my colossal, colossal blunder. The S.I. guys delete the BBQ reference and end up promoting this dashed-off piece of writing quite heavily. Still, despite my successes, they regard me with somewhat more respect than a precocious intern might merit. My previous work life isn't at all acknowledged and I'm not happy with ESPN. ESPN is not thinking about me. The scoop is this: As is true of the athletes who grace the cover of *The Magazine*, I am the software, not the hardware. Not now, not ever.

KIM, *THE MAGAZINE*'S PUBLICIST, GETS *AMERICAN JOURNAL* TO DO A SEGMENT on Michael Jordan's past-life prison freak show. After I recite my sound bites outside the Garage—the magazine office's central space—the flack, the producers, and I stop in our tracks, following the office workers' lead. Everyone stares at the tall man making his way to Max's corner of the floor. It's David Halberstam, the boss's very good friend.

"That guy is my favorite writer in the world," the producer muses. He turns to Kim, excited. "Do you think I could talk to him after we get some B-roll? Donnell, perhaps you could walk along that wall, toward the camera. Not too fast though."

What do I know from B-roll?

I'm pimpin', cold puttin' it down with soul as I stroll along *The*

Magazine's magic carpet. Soul in my stroll, muscle in my hustle. It's Donny Shell's national TV debut. Uncle Ricky would be proud.

"Oh-kay," the producer says once I've gone the distance. His cameraman drops the recording instrument to his side. The producer rubs his goatee while he studies the mock-hardwood patterns on the Garage floor.

"See, the problem is," he says, "you look like you're gonna kick my ass."

"Oh," I say. Dang. "Okay, um, let me try it again."

I do a couple of pinched-butt-cheek B-roll strolls; the *American Journal* crew moves to my desk and shoots me pretending to work. Call me paranoid, but the cameraman seems to be willfully avoiding the copy of *Ego Trip*'s last issue that I've positioned as a design element.

I AM HEATED.

Hollywood Basic was never a Disney property! And there's probably not one person in the company who knows the meaning of Raw Fusion! That early Sports Info infatuation is long since gone. Now I'm cultivating something other than hipster disdain. The workplace proletariat is smart and refreshingly devoid of casual insanity. But the kids are mad mallish, straight-arrow, and I feel like I'm in the station house and I'm holding funk.

The whole cop vibe comes from a handful of S.I. guys. They show irony-free admiration of black jocks they call throwbacks and tend to have developed writing careers so they could hang out with sports stars. They *love* Bill Romanowski.

Looking up into the scoreboard, I take the broader room's measure. What have I entered into? An orifice. Or an office, er . . . officer. Officer, *officer,* offisah! Overseer!

On this green day I stand up from my cubicle, peruse either surrounding aisle, and say with only slightly veiled disgust:

"Awfuck. This is the straight-up jock lunchroom table."

One Rolodex over, on my side of the aisle, Brown Mark clicks to a new Web page and scans the monitor before him. But he's talking to me.

"Dawg, I know you feelin' yaself, but"—and here Mark wheels on me, grinning—"come on now. Not everybody's tryin' to hear all that mess. Not everybody gets to act like the King of One Hundred Twenty-fifth Street. Some of us gotta work."

This I don't take personal. It's his *turn*. Residence in our cubicle quadrant equals membership in the 125th Street Neighborhood Improvement Association. The nabes seem to have assigned turns to tell me to pipe down.

Mark takes his responsibilities quite seriously, as he's crazy dignified, a Jamaica native and Howard man. When I play him King Tee's "Super Nigga" and bump my head like it's the first time I heard that shit, Brown Mark listens attentively and says, "Yes, but couldn't they have called it 'Super *Brother*'?"

And I just don't know what to say about that.

Like AG across the way, Brown Mark is a writer-reporter, which is a step up from scrub on the job description hierarchy. Our aisle is arguably the blackest strip of office space in mainstream magazine publishing. Rounding out our quadrant, Young Eric plays the gentrifying white yuppie to the max. A few weeks after the mag launched, he asked Traceye from marketing the difference between Sean Combs and Puffy Combs? At once it was clear that this guy would live pretty much isolated in our neighborhood and that he would be headed big, big places with ESPN.

And I am the King of 125th Street.

One cubicle a block up from us is Classy R, senior editor and den mother of the Negroes. The R-uh's hair is done up in a straightened fashion that is stiff and frankly matronly, and Classy R is a bit self-conscious about it. She's uncertain of where to go with her style. We're roughly the same age. Unofficially HNIC—is there an official way?—Classy R flutters on the periphery of the S.I. set and rooms across the cubicle street from O.G. Sports Info cat Jon, a live-in landlord.

Pan back a cubicle.

AG, diagonally across the aisle from me, is whom I talk to most. I notice him looking over one of my shoulders or the other at the stuff on the wall. On my left are two Sambo figurines, one man, one woman. I call it my tribute to blacks in entertainment. I want it understood that I'm not here to entertain anyone. On the other shoulder, a makeshift photo comic in which Big Pun and AZ read copies of *The Source* issue with my Ice Cube cover. They say, via an adjacent thought balloon, "Damn, when did *Source* cover stories get this fat, yo?" Stacks and stacks of stuff on broken computers and books and stuff make my art collection difficult to see. So people keep looking, harder.

AG wonders how my desk manages to look war-torn when my black ass exists in the office primarily as rumor.

"Dandy Don, you got everything there but a car up on blocks," he says. "I'ma start calling you Rollo."

Great. King Rollo.

But AG's cool, an Altadena Negro. AG played pro football for five years and has personality. You forget AG's a pro athlete. But, because he's my age and went to Stanford, at first I thought AG was my opposite number.

AG, because I asked him, is retelling this amazing anecdote about training camp.

It takes place in the years before he made the Canadian football circuit. After a night spent awaiting The Turk's knock, he sought out his sagely old-school defensive-backs coach. AG wanted to know if he was gonna make it. The team, his career, his life.

"Tell ya the truth, I've never been sold on you Notre Dame–Stanford boys," said the team's HNIC. "Gimme one of them niggas from one of them small, black, rural colleges, one that maybe didn't wear shoes until he got to school. One that might have *taken* the pussy once or twice. That's where the real football players come from."

AG didn't last to the start of the season.

I've had him tell that story throughout this first year and laughed hard and loud as ever because I haven't heard this most American of sports so purely distilled. It's funny 'cuz it's true.

———

LIFE IS VERY DIFFERENT NOW, WHOLLY UNRECOGNIZABLE FROM THE decade since college. Whenever I do media, I'm introduced as "sportswriter Donnell Alexander." Old Cali crew Mina and Ernest speak slowly in our phone sessions, special-ed-style. P-Frank now treats me like a sucker, as though he writes my lyrics.

And I repeat like a mantra: I had a good run. For a minute, I was someone.

Because Donny Shell is very cool, I hit my marks, because I am at heart an unassuming guy. I really want things to work and believe there's a really refined sort of revolution to be promoted once I finally get in the game. So cool is the rule. I don't propose stories about, say, steroids in pro football anymore. It's now comprehensible that Disney's mammoth pro football contract inhibits coverage, mos def. I'd be better off pitching a piece on the correlation of MLB herpes outbreaks and star pitchers who can't get out of the first inning. No matter how many 'roid rage outbreaks underline lurid headlines, that story isn't gonna fly.

THE EDITORS INSIST ON STRATEGY SESSIONS SO MUCH THAT THE WRIT- ing staff refers to our gig as *ESPN The Meeting*. Max and the rest of the S.I. guys think entourages are the next big story. Penetrate the entourage of Allen Iverson or Marcus Camby, they say. Be our man on the inside.

They think the entourage is the ultimate metaphor. First off, I tell them to recognize difference: I do entourage time in LA, Miami, and Manhattan. Occasionally I'm with mine. Understand that running with the Chicago Bulls is much different from late night at the Viper Room with Medusa. Backstage at Family Values isn't the same as backstage Chris Rock's tour. It's the individuals, not the genres, that make the difference. Let's not generalize for the public. Hey, here's a story that tracks: It's about the ultimate hangers-on, the American sports journalists. We're remarkable in that we hang out, fatten our wallets off, and only have to pretend to be down with the player posse's general concern.

But no one at the wood table so shiny and long wants to talk about that. Apparently, last night Rachel and David Schwimmer were antic and touching.

I begin seeing the whole Disney thing as a personal irrelevance.

That's how I'm livin', too: there's my job life, a distinct subset of my work life—with hard boundaries. There shall be no overlap. Fuck a job. The less you're in my mix, I tell the editors, the more I can focus on my work.

I am not on the team. I need a producer, not a coach.

You give me money, I give you stories.

I give voice to this philosophy about once a week, usually perched on my 125th Street, ergonomically correct chair.

Still, I am a squirrel just tryin' to get a nut.

14.

License Like a Muhfucka

R EAL STRUGGLE LOOKS—ONLY LOOKS—LIKE THIS:

Snow still clung to mountain peaks on the morning that the girl who would become Grandma Geneva sighted Arthur striding down toward the Jenkins shack in the holler. She had already swept a winter's worth of dirt from the porch floor and was readying her mop water, fixing to bring those hardwood floors back to their natural blond. It was the first January Saturday after the war, and as she thrust out her chest to the cool, clear air, Geneva set her eyes on a middle distance. And there he was.

Arthur's uniform and dangling medals couldn't have impressed her more if he had been Douglas MacArthur. He moved closer, each step treading away the memory of their silent fighting, filling the lapses in his correspondence. And the girl's heart swelled. Geneva was sixteen.

Arthur squeezed tight this young sunflower. He breathed in the homeliness of her just-pressed hair and melded with Geneva on the porch, turning her straw-colored baby fat to warm, soft butter.

When they walked though the front door, still ajar, gently encased in mild Appalachian air, Geneva Jenkins's family gave a start, then gathered round.

Papa, half from Cherokees, half from slaves, pumped Arthur's mahogany hand, working it with an awareness of the Graham family's relative prosperity. Graham's Farm, high up on a flat stretch of the mountain, was about the finest ag outpost you would find among the black folk around Kimball, West Virginia. As good, really, as anything over in Welch. Not anything like the long days down here in the holler. In Papa's strongbox sat the engagement ring he'd bought with $50 Arthur had mailed from the Philippines.

Mama hugged Arthur, then stepped back for a look. West Virginia black Cherokees like her worked their asses off, knew nothing of ease, and even in uniform, Arthur came off laid-back. Mama studied the image he cut, 'cuz in it was a quality she never saw in stern Papa. Mama had liked the idea of this young man from one summer day in '44. That's when Geneva had come home from her cousin's party raving about some handsome soldier on leave. Arthur had been all over; Mama's little girl was a hillbilly. Although her daughter's birth in Val's Creek had been followed by moves to Big Stone Gap and now Kimball, a painful sameness jaundiced her mornings, the helpless drag of being about nothing. Arthur looked as much like Somebody as Mama felt likely to see.

Arthur, Geneva, Mama, and Papa sat down at the kitchen table. And as easily close as girls who slept three to a bed might, Ethel, Edna, and Geraldine, Geneva's sisters, gathered about. Arthur produced from his uniform pockets a knotted kerchief. Excited chatter rose, then faded as he spread out items one at a time across the wooden surface.

"Dang, Arthur, you comin' in here like Santa Claus, all late," said the youngest, Geraldine, sandwiched between Papa and Arthur. "What you got?"

"You mean, what's my girl got?" Arthur dug into his pockets. "I picked Geneva up a li'l somethin' whilst I was out in California."

"California!"

That was Papa. Arthur held up two rings and then a bracelet to the light.

"They call that the Golden State," Mama nodded toward the younger girls.

"I see why," said Geraldine.

"It's not much, but I saw these and couldn't help myself. I figured Geneva would care to have them."

"You like these baby?" Mama asked.

Geneva shook her chin twice, hard and forceful.

"I'll tell you what," Papa announced, standing in a gesture of final evaluation. "You'll be hard-pressed to see finery like that up in Charleston."

Geneva struggled not to squirm in her chair, to keep her body off Arthur. She tried to remember that she'd been mad. The engagement ring, estranged from her emotions by that correspondence spat, stayed locked under her father's watch; the bauble hardly seemed real to her. More importantly, Arthur had picked up this jewelry in Los Angeles, a place that in Geneva's mind was as far away as stars in the lower West Virginia sky. Just seeing all these new things laid out on the table was a thrill in itself. While her sisters buzzed with fascination and fingered the twinkly trinkets made of brass, she felt the gentle onset of a swoon.

She grabbed her mother's hand, leaned in tight, and whispered, "Oh, Mama, I want to get married to this man."

Not thirty days after that, Geneva Jenkins took Arthur Graham's name. Nine months after that, when the little girl Art and Geneva named Brenda Lee came gurgling into the world, Kimball busybodies checked the calendar to make sure no funny stuff had gone on before the minister joined this couple together.

ARTHUR HAD BEEN BROUGHT UP BELIEVING THAT THE ROLE OF CHILDREN was to serve the family's greater good. Back when he was sixteen, county lawmen had come knocking at the door of his father's home. As the ten other Grahams looked on, officers ransacked the property, tearing into every doorway and enclosed compartment. Someone had spilled word about the moonshine, Arthur's daddy's sidelight. When the deputies finally unearthed a still, the room went silent in the wake of accusation. Arthur stepped forward with a simple "It's mine." As the oldest boy, the responsibility was his. He said the still was his secret, nobody else had been aware. Arthur knew that, at sixteen, he'd only do a few months in jail before coming back to the farm. If Daddy went, the bid would be a lot longer, and there might not be a farm to come back to.

He quietly did the time. According to how he was raised, heroism had nothing to do with it. This was just what you did to keep a family together. There was never any question whether his children would get to know this. He instilled the value in his firstborn child. Brenda was cleaning and minding babies before she was old enough for school.

When the coal companies began doing the unheard of, laying off miners, Art drove up North to jobs his brothers arranged for in Ohio. Geneva chipped in with housekeeping work found through good fortune and family fortune. These days the young mother was moody. Arthur had confessed that, way back when he'd let Geneva's letters to the Philippines go unanswered, he'd fathered a child with a local girl. A sense of betrayal nearly ate Geneva alive.

Considering the mood of the house, every little bit of labor Brenda committed to counted.

No matter how tight a household Arthur and his now twenty-year-old wife ran, the Grahams only seemed to get further behind. Kimball, like Welch, Val's Creek, and a hundred other dots on the map of West Virginia, was a company town. It was a place where coal men with clean fingernails had it so that your assets running at a distance behind debt was a lifestyle mandate. And with the arrival of young Sherry and Roger, making ends meet became less and less a reasonable dream for the Grahams.

Contacts in Cleveland took a liking to Arthur during the extended shack-ups with Tommy, his brother. There was always work to be had up there, plus that lakefront town rocked at night. LA ain't have nothin' on this. Arthur brought his family up North in 1953.

In Cleveland, the Grahams learned the difference between being poor and being ghetto. It wasn't a lesson they were prepared for. The five family members lived in two rooms, sharing a kitchen and bath with another family on their floor of the rooming house. Their food-stuffs had roaches and rats. Home wasn't the biggest problem though. Classrooms were crowded and sickly. One morning, Brenda and Sherry, ages eight and six, were mugged on the way to school. There was, too, the day Geneva returned to the apartment from a grocery store run to find five-year-old Roger playing in traffic. Brenda had been left in charge, so Geneva beat her butt hard with a belt after bringing the boy inside. Grandma knew, even as she handed out the thrashing, that the incident wasn't fully Brenda's fault. If they'd been in Kimball still, hills would have rolled where now cars ran.

It was Arthur who had wanted out of West Virginia, but even he had to admit that Cleveland wasn't working. But he couldn't go back. The Grahams stomached the ghetto for five years.

In the spring of 1958, Arthur took one of the fishing getaways that helped him cope with boardinghouse life. Northern Ohio had never looked better than on this expedition he took with his pastor on a route he'd not taken before, west along roads that caressed the contours of Lake Erie. Art had been an expert fisherman since childhood, and the Great Lakes were legendary among anglers. This area had an almost resort quality to it. The lush, untouched green life surrounding Erie's edge was married to an orderly agricultural sensibility. And by the time the pastor brought the car near those docks where perch supposedly bit better than anyplace else in the world, they had entered into a bona fide city. A smallish one, but one with all the amenities.

Sandusky, Arthur's friend explained, was the biggest municipality between Cleveland and Toledo. There was money here, too, as Sandusky featured prime lakefront property. Had a couple of develop-ment deals gone differently, it might have become Toledo. Now, though, the place was known as the home of Cedar Point, a major amusement park. Arthur remembered it now. The kids bugged him to take them there all the time. All that day and throughout the night, the Lake Erie perch bit like Arthur could not believe. It seemed he hardly had to leave his line in the water but a minute. Catfish and bass were taking the bait as well.

He was working two poles at a time. With downtown in the immediate distance, they stayed out on the docks all night.

The sun wasn't even fully up when, beer in hand, Arthur surveyed the locale: this is what he had been thinking, what he'd been dreaming of. Nearby, on a street called Perry, he saw apartments that hardly looked different from where they lived in Cleveland. It was clean though. Black people could live here, the pastor told him, and for a heckuva lot less than in the big city, that's for sure.

That settled everything.

Perch are what you call a good-eating fish, sweet and tender. Bread them up, and they fry well enough to melt in your mouth. It was Sunday night when he got back to Cleveland, a couple dozen perch in tow. Pans clattered, grease splattered, and in minutes the whole house smelled precisely like one of those downtown soul kitchens. It sounded like a lip-smacking convention when Arthur cleared the air over a dinner table filled with Grahams:

"We're moving to the town where the amusement park is."

Not one person at the table complained even a lick, and no one considered their move part of a greater struggle, even though that battle to escape bottom and—maybe—become mired in the middle defines us all.

ISN'T THAT SOMETHING? I TRULY AM LIKE THIS ALL THE TIME—SWIM-ming in my own history—even without an editor. (Actually, no editor was ever assigned to this project.) (So *that's* the problem? you say.) It should be acknowledged that the basic premise of *Ghetto Celebrity*—the whole nigga *Zelig* thing—is bitten from 1997's "Bomb MC," by the Colored Section, a jam that clearly none of y'all were ready for.

For real reals: I don't give a mad fuck. 'Cuz at this point I am feeling myself, like, totally. Ain't nobody bad like me. Like that. I propose that if humankind is going to be programmed like machines, we ought to be funky machines, silicon-based life-forms with some stank on 'em.

In fact, in the continuing spirit of improvisation, I'ma do a song about virtuosity in the form of Donny Shell, the true MC and crowd mover. The man, the myth. (Somebody put a beat on there. Bang on the table if you must. Yo, if you're freeloading at Barnes & Noble, get the cashier to beatbox for you. Tell 'em go midtempo, 'cause that's how I feel this rhyme. It's about rhyme you feel this time. Your eye on these words, your word against mine.)

One, two. One two—
Now . . .
Time's gone and the rhyme's on
Better be there with bells
'Cuz I keep my word in dresser drawers
at finer motels
Crackers won't dine on me
And I'm not tryna be
Just Another E
True Hollywood Story
And,
I'm past sick of thug niggas who be thinkin' I'm shook,
When inside I'm spinnin' vinyl and reading a dirty book.
Ay yo for 35 years I've tried to write my life
(Right my life)
To my delight
You don't hear me doe:
It's been a rite trife

Black niggas—Treat each one individual
Most of us is drownin'
Some of us is kinda winnin' though
Coach Dave I need a blow 'cuz I'm feelin' mad winded
Zadie Smith is on the stage and yo that bitch is light-skindid
It's cute: She's eatin' pussy
How 'bout a nigga like me?
Buck-ass, dick out

Bangin' white chicks naturally

It's straight catastrophe

Pure disorder

When I'm on tha set

Test right-wing snatch for moisture

Then see how deep shit can get

That's why:

I cold sick of thug niggas who be thinkin' I'm shook,

When inside I'm spinnin' vinyl and reading a dirty book.

Ay yo for 35 years I've tried to write my life

(Right my life)

To my delight

You don't hear me doe:

It's been a rite trife

Cops say: Coke on the CD case

Bio: Smack in his DNA

On the low Colin Powell's like,

"Nigga, ain't you got nuttin' to say?"

Bourgeois agent ignores e-mail

And my momma won't call

'Cuz they think I type the shit

That cause our people to fall

Whatever though

I'm better yo

Advance me any more

And there'll be no keepin' score

'Cuz this the shit you adore

Keep y'all askin' for more

(It's buck muhfuckas!)

Watch ya step

Gimme 'spect

And check my metaphor

'Cuz:

I cold sick of thug niggas who be thinkin' I'm shook,

When inside I'm spinnin' vinyl and reading a dirty book.

Ay yo for 35 years I've tried to write my life

(Right my life)

To my delight

Still you don't hear me doe:

It's been a rite trife

Don't ever fuckin' tell me I ain't ghetto.

Speaking that which isn't glorious is my contribution to the struggle. It won't be Jesse Jackson who gives full disclosure to the awful urgings that urge us all on. And it won't be those porters in the airline terminal who won't ever ride the plane. It won't be them that do the dishes, but never have the pleasure of dining in even a three-star grub joint. Nuh-uh. It's gotta be me, because I made it with the permission of no one who had authority, and my mama told me to speak my truth.

15.

a nickel and a nail

YOU GOTTA HAND IT TO AG, HE HITS ME WITH THE INSIDE DOPE. HE'S GOT it like a mythic Jack and Jill Open House up here on 125th Street, telling me shit I never knew.

Rocking a beret jauntily back on his crown, recalling junior year in Palo Alto, my man is explaining the class act thing.

That's what they used to call AG, "a class act." They call cats like Cal Ripken that, but with black ballplayers it's deep euphemism, usually reserved for Ivy Leaguers and such. Grant Hill types. Class acts. AG despised being categorized that way because he knew being tagged as such only signified management's and the sports entourage's comfort with him. He felt like it demeaned everyone else, while setting him on his lonely.

A nice Pasadena Catholic school got dude on the class act path. But Papa AG made his bones selling liquor in Compton. My cubicle neighbor wasn't born yesterday. He knows the system insulated him from sensation that knows no caste, and he understands the beginning and the end of our differences.

AG scratches his nearly smooth scalp underneath the beret. "They never knew me. I'm buck-ass wild."

I really had thought he was my opposite number. That first spring of lunchtime hoops at Basketball City, AG and I about came to blows. We were in a cab that pooted along westward on Thirty-fourth, me, Guff, and some random S.I. wanna-be, getting ready to turn down Seventh Avenue. Maybe free agency was the debate, something about the merits of playing where you've set up roots. AG was up front, fist on chin by the power windows, and set a middle-distance gaze upon the Chelsea masses. For the gig, he'd relocated from Atlanta.

Our driver turned down Seventh Avenue.

"All that counts is getting the money," interjected AG. His wife had died unexpectedly the previous fall. New York had failed him as a stand-in for Atlanta. Sometimes he mourned publicly. This time, AG merely declined to alter his stare. "Nothing else matters."

It goes without saying that I was stoned at the time. Manhattan never sees me straight. Manhattan is a nightmare straight.

"That's bullshit," I said. "Don't make your issues our issues."

Then, on the Basketball City hardwood, AG said fuck you, first opportunity—before the ball was inbounded. We were choosing up teams.

"All I know is," he said, "I want to guard *that* motherfucker."

Which is funny, 'cuz I suck. I told him I couldn't wait and we went chest to chest, pushing and woofin'. Brown Mark separated us. I was not mad—our shoving match seemed to be pushing me a lot further back than AG.

We both seethed as the game started. Right off, I stuck a J from the top of the key, without taking my eyes off the enemy. I looked in his eyes as a shot and hissed, "Bitch." Then AG used his superior athleti-cism and conditioning to turn my scattershot warring into my team's demise. We cursed and dipped shoulders into each other through three games and started up fighting again in the locker room. The fracas ended when I shouted, in a way both unjock and thug-free, "I thought you were my *friend.*"

And with that it was over. Sometimes you gotta fight if you want to be tight. AG knows this from his days with the 'Niners. He has a game ball.

"Another inch," says AG, who's just under five-ten, "and maybe I go to the Pro Bowl."

"Yeah, well, another inch and I'm a porno star," says I. "Nigga, I ain't tryna to hear that shit."

AG loves that I'm crazy. Or rather he loves that I don't care if they think I'm crazy. He loves to think that I think that.

When we opt out of working and *The Magazine* bustles all around us, there's a *Grumpy Old Men* aspect to our social protest. We're both tired. Our shared desire, or so we say, is to have shtick, that's when we'll know we've made it. We're both pushing thirty-two and are black granddaddy tired and want to be like Jerry Seinfeld, lauded.

AG caps the class act talk by handing back my *Best of Earl Grant* jewel case. He flips past the cabaret singer's buck-dancing, crowd-pleasing, chicken-grinnin' cover pose and zeroes in on a small inside picture. Grant's chillin' hard, toying with a white poodle, sitting in a white convertible Cadillac. He's got his shades on. Clearly, the nigga was in France when the picture was taken.

And you know he got paid, on the under.

"That's what it's all about, right there," my man says.

You have to hand it to AG. He really is a class act.

BECAUSE A DAY WITH ALL THE SPACE HEATERS ON IS MARKED FOR WRITing about the Delbert in me, a day for getting up at four, Amy will trudge off with Forrest to school. The kitchen smells vaguely of marijuana. A hippie speedball, they call this, java and a joint. I'm on the floor and stretching sideways, coffee cup in hand, Icewater mixtape in the makeshift boom box.

A few minutes after seven, my wife passes through. Soon the boy will be out looking for his juice.

Like most every morning, Amy is wearing my Organized Konfusion T-shirt and panties.

I say, "Hi, Booty." But my heart isn't in it and she feeds off this. Amy makes a face like something stinks.

"You've been in town for a month now, so you can't use traveling as an excuse. At least do something about that stack of dishes, Donnell," she says.

Her belly seems bigger to me, and I'm sure she isn't pregnant. The difference isn't measurable, yet it's unforgivable.

Cannot believe we're not fucking. Can't believe *I* don't fuck. I wonder, if you pass up a three-way, and you never thought you'd pass up a three-way, and you aren't especially in love with your wife, does that signal a kind of sexual dysfunction?

"Juice, Daddy."

Forrest is up. I run my hair through the cornrows the mandatory and profoundly expensive nanny has given him and kiss him on the lips.

"Open the fridge and I'll get you the juice."

I climb to a standing position. I work in the predawn hours with no pants on.

Most of Forrest's wants are simple enough that his speech suffices.

When my mother wondered aloud whether my boy is autistic, she threw in a mention of his resemblance to Nephilim—the wicked offspring of angels who in the Bible mated with humans. Amy says it's important to remember that Mom's been pretty ill lately.

My belly is huge. I am 220 and can hardly see my penis anymore. Amy comes out of the bathroom naked and, okay, she's not that fat. You know what it is? It's her lips. They seem to be in recession. Yes, I bet you could map the trajectory of our tension by measuring her lips in photographs. They began receding in California, when I told her we really had to do this New York thing. When I got back from my first playoff road trip, there seemed to be nothing left of Amy's lips, and by the time *Gear* fired her, on her birthday—when she was staggering weakly around the apartment—she was straight up in lip deficit. Now as she prepares to be inducted to the Condé Nast fold, Amy actually has indentations where lips should be.

That heavy-lidded pair of emeralds, though, are exactly where they belong. When we're not speaking, her eyes are the reminder. They say just enough, like our son.

Do you think that during even her worst feelings of betrayal in SF she felt as hateful toward her man? Amy used to despise it when I'd say the institution of marriage lost utility as people stopped living in villages. She always thought other women were the biggest threat to us. Turns out the problem's career. Our disarray swirl and indefinite climb had not been a part of the bargain during those bike rides in Chico.

THERE IS ONE WOMAN, THOUGH, WHO HAS MY FANCY, UNRESTRAINED. And I would just like to state, for the record, I said to hire the middle-aged Jamaican nanny, the one smelling of Old Spice and shaped perfectly like a pear.

Our family landed in Brooklyn because, stepping off the third F-train stop beyond Manhattan, the air felt relatively country. Cobble Hill is one of those places that's deemed hip by people who keep track of such things, but the area literally teems with buzz-harshing yuppie smiles. Menacingly flat, the smiles reduce my quality of life, harshing worse even than the Caribbean nanny army that raises white-climber spawn.

But what do you do when all the agency sends over are women from Jamaica and Trinidad & Tobago? I can't say for certain, but I do know that you don't hire the gorgeous one. You don't hire the model from *Black Hair* who has an assortment of high-end extensions and cheekbones that make Grace Kelly look pie-faced; who's five-nine and has more subtly varied shades of brown than Crayola might contrive if Louis Farrakhan were named CEO. Ext-nay to curves, dewy/doe-ish Latin eyes, and soft Trinidadian lilt. Don't even open the door. You scream out the window, "Position filled!" A down-home black chick would know this.

But, hell naw, here's Amy, with her comparative research and thought-out rationale: "She just seems more energetic and interesting."

I might as well hire a service to deliver problems to my stairwell. "Hate" is pulling up fast on the list describing my feelings toward Amy.

And of course the new nanny, Patrice, is indeed brilliant with

Forrest. She's understated in her genius, just like my son. The two chase each other around the apartment, as if they are peers in spirit. But she can flip it, bantering with me as she guides Forrest through living room art projects. The nanny braids his hair straight back just like Spree. Patrice is a constant reminder of what black beauty is about. I say cultivating camaraderie with her is for Forrest, but it's probably for me.

There's a very good chance this episode is about me. I am newly blessed with perception into the phenomenon of fathers who fall in love with their children's caregivers. In the stay-at-home dad's case specifically, the role you have in the raising of your child gets confused by this other adult presence. This *loving, tender* presence. Peep the walks to the park with the father holding one of his son's hands and this statuesque woman holding the other.

Patrice has been in the country for a matter of months and finds insight in all I say. Then she mocks me in a fashion that's giddy. Some days, just leaving the crib is a struggle, and my new friend and parenting understudy magnifies the actual mother's natural flaws and her, uh—fucking hell, let's just say it—age.

Of course nanny-courting is utterly despicable. I've told as much to Amy. That happened when we were on speaking terms. Yeah, that time. "Amy," I said, "fucking the nanny—oh, did I say *fucking*? Jeez, I hadn't thought of that—is a mistake that's comprehensible, but it's something that you *just don't do*. As a parent you make choices, and the very idea makes me sick.

"Sickens me," I say.

Today, Patrice is crouched and leaning forward, peering into the refrigerator while Forrest naps and I'm just out of the shower, fastening my paisley-brown robe, the one suffering from static cling. Today the shiny, ebony extensions blow to shoulder-length, fine and swept straight back in a fierce flip. The girl's blue jeans are tight enough to provide an anatomy lesson in braille.

I space while Patrice rises, then turns, smiling natural innocence. She asks if I'd like a bite of her mango.

I quiver like Benny Hill trying to give up cigarettes.

"N-nuh-nuh-not right now," I say, then scramble to place a pot holder before my newly chubby crotch. Then I return to the bathroom and don't come out for a good, *long* time.

Nope. I don't condone it, as that comedian says, but I understand.

SOME OF THE PEOPLE WHO RUN *THE MAGAZINE* AREN'T IMPOSSIBLE. Skipper, the Disney VP who really runs the show, seems to have my back. The North Carolina native and Jonathan Swift expert drops practical wisdom, like "There are no five-eleven-and-a-half-inch men." And I—previously 5–11^1/$_2$—think, "Oh, yeah, lose the driver's license!" and immediately round up. He gets me playing defense at Basketball City. It's him who keeps me remembering that sports don't suck.

At perhaps the one hundredth special meeting in a little less than one year, we toss around names for a new section that will showcase "Something Else," my new column. Max mentions "The Life." Heads nod in assent, but I feel I oughta say something to these rubes. You really should know, I say, that where I come from *the life* connotes a down-and-dirty place. The middle-age stares around the table are dull, silent, and unnerving.

Then Skipper pipes up:

"You know Dah-Nale, it iddn't necessarily a *bad* thing to have those connotations."

My kinda nigga. He says my name right and everything.

I TRY SHOWING *THE MAGAZINE* BRASS WHO I AM, TAKING SENIOR editors to hear The Roots jam at Wetlands and LTJ Bukem spin at Vinyl. Breaking in the office, I mention to the latest kid Max has hired away from Time Warner that Cake played at my wedding. Or I repeat the old gag about how I got so smart without finishing college because, while I didn't really go to class, I did do bong hits with kids who went to class and had meandering postcoital conversations with chicks who went to class. I'd pause, then chortle that the sort of attention you get in those locales beats the fuck out of a Top Ten education. Pausing is crucial because Gen X yuppie progeny need perfect syntax to groove on rebellion. I'm accessible, if not Al Roker, but the communication fails to rise to editorial's top echelon. I remain unreal, a hipness machine through which Disney hopes to manipulate the masses. *The Magazine* is, my faux-hip sentences vouch, so down. Downer than *Sports Illustrated*, which is to say "down" with a trademark symbol attached.

After a decade dishing raw scoops, I, Donnell Alexander, have become a tool in the selling of cool. And mostly, I wish I were dead.

Because the top editors have a really fearful notion of what cool has become—or maybe they mistake my dreadlocks for braids—the only features I'm assigned are profiles of athletes they call "troubled." Fine, I guess, but these cats are impossible to pin down for interviews. Not that this jock substratum was ever much in my Rolodex.

Call me a jailhouse lawyer, but at least I'm not a narc.

What would you have me be? If I've always done things this way, kept my mistakes around me like wallpaper. The biggest ones are the best of all I've had, and I'll take a loss to get wins later. I want to buy the world one day. All those things that irk and confuse and worry you, they're like a warm blanket to me. I would be lost without them. The real deal isn't ever something you would have me be in on, but know that your attempts to bring me around? To make me into you? They've long played out. Dead tired. I wild straight from boredom. Spin at the sigh of disappointment, kick on each resignation ploy. Step, bend, twist. When the time's right, you'll see my routine.

When I give those looks, the ones that unnerve you, I'm looking up to you. You know? You don't like the way I see you, so my gaze seems strange. Don't hate the messenger, I didn't make you. Do remember, I am looking up to you. It's all I can do. It doesn't mean, though, that I feel mired in disadvantage. I can take you or leave you, and I'm not stupid. That makes me your worst nightmare, unimaginable.

Understand that you can't possibly have the map for what I will turn into. Only after you've done this will my unknowns not register to you as wrong and final. You might embrace my mistakes.

Invent some faith now—you don't want me to be wrong.

The game's rules, each day's faces, changing, like the build-ings—outside then in. All is running past me. Revolving doors and subway stations. I let go what I knew of the world and adjust to this film that's been switched midreel. Damn coherence, I get to move in a new way. What more could one ask of a wormhole? I'm all done, done with all the schools and with each and every city, because cities are intense collections of people who've generally agreed how things ought to be. They are a menace worse than Boomers.

That's why with all the pageantry, I still couldn't tell you what you want me to be. 'Cuz what you want—what you think you want—is like starlight. Gone, visible only as illuminated rumor.

The latest malcontent: Albert Belle. The call comes from Wulf, Max's second and the editor most obviously offended by my existence. The assignment gets me inside Thirty-fourth and Madison, on the phone with Terry Belle, Albert's twin and business representative. The idea is to arrange an interview with the reclusive and mercurial guy I named my son for. As was the case with Sprewell, I think I can redeem him in print.

Terry don't know, don't *care*. He is to negotiating as Shaq is to three-point shooting: Rigidly out of place, a charged ion. The Belle negotiating strategies are articulated by telephone over about ten days.

"Albert is one of the all-time greatest hitters. It's going to be my pure pleasure to help put him into context."

"Yeah, well, Albert needs to review the article before you turn it in," Terry says. He's got the hard-core Louisiana accent. And he's tack sharp. But no wonder . . .

"That's not gonna happen," I respond, "but I'll go over all the facts with you before we go to press in order to guarantee accuracy."

"Guarantee me a cover."

. . . *his brother's reputation is so fucked up.*

"I can't officially guarantee a cover story. But I will say that, if you give me the access I need, I will get you a cover-quality article."

"Okay, we'll think about it."

Twenty-two hours pass.

"Thought about it. Albert has to be paid."

He seems serious, so I laugh into the receiver.

"*The Magazine* won't pay Albert Belle to be in it."

"Then you don't get my brother . . . Wait then." Terry has a brainstorm. "Get him in one of those cool commercials for ESPN, the network."

Is this how Garnett and Marbury got in the mix? Doubt it, but couldn't really know. This cat has no idea how deeply he has me in the palm of his hands. I'm thinking I should surrender some dignity and mention Forrest's middle name.

But I don't.

"Christ, Terry. That sounds fairly impossible."

"You can do it. Albert will donate his pay to charity."

"Let me get back atcha."

Sheepishly, I report the request to Wulf, who bumps Belle's request up the corporate chain of command.

Stunningly, ESPN is willing to make the swap.

Days go by, flight's booked, I close both bedroom doors behind me so my son can't kill my packing. The car service will pick me up from the office, at eleven. I'll check voice mail, first thing . . .

Aw shit, there's a message from Terry Belle. Deal's off. The stated reason is as indistinguishably capricious as any of the dozen other stipulations, denials, restrictions, and goose chases that have been laid out before me. Desperate, I do some shit that I never did even when Death Row Records' petulant, arrogant flack, the one who made me chase my tail for that Nate Dogg interview, had me pinned.

I beg.

I dial Albert's brother up and beg. I put it on my son that no other cat's gonna come through like me. I don't tell him Forrest's middle name.

"Terry, if you could just let me talk a minute with Albert . . ."

"I *am* Albert," the voice on the other line says. I feel myself making O'Shea Jackson eyebrows.

"What?"

"When you are talking to me, you are talking to Albert. I am Albert!"

Now that's some retarded shit right there. Turn up the showers 'cuz I am done, right here in the middle of Sports Info.

"Nigga, please! You ain't Albert, but you *is* out yo' muh . . . fucking . . . mind!

"Man, nigga?" I ask the receiver. "Nigga, just, just, just . . . nigga, *please!*"

I slam the phone down, dig roughly through my bag, and snap on my army coat. I cuss and kick things.

No one looks up. Keyboards click-clack.

The mad-mallish Sports Info set strenuously watch the product on their monitors, the financial bottom line rolls across a dozen TVs. They watch the paint dry.

I lecture my lady Sambo figurine. "These niggas is either well-paid sandwich-board salesmen or completely insane. Even the fakest gangster MC said *something.*"

Aunt Jemima watches, oddly touched.

In my heart I'd like to be the Ernie Banks of sports journalism, and they make me be the Dennis Rodman of this shit. This desire just seems so simple. I want to pay pure homage to a home run hitter. Please let me be Peter Gammons just this once, please let me have the tools.

Ugly as it's all gotten before, never before have I been so bruised by the everyday fight between my work and my job.

AT HOME A PATTERN SEEMS TO BE DEVELOPING. THINGS ARE COOL through the fall, but tensions with the wife resurface after Christmas, at that lurch between the NBA All-Star Game and the Super Bowl. Around the same time last year that we left LA, our rapport takes a subtle change in tone.

"Fuck you, Amy. And fuck all your fucking loser friends!"

This is what I say at the most insufferable times, when my wife announces that her friends disapprove of how I treat her. There was a time when Nona and these other people were my friends, too. They don't know what I go through. I've become a caricature of all those black daily reporters I used to mock, the ones who sit around bitching about white folks all day. I make nearly eighty thousand pretax dollars a year, and my spouse makes nearly as much. Most people I know think this means everything. Yet, I'm a dead man walking. I have been robbed of my hipster shtick and am being slowly beaten to death with it.

Maybe I should believe my old brainiac colleagues' intimations that I'm no longer a serious writer. If quantity's a decisive factor, then, yes, I'm out, because I hardly ever write. I apparently have all the time in the world, so Amy wants to know why I can't make her breakfast like I used to. She doesn't understand that my new friends are sports guys, hard-core drinkers, and it's damn near impossible to get up early and make someone else breakfast when you've had fifteen brewskis the night before.

"Bitch," Amy gets told, "you are burning equity by the day."

I tell her about my plans to secure preliminary funding for a start-up called *Joint Custody Today*.

"You're like my mother, Amy." I say this in the Mafia lighting of our railcar hallway. "You could only take me so far. You are extraneous." She slumps off to her Condé Nast job with tears streaming down her face. The neighbors must think I'm whippin' that ass. That's where gentrified awareness deceives them. Amy, like only Johanna and Brenda Graham and a couple editors and sensitive rappers, learns the pain of being knocked with my most lacerating words. Brutally violent sentences.

Soon Forrest will be three. He knows what's up. I give him talks about how Daddy knows he shouldn't call Mommy bad names, but that sometimes Daddy falls short of his goals. This doesn't make Daddy a bad person. Daddy's first impulse is to hit, and that would be really, really bad.

"There is no hitting in this house."

THEY DON'T HAVE PEOPLE LIKE ME IN THE RESPECTABLE PRECINCTS OF Trinidad—not outside captivity, not in broad daylight. Patrice is stunned by my lifestyle. I'm here at the apartment all the time, usually dressed in that paisley robe Amy bought me six years ago, when we became engaged. And when I do leave for the office, I smell of reefer.

Home for Patrice is from something like a suburban setting, and where she comes from people know how to behave.

But she likes me, in that little-girl way where she pretends not to like me. There's gratuitous eye-rolling and playful digs. Then, seasonally her affinity comes out as a full-blown crush. She muses longingly and under her breath or too loud, when I've dropped out the background noise on our banter by—out of nowhere—lifting the needle from my vinyl.

Mostly though she takes luminescent potshots. I'm on the couch watching *Ricki Lake* when she breaks from playing ringmaster to Forrest and the boys in his play-date bedroom.

"Why don't you get a job?"

"I have a job. Can't you tell I'm busy?"

"Yeah. Busy smokin' up all that weed out on the patio?"

"That's right, *busy smokin' that weed*. Busy trying to keep from killin' somebody. Tryin' to keep my sanity."

"I don't believe there's enough marijuana in New York for that. You better go buy some more."

I mutter, maybe audibly, "Busy tryin' not to have sex with you."

"Humph. You definitely need to go buy some more." (Definitely audible.)

It's funny because Patrice finds me goofy as my sister does. But our vibe differs completely from what went on with Gaye. Patrice is far from my sister. It's more like that teenage flirting with distant, taboo relatives. And it is, if possible, much more inappropriate.

16.

a class act

IT EXHAUSTS ME, THE SPEED OF THE CITY. NINETY-NINE PERCENT OF THE populace probably ain't had methamphetamine, but they're all doing speed as a hobby, at least. Myself? I'm strung out, strung along, cowering at the crib after dark. You'll catch me at the Kit-Kat Club or Madame X or a Brooklyn house party every now and then, but I pass on the hard-drug trappings of NYC. Not tryna calibrate how to score a seat at the elusive quality Broadway show. The taxis speed right past me. And there shall be no dates at the Tunnel. My wife is just too white.

Manhattan operates on a pure grid format, and tabloid wheels get the city on message before the sun comes up. There's a surfeit of Donald Trump niggas who mistake being good at business for being a good person. The bottom line is always visible.

I wake up early and wonder away the long wait. Hot 97's rented out their airwaves to Bad Boy once more. Does Puffy Combs have investments in the prison industry? Coffee brews and I shudder. I wonder, what am I waiting for?

God though, one blessing makes up for the crud: The NYC Ladies' Dance. I turned pro in voyeurism a dozen years past, so know this isn't made up: if you have vagina in the 212 or 718 area codes, public undulation is in your repertoire. Excepting only maybe the infirm, females in New York fairly shimmy up and down the island of Manhattan, vamping hard at either tip. I've never seen anything like it, this intense expression of style, for we aren't talking about women. These are females with self-possessed verve. They are *ladies,* and they fucking shake it in the city.

Somehow I don't mind that the framework for the dance is routinized as everything else here, based on weather. All the overpriced barflies who flipped, trading in "Take back the night" protesting for *Sex and the City* sluttiness, won't make me mind. The heavy coats come off in March and mark a surging reemergence of the feminine. Every thang's unfroze, with no Santa Monica pose. Broke, overweight, and oblong chicks alike are in on the act. *There's cellulite in them thar trousers!* Down under the scaffolding, the Rubenesque is presenting her plush booty through snug uniform pants. A harridan rocks out of her business blouse, doing her thing as she's doing her thing. And all the best women have scars on their legs.

By July, you can see a bare breast a day if you seek it out in the Village. Which is nice. A great man once said, stolen naked is gold naked. What then is the value of casual naked, token-effort-at-concealment naked?

Methinks it's platinum naked.

Manhattan ladies in summer office gear straight work that line between admiration and desire.

You separate the women from the girls in August. One set has all-the-time panty lines. Then winter fashions, complex and amazing, come, and the striptease is done.

Nature's finna call the tune. It's not yet March and I'm ready to get to the fresh part of the grind, the one that a nigga like me don't mind.

Women disappear into revolving doors all up and down the island of Manhattan. Up each elevator floor, they lose a little life. The city is lessened. Every office tower is a chamber in New York's big, cold heart.

IN AND AROUND THE GARAGE, THERE'S FRETTING AND MOVEMENT. I AM far from the seventh-floor hub, in a corner office, the one that belongs to the editor in chief.

Working for ESPN is like writing with a condom on. Career jail. I type in a reference to Eminem, and the word is cleanly deleted before the page goes to press. Observations that are the exact opposite of my take are added beneath my byline. I'm told that the word *Bauhaus* can never appear in *The Magazine*.

The chasm of sensibility is deeper than the assumption that style and content are separate, and how badly matched I am to ESPN is only obvious in the intangible. My strength as a writer is gray areas, so I'm of limited value in this black-and-white world. No article longer than two hundred words will run exactly as I want. And exactly is all I want.

They want me for my pop references, a fact that's generally understood.

"You're paid as a consultant, aren't you? I assumed that's why you're never here," asks Traceye from marketing. She's a Knoxville College grad. Knoxville is to Howard as Brown is to Harvard, and Traceye is the only other junior college alumnus I'm aware is on the payroll. The only way I could get more ghetto than her would be to add an *e* to the end of my name. She watches, aghast, as editors hover around my desk, cool-checking senior writers' prose before moving it on.

Traceye's bright, but clearly ignorant, and I tell her, nope, no such cheddar from The Mouse. My means of payback is to devolve into something out of *Dilbert: Banned from TV,* arranging trips, and journalism, based on the likelihood of bad weather in the tristate area. Escaping to Chi-Town and the Sun Belt, I throw hotel room parties and run up truly shocking tabs. My ESPN voice-mail service functions mostly as a storehouse for my freestyle rhyme rehearsals.

But you can only punish so much from afar. I go to Thirty-fourth and Madison so I can:

- Provide visuals for skipping 85 percent of all meetings.
- Place Kool G Rap's a cappella performance of "It's a Shame (What I Gotta Do to Get the Money)" as a voice-mail greeting.

- Not only have pot delivered to the office, but smoke it in the john.
- Advocate the legalization of marijuana on the network's nationally broadcast Sunday morning radio show.
- Destroy $10,000 worth of computer equipment.
- Sneak into print writing that engages the issue of homo-eroticism in sports.
- Resign loudly and repeatedly, from my lair on 125th Street.

I may be the worst employee in Disney history, and this acknowledges the storied worst of Quentin Tarantino. This time I mean it when I quit. And Max knows this.

My dealings with Max are awkward, in no small part because he's among the least comfortable white guys in nigga company I have ever known. That shit might play with all the Uncle Ben motherfuckers they hire over at Max's old Time Warner job, but I'm not feeling it. Also, the writer-reporters call him Austin Powers. He reaches unnecessarily, raiding his pop culture storehouse. It's as if my gig is run by Crispin Glover's jock-sniffing father.

Max is John by birth, but he asks everyone to call him Max because of how laced the spot is with Johns. Shit, I call that muhfucka John, 'cuz there's only one Donnell up in here. And I have in my pocket a freshly procured hit of ecstasy—Calvin Klein—that I'm holding out as a reward for standing my ground. The dose costs $60 and ought to be exquisite, a sure bet to rescue tonight's first-anniversary party for *The Magazine* from guaranteed pockets of the mundane. I finger the tablet deep inside my freshly pressed slacks, the one sop to formality I'll allow.

Maybe I should have taken the E before. Then for sure I would be honest in dealing with this cat.

No, I want to do this on my own. It's just me and John/Max now, and he slides shut the door behind him.

At issue is the latest installment of my column, "Something Else." The hoops lockout has ended, and in the column I harshed on NBA management for manipulating the images of their employees as a means of improving corporate's bargaining position. I wrote that the extended Sprewell-Carlesimo media clusterfuck was as much a product of racist character assassination as was the whole baggy-shorts outrage and cornrow hand-wringing. I offered up that Tom Chambers, who is white, punched a strength-conditioning coach in the same month as Sprewell's East Bay misdeed. News media hardly picked up the Chambers story. Apparently what the sporting press does best is parrot the perspectives of management.

Someone at the top of editorial deleted the entire Chambers reference.

I tell Max, "We're at cross-purposes, John. We might need to call the whole thing off."

"You just need to relax," Max says. "I want you to succeed. I want to promote you. I want to put you on the network. But you need to understand that you're not a finished product. You need a coach."

"That's where we disagree, John, I don't want a coach. All I want is for my shit to be as little about you as possible."

I try picturing myself on *The Sports Reporters* with Mitch Albom and Bill Conlin, talking about Iverson. And it's not just now occurring to me that ESPN is never going to let me get on-air shine like Stuart Scott.

"That's interesting," Max says, "and I'll think about it. But to some extent, it has to be about the team. You like team sports, right?"

"Of course."

"Look, earlier today I came up with an idea. LeBatard and Friend are here. Everyone from the network is in from Bristol."

Minutes before this meeting, I'd heard Steve Bornstein, who was just named president of ABC, would attend the anniversary toast.

"I thought maybe we could do this thing to maybe bury the hatchet. It would be a public show of good faith. Will ya hear me out?"

Max has in mind a dramatic performance, a skit we'd perform before everyone clinked champagne glasses. He'd thank an individual department, then I would do the hip translation.

It is so *stoo*-pid. So I decline.

Max asks me again to come up with something, annoyingly presumptive as usual. Then I finger the ecstasy.

"Well, I'd want to be introduced as . . . um, yeah: Tha Ghetto Communicator."

"Ha ha HA," says John, clapping his hands and pitching forward in a way that's over-the-top and phony. "I love it!"

"Okay, I'll do it, as long as I get to do the script. How long do we have, forty-five minutes?"

"Thirty."

"See you in twenty."

ON THE WALK TO MY DESK, CALVIN KLEIN CALLS MY NAME. HE SAYS, with androgynous allure, *there's still time.* Still time to drop that hit and be giddy instead of tense when you do that show with nasty old Max.

I flop atop my whassat desk chair, click on a Word file. The office grows noisy with spouses and elsewhere-based Disney hotshots in for the party.

By the time I finish, Amy's in the house. Back in Cobble Hill, Forrest is having quality time with his nanny. The car service we'll call to carry Patrice back to Flatbush later this night will clean out our extra funds.

I hear my wife talking with AG. I tell her what's about to pop and she's stunned silent. It sounds just that wack. We've gone from calling a truce to remembering what we see in each other, and Amy knows me enough to see apocalypse if this stunt goes wrong.

I print out, then sprint out, tracking Max down, taking office corners like Cris Carter on a down-and-out.

THE SCRIPT I GIVE JOHN IS PLIABLE, YET DEFINITE. HE LAUGHS ALOUD while scanning the brief routine. The man will go a long way to appear down.

Dan LaBatard and Tom Friend are indeed in and squeezed into the

Garage. I give them dap before sliding in to link arms with my wife. Amy asks what I'm going to say, exactly, and I tell her the script is metaphoric of my entire Disney experience. An Amy eye-roll beats her stifle cue, so I keep to myself the skit's reference to Bobby Benigni's guard scene in *Life Is Beautiful*.

John stands in the light, on the far side of both the crowd and the open Garage entrance.

"And to help me acknowledge everyone in a hip fashion, I'd like to introduce Tha Ghetto Communicator, who this evening will help translate my words."

I pass my commemorative flute of champagne to Amy.

A wee collective inhale, just a little suck, withdraws from the crowd when I stomp out to stand next to the boss. A bunch in back chatter as-is. I'm trying to pimp as if I might avenge the loss I took in the back alley with Rick. Among the senior editors in front, the ones who know me, there is a shared horror. They seem stunned by how badly this might go. I catch a glimpse of the ABC honchos.

John gives a stilted spiel about how great the first year was. And it has been remarkable. Buoyed by a dozen ads a day on ESPN channels, *The Magazine* launched bigger than any other book ever. Distribution is only climbing. Over at Time Warner, Max's old cronies are running scared, fearful of looking square. The appearance of hipness has become a money matter, so every third issue of *Sports Illustrated* jacks some element of our book.

John turns to me. There's a beat. I raise my chin and narrow my eyes, then thump my chest twice with my right fist, thumb side in.

"Respect," I say.

Fascinatingly uncomfortable laughter leaks out around the room. There's no more chatter in the rear.

I got one hand in my pocket. Calvin Klein has become a talisman.

"To the production department," the editor toasts.

"To Willis's shook-ass crew," I interpret.

My voice cracks, barely discernibly, on the word *crew*. Is this something I can really do?

The hip crowd laughs though, and that goes a long way.

"And to John Walsh and John Skipper," John continues, "the great white father and the great white leaper."

Walsh is the genius behind *SportsCenter* and an albino—God is an albino!—and Skipper's tight. I saw him sign in at Basketball City with only a vertical line beneath a dot and a horizontal line next to that. John Skipper, a true player for real.

So I'm kinda caught off-guard. These are great men. I look down at my notes like I don't know what I'm supposed to say. Then I survey the crowd.

"And . . ." I gesture grandly, sweeping an open hand toward Walsh and Skipper, who are in front of *The Magazine*'s throng, ready to clink.

"And, to the plantation overseers "

Alright then. There are hushes and there are hushes. This hush is remarkable not for the purity of its quiet, but because of the very fractured nature the problematic silence represents. In the sonic drop-off there are nervous titters, carryover guffaws, mostly from the ad folks, who think I'm a hoot. Traceye from Tennessee silently mouths, "No, you did *not!*" and there is at least one genuine laugh. It's fucked up and I'm proud. Just a little something to reflect on at all the anniversary parties from hereafter. I am so outta here. The skit peters out, as will the absenteeism, exorbitant room tabs, and watered-down journalism. But I am so out of here.

I step back to my wife, pull CK out, and wash that nigga down with champagne. Shit is ill, but it feels good to once again write until everything's been said, until I've said everything that's in my head.

THEN THINGS GET TRULY ODD. AND REALLY HARD.

It is June. Mom is sick, sicker than ever. Through the decade she's been in the hospital twenty, forty, two thousand times, but she's never asked me to come home. Not even from Chico.

When the call from UC Davis Medical Center rings at 6 Strong Place, she won't ask. But the doctors are about to put her on a breathing machine. She'll be intubated, induced to a light coma. She's had a nurse dial my number first.

Mom's voice is high and feathery, almost pretty and not quite there.

"Do you want me to come home, Mama?"

"No . . . don't. I know you got money troubles."

"Yeah, but, do I *need* to? I mean, is this the one?"

A voluminous pause comes right here.

"Yes . . . I think you better come home."

I make the deal to fly out the next day through Disney Corporate Travel. Their rates are cheapest. My chest is pounding, and I don't jet until morning.

Around the block at Cobble Hill Cinemas, the new *Star Wars* flick is on. I haven't seen it and so decide to kill some time and clear my mind. Young Anakin Skywalker, preoccupied by the opportunity to become a Jedi knight, realizes only after walking away that he's never going to see his mother again. He turns, and his mother calls out, "Don't look back."

Instantly, in the overstuffed, prepubescent matinee, I am weeping like a self-conscious playground wuss, with sniffles and snorts. A prepubescent Brooklyn Heights princess in pleats keeps turning around in her seat, fascinated by the unshaven man who's dabbing at his eyes with a Paris tee. I hocker and glare. *Nothin' to see here, bitch.*

I think of the first *Star Wars*, the night out at Cinema World. It was one of our last times together without conflict, just me and her blowing down Perkins Avenue in Granddaddy's plum-colored Buick. I nearly talked Mama's head off. The movie was the best thing I'd ever seen. I no longer wanted to grow up and play pro football.

More than twenty years later I wonder if a Jedi master is what my mother wanted me to be.

SACRAMENTO AIN'T SO COOL WHEN YOU'RE THIRTY-TWO, HAVE NO National Rental Car, and the temperature is over one hundred. I bunk with cousin Leah, two blocks from where Sherry, her mother, lives, three from my mother's apartment. All of the Graham women live within a mile of each other. Angie, Sherry's other daughter, is on the far side of Johnson High. Aunt Marlene's just off Broadway. All remain cloistered as though Arthur had never ventured north. Grandma's suddenly old from the stroke she suffered a few months ago. She's no longer mistaken for Lena Horne and gets around with the use of an aluminum walker. The Graham men are nowhere to be found.

Brenda Graham is balding and one hundred pounds overweight and has been that way for half her life. Her decline was set into motion by me. Or him. I'm sure of this.

It's weird now because I've already gone to the hospital, along with Gaye and Robby. My sister's younger ones stayed at home. Mom was unconscious, in a middling way in which her groggy eyes briefly opened, showing fear and recognition. Then she was out again.

But it's nice now, because Mom is gonna survive this and we're all back at Sherry's place. Me and Gaye's older sons are in Grandma's room, watching San Antonio and New York play for the NBA title. Robby and Ryan lounge all over me. They're both mad tall, especially Ryan, whose height at age eleven is a shade under mine. He's starting to behave these days because Aaron, his father—the kid I nearly shot in the Sac City era—is about to be released from Pelican Bay State Penitentiary. Ryan talks a lot about living with his dad.

I tell the boys New York stories, like how I told everyone at the magazine that the Knicks would be in the finals and everyone bet against me, and how, after Larry Johnson hit the four-point play to beat the Pacers at the Garden, I yelled at my old friend Mike, the Fresno State Sports Info guy who covers hoops for the *Times*, about his relentless riding of Sprewell, and then Mike penned a column without precedent, a column in which he admitted he was all wrong. And they, too, think it's interesting that this week, after being profiled by me—and having his relationship to Sprewell depicted as a dream scenario akin to Malcolm X affecting Puff Daddy—LJ, who doesn't do interviews, announces to the media that the Knicks are the "rebellious slave" team. And the press goes berserk.

Robby and Ryan think I've got rare skills.

We watch the game on the bed, on the floor, in a chair. Robby and Ryan use my legs for pillows, but the scene is tough again because Pops, Gaye's husband, keeps coming in to take the game in with us and I am secretly planning his murder.

Having such beef is wack because the family is so fragile right now. But I have decided to wait for just the proper occasion. I will make my plot known soon enough, because I want him to sweat out the last days of his life.

Right here I am polite. It's easy. Like every gangster I've ever known, he has been nothing but humble in my presence. (Except for that one punk from Mobb Deep, but he ain't know no better.) Delbert, formerly homeless and now the counter guy at Oak Park's premier African store, is this way. Gangsters understand that I am the same as them, only much, much better. But what Gaye's husband doesn't yet know is that he's a dead man walking. Medulla oblongata, take yourself out with no pain, I will relay to him. That is the painless way.

Because he has tried to molest someone in my family.

Gaye's husband Pops has committed this act because he is a gangster, and molestation is what gangsters do. Sexual molestation is only the most base form of the way thugs molest, bother, and exploit. And they always destroy their own, in the name of the family. It's insidious, this victimization. Pops has infiltrated the fabric of Gaye's brood, assuming a paternal role with his rock money and manipulation of my sister, and the youngest ones will always resent me for taking him off the planet. It will be painful, these hard feelings, but I know better.

If my father had stayed around, my life would be more regularly painful.

Right now, though, a few minutes into the second half, I'm not mad. Snacking on Kool-Aid and Doritos, I buoy myself with irony. All this perceived power in my world of words and I can't protect my family. I broke down and cried about it once in the office of the *LA Weekly*'s editor, but she never quite got it. She was a Quaker product and could never know how tortured I was that I might, say, define cool for America's intelligentsia and admen, but couldn't make things alright for my little sister. It is too funny.

And it's hard because people will read this and think this—molestation and disease, thoughts of avenging murder and fears of poverty—is hard, maybe as hard as it gets. In truth it gets much harder. My people were always among the lucky ones in our hood: progeny of Graham's Farm, Mr. Hots' grandchildren, people on the verge. The deeper you get in the hood, the more children suffer and assume it's their birthright. The drunkest Indian you can find will confirm this for you. Give him one day at ground zero of any given U.S.A. ghetto and he'll say, "Thank God we got reservations."

Mom returns to the duplex later that week. I show her and Grandma video of Amy and Forrest at the playground in one of our recurring placid moments, along with footage of Patrice giving my son a bath. Then I fly into La Guardia, get a ride to Cobble Hill by using a car service voucher from ESPN. The phone rings. It's my mother. Grandma's suffered a fatal aneurysm. I turn around and go back home, stunned and glad for my distance.

"DO YOU THINK AALIYAH IS SEXY?" PATRICE ASKS.

"What? Yeah, I dunno," I say. "I mean, for sure."

"She has great abs."

"For sure."

Chicks from Trinidad and Jamaica push a platoon of strollers along Cobble Hill's bumpy sidewalks, loving the kids, disciplining them, and instilling in Wall Street blue bloods a taste for jerk chicken and rice and peas. Little towheads suck their teeth to show displeasure, just like Yardies.

The woman we employ is on the couch, holding Forrest between her legs while she braids his hair. It's rare for Patrice to be inside on such a fine summer day, but the reason lies to her left, sleeping on a small folded blanket. Jetoye resulted from a flash period of wildness. This fake don from the Bronx got Patrice fat. When she didn't abort the fetus, dude was out.

She is shockingly beautiful. She's tired, and buzzing just a bit from the motherhood high.

I'm home, reading through Nexis-Lexis files on CWebb, and sitting in the rocker I hand-stained for Amy three years back. Back then she found my uneven paint job adorable. It's not certain what she'd say now.

In days Disney Corporate Travel will put me on still another flight to Sacramento. Forrest has his head down while his minder pulls together a row in back. He grimaces but holds back his tears. He won't hide my luggage. He will stand mute with his ear to the phone when I call from the coast.

Jetoye, three months old, begins rotating her fist, still sleeping, and the motion elicits a cry. Patrice is on her in an instant. Forrest is done.

When Patrice takes her right breast out, Forrest is still getting to his feet. I know she's taken it out because, from the corner of my eye, it's clear the cup of her bra is beneath her hand. Deductive reasoning is all we have to go on. I cannot peep her nipple. That would be just too much.

Patrice coos about how much she loves breast-feeding. It's been a much bigger thrill than she ever expected. It's deep, she says. I bet, I say.

I'm pitching *This American Life* on how not to fuck your nanny. 'Cuz I could do that as a book, dog. One May day before Jetoye arrived, I told Patrice that I dig her so much that only my son can have her.

That's not brought up again. As sleepy Jetoye suckles, we discuss Forrest's schooling. He's still in the Montessori classroom for kids with speech issues. His verbal communication has improved. The freak-out factor has lessened—for me, not Amy, who always took it as it came— and I'm not anymore secretly dogged by the prospect of having a little yellow child on the little yellow bus.

Still, I wonder if all of this intervention is a bourgeois means of micromanaging the parenting experience. They didn't do that shit when I was a boy. And look how I turned out.

"Why do we have to make these kids reflect the adult thing so early?" I ask the nanny. "I mean, can't they just take in for a while before they spit? What's a kid got to say, really? My friend Jennifer told me that in Africa, they don't make the kids do anything until their fifth birthdays."

"But this isn't Africa."

"Touché."

Patrice chooses her spots well.

And then she does that laugh where she pretends her dignity isn't under armed guard. Her guffaw is as muted as a dam break.

I have to ask her, "You think I'm pretty terrible, don't you?"

"Hey, it's your house. I just work here." Jetoye has fallen asleep in her mother's cradling arms. Forrest is entranced by Cita on BET.

"No, your opinion matters to me. You do think I'm awful, huh?"

Holding her little baby tight across her front, Patrice does her best to withhold from her eyes the quality that her mother has described as being "too daring." For this to happen, the nanny must point her head at an angle away from me and maneuver around in her lids so that she is looking at me in the most intriguing of ways.

"What does it matter what I think? It's like I said before. You just seem too much like a fox."

"See now, that's an answer right there. You could've said no."

'Trice's dam breaks, eyes roll.

"That's cool, but I'll tell you what," I say. "I may be bad, but every day I'm not chasing you around here nekkid, I give myself a firm pat on the back. A lot o' niggas would not let you rest. Like my father. That motherfucker would have been on you before Amy got to the Bergen train stop. Shit, you may think I'm bad? Well, maybe. But I'm better than my father. And my son's gonna be something else. There's not one other thing that counts."

IN SACRAMENTO, THE BACKUP SINGER FOR BLACKALICIOUS RECOGNIZED me when someone backstage at the DJ Shadow show said my name. I was there to squash some obscure beef with Shadow.

"Oh, my goodness, *you're* Donnell Alexander? You used to be incredible," she said. "Whatever happened to you?"

Whatever happened to me is that I went to work for Disney and fell out of the real world. I'm here for the CWebb article, and this time in Sactown, all I want is to get the story and avoid my father. Of course he's not to blame for Grandma's death, but since moving East my tangible regard for him has diminished. In my eyes, he stands for death, or at least decay. He has been fading since relating the flag hustle. I haven't wanted him as my father anymore. For only about five weeks total, Delbert has been in my direct presence, and the effect is omnipresence.

CWebb is dependably easy, and our interview along the Sacramento River seems to be the first break I've had in years. Jason Williams and the ballers' dogs and a photographer are there. JWill's girlfriend hangs out and has fun, and I'm home.

Before I skip town, Gaye shows me a picture of our father. Delbert is sepia and he carries an Old West rifle. At first he's unrecognizable. I think the image is of a buffalo soldier. Turns out, he's had the photograph taken at an outdoor mall, copied it a hundred times, and peddles it in a store where African oils and *The Final Call* are sold.

Something clicks. It's obvious: this is the very same image he once sold me.

BACK IN NEW YORK I GIVE A SPEECH, ONE CONCERNING *THE MAGAZINE*'S alterations to my CWebb profile. Many, primarily residents of 125th Street, consider it my best on aesthetics and commerce. Others think of it as naked sedition, prime evidence of why I should be, at least, fired:

"Raw cocaine.

"You people seem to not understand that there are people in the world who have had raw cocaine," I say to Gary, a studious senior editor. "Not everybody deals in that weak shit. There's a range y'all ain't even knowin'. You put that weak shit out on the market, and people remember it. I'm telling you, you're engineering your own demise."

When the CWebb story went to press, consensus was the piece made Top Five for *The Magazine*'s brief history. And I had felt good about the copy. But they changed the Prince/Bone-Thugs reference "this is what it sounds like when thugs cry" to "this is what it sounds like when *the* thugs cry," and I am through the roof, doing everything but stand atop my desk.

"This isn't personal and it is not politics. This is strictly business. Sometimes you have to give it to 'em uncut."

This mostly just woofin'. I am waiting for a deal to go through with Vanguarde Media that would have me editing a magazine. Now, more than ever, I could give less than a fuck about what anyone in the Disney food chain has to say about me. See, no single force can make or break my career. I can actually afford to send money and presents to Mom, Gaye, and the kids. Amy doesn't hate me. I have options and the truth is a freewheeling thing.

"This magazine is too watered down. Not only do we not get it raw, we come up short like we've been cut five, six times. This is light weight."

Then the CWebb issue hits the streets, and the shit hits the fan. He is still contraband as Sprewell, but I wrote without apology about how people outside the sports establishment think he's a good kid who happens to be growing up in public. Along the way, I quoted a couple of players dissing commentator Bill Walton, who, it turns out, is Max's best friend.

Max and his lieutenant Wulf want me gone, and so two days after Skipper is promoted up the Disney ladder—and *his* father dies—Max places a letter in my file. It's near total fabrication, an indictment. It's not a warning, but is designed to make me quit. Of all the shit I've pulled, the memo actually accuses me of a thing I didn't do. It says lacking good ideas. It shows me the door, then says no one will mind if I use it.

`The backroom civil war at *The Magazine* is over. The new Up South won.

"HOW CAN THEY SINGLE YOU OUT FOR ACTIN' CRAZY?" ASKED CLASSY R. The R-uh is still den mother of 125th Street and reigning HNIC, but her hair has flourished, stylishly woven into braids. They reflect her powers of political negotiation in an S.I. world. "Believe me, there are writers here who act a whole lot crazier than you."

Classy R is just being nice. But the point is moot. This is no place for Donny Shell. It's front-runner culture. If Webber's team were winning, the work would be just swell.

Nobody enjoys being beat to You Can't Fire Me, I Quit, and though I hate the gig and have plenty of offers, I'm bugged about how shit went down. So, I write my father a letter, even though I fully know there's long been no map from where I am.

FIGHT THIS GENERATION! FIGHT THIS GENERATION! FIGHT THIS *generation . . .*

It's meaningless, this song. And in its meaninglessness, the song is everything. Sometimes it gets no better than hearing fuzzy guitars throb and argue while a smart-ass punk does his best to cut through. I am sitting on the life-size windowsill of my room at the Adams Mark Hotel in St. Louis, smoking the last of the three joints I sneaked up on the plane. Usually I wait to score until I'm in the destination city, because my dreadlocks get me security-searched like nobody's business, but I make an exception this time. I'm not trying to be stuck in The Lou without no funk this time.

In the days after the Max letter surfaced, Gary, the studious editor, ran this game: on your way out, win us an award. He says this right after admitting that Max and them never submitted the Spellman story or any of my standout stuff for competition. *The Magazine* craves writing awards because critics correctly surmise that its words are window dressing for images. Turns out that, even as these cats have wussed out on giving me light, they scratch their chins and say, "I can't believe that Alexander piece never won an award." They are gifted with denial.

Gary maneuvers to squeeze one last work from my jones for story-telling craft and fuck-you gestures.

This is big pimpin'.

And popcorn that I am, I try. High above the Mississippi.

I ALWAYS HULD DELBCRT'S LETTERS A LONG TIME BEFORE OPENING them.

It started as a sidebar, this amazing tale about a Carolina kid who did everything right: went to church, listened to his mother, said no to alcohol and drugs, and earned his undergrad degree and eventually a master's. Then Leonard Little went to his first NFL training camp. Caving in to peer pressure, he attended a benefit in a bar, here at the Adams Mark Hotel in downtown St. Louis, following two-a-day drills. Little and a barfly who sat by watching swear the linebacker had just three drinks—maybe the intense practices altered his body chemistry?—before he got in his 4 X 4, drove a couple of blocks, and in a low-speed collision adjacent to the Arch, killed a suburban mother.

My last ESPN premise is that it takes a lot of practice to drive drunk. I've driven at the Leonard Little level of intoxication countless times without consequence.

But that's where I'm wrong. At home I have a wife who is not DOA, but slow-mo roadkill, an angel eaten up inside. It's a crime that she's paying for my ambition. All she ever wanted was the stoner dude she loved in Chico. She had a notion that she could hold him down. She didn't know his battles, never mind wanting to join them.

Fight this gennarashion! Fight this GEN-ER-A-SHUN!

———

OUTSIDE THE PICTURE WINDOW, YOU GET ALL THESE LIGHTS. THEY'RE IN the building across from mine. It's a grid pattern, maybe thirty rows from ground to sky. And inside every other one you can see the silhouettes of people, maybe men, perhaps women. They are without gender and without race. Lifted as I am, they all appear to be dancing or contorting in a giant Twister tournament. Every window seems to showcase a party. For a second, I wish I were there. But I've been in those rooms before, being spied from an anonymous distance, and I can tell that it's not so great where they are. Those people are looking back at me, lusting after the silhouette of my cool party. There's no point in wanting in.

The next day, I'm down the street in St. Louis's Trans World Dome. My first live NFL game, Vikings against the Rams. I walk into the playoff locker room of the soon-to-be-champion Rams and watch Leonard Little. He stands on the fringe of celebration, his pain all but forming a force field around him. I am feeling him.

There's a saying in Hollywood that after a film's funding reaches a certain number of millions, you've got to start putting black hats on the bad guys and white hats on the good guys. It works that way in journalism as well. I was a good investment before *The Magazine* hit the million mark in circulation, but beyond that mark my presence in its pages only served to confuse. And I was such a hard case that these crackers weren't trying to keep me around.

But I'm most fascinated by the fact that I care.

I READ DELBERT'S LETTER ON THE FLIGHT EAST. THE CORRESPONDENCE is the second in a series. In the first one he told me that he had wanted to name me Hakeem, meaning "wise one," but that my mother wouldn't go for that, it being 1966 and Sandusky and all. My father was the one who came up with Donnell, which is Irish and means "dark and brave."

Whatever, 'cuz now he's on some inspirational fare. He's got it in his head that, of all the Alexanders born of those sharecroppers who sneaked away from their subtly masked captivity at the end of the nineteenth century, I'm the one closest to fulfilling their destiny. He pinpoints this as the source of all conflict in my writing life.

"They fear you because you're their replacement," Delbert wrote.

My father is such a fucking idiot. I ain't a replacement for shit. I am newfangled roadkill. However, I feel optimistic that my patented blend of passivity and pointless punk-rock protest might, through earnings, one day be extinguished. It won't be Forrest's concern. I will give Delco this though: My father has major-league clues about fixing in the mix. Ever on the margins, he's managed to remain in the game. Here's a good laugh: "The Life" that housed my column is going to be a show on ESPN. That means that in an obscure but powerful way he's involved in the fame he always craved. The germ of his ghetto celebrity will be beamed into homes around the globe.

And being TV, the medium will make him look tall.

WATERED DOWN AS ESPN TURNS MY LITTLE STORY, IT HITS BIG. ACCORD-ing to form, here would be an excerpt proving the robustness of my prose, but Disney owns the rights to that work. I can't afford to tell you. I do have these:

> For all the joy and laughter that sports has given me, it had only made me cry once. It was when Len Bias died. I was ten years old. Now that I have read "Head On" by Donnell Alexander, the count is two. I can't remember being moved this much by an article of any kind. Thank you.
>
> *Zachary Browne*

Congratulations on the May 2000 issue. I contend that it is without a doubt the best magazine that your young publication has produced. The articles on Larry Walker and University of North Carolina vs. North Carolina State University were very good; however, I believe your article on Leonard Little (Head On) deserves the most praise.

Evandeaux@555mail.com

I lost my dad 10 months ago when he had a massive heart attack while umpiring a summer league high school baseball game. I found Leonard Little's story to be very inspirational. The tragic accident he was involved in will be something he will never understand, but will overcome. His mistake should be learned from, but his faith admired. Donnell Alexander, thank you for such a meaningful article. It's a story all of us can learn from.

David Gulley

All of us. The humanity, how it tingles. Exiting *The Magazine,* I felt like Snoop and Dre walking away from Death Row—banged up, but with incontrovertible evidence.

"WELL, DANDY, YOU'RE A MARTYR NOW," MY MAN AG TELLS ME AS I PACK up my Manhattan life.

Here is one sportswriter who would not take it anymore . . .

"Yeah, that's me. I'm like Tupac and Jesus."

"I mean it, man. Now that you're gone, you've attained that status."

"Fuck martyrdom. It's totally overrated. I'm almost offended by the assertion."

"Whatever. I was talking about it on ESPN Radio this weekend. You know how college players get drafted and when it doesn't work out, they call it a bust? You coming here was like a blitzing linebacker being drafted by a team that only rushes down linemen. In that case it's not the player who's at fault, it's the system. Shit like that happens all the time."

"That's really interesting," I say. "Not sure what that has to do with martyrdom, but it's a nice thing for you to say. I did my share of dirt though."

"I know. Everybody knows. That's kinda the point. You're a class act."

"*Now* you're outcha mind."

"A throwback."

"Nigga, please."

It's always funny when you call AG "nigga," 'cuz he has only trace amounts of the quality in him. It's as if someone sucked out the poison.

I DIDN'T TELL AG THAT I'D CHANGED MY MIND ABOUT ESPN. THE BEEF didn't start with these niggas. They were doing basic commercial art and I was doing, well, I'm still not sure what the fuck I was doing, but it was some sort of experiment about retaining and projecting myself. They were doing a business, and my presence didn't just fuck up the template, it probably caused seizures among various members of ESPN's audience. Besides, they put me in the mix. I mean, I went on Fashion Television, dog. And Big-Pimpin' Mickey got me to New York, got me defined as something other than a critic, exposed me to game. I'da called off the whole beef for the price of a personal assistant.

Just one thing is inexorably extra: What part of the game was penalizing someone for being ahead of the curve?

In the paradigm of capitalism, patriarchy is pimpin'. ESPN is *LA Weekly* is Delbert Bilal. The realization makes me ruthless. Fuck yeah, I'd get in bed with either my father or the for-profit Left or Mick the Fat Mack, because if I did, I'd do it with the prospect of them *woikin'* for me. To pimp the pimp would be a dream come true for any ghetto bastard.

"GAYE NEEDS TO GET HER ASS BACK WITH MY CAR. I'M TRYING TO CATCH a plane."

"Don't cuss so much in my house, especially with all these kids around."

Mom becomes more insanely religious the worse her health gets. She knows Gaye's kids do every cussword in the book before breakfast. All five are among us, in Robby's room playing video games or here in the front room. Destiny flips through the CDs in my open suitcase, and Little Tiaree, now almost three, gets caught up in the tubing from Mom's oxygen tank.

Gaye always pushes it to the limit, but this time she has at least said it's important that I wait. What's the big deal? I know she won't be bringing Pops by because I've marked him for death and he steers clear of me.

It's been a great trip to Cali, all on Disney's dime. I got them to front me five grand for a freelance piece that maybe I'll do and maybe I won't. Fuckers.

My writing life is my own since I scored an Internet side hustle, consulting, and do penance at a nonprofit Web site devoted to media awareness. I'm flexible as ever, not stressed-out, so Amy and I have loved like we've never been unhappy during our week in southern California. Forrest's digging it down there convinced Amy that every-thing can be normalized if we can just get to the West Coast, home. And I've been up here, at my man Rob's wedding, since putting my wife and son on a plane. Shit's so busy that I haven't even had time to see Delbert. I'm ready now.

I wish Gaye would come on.

"I swear to God I'm gonna miss this plane!"

My rental pulls up. Ryan throws my bags over his shoulder. I don't even recognize who it is riding with Gaye.

———

IT'S DESTINY AND RYAN'S FATHER, AARON. I HAVEN'T SEEN HIM SINCE before I left City College. After Aaron got transferred from Folsom to Pelican Bay, his kids didn't see him either. Now he's fresh out of prison, and the bloom is still on the rose. Ryan's beaming on the porch, looking just like Aaron, who's grinning in the car. The feeling of relatively-simpler-times reunion is in the air, and I'm more glad than ever that I didn't shoot him.

In the driveway, we give each other huge hugs.

"You done got big," Aaron says.

"Shoot, man, you the one!"

It's all true, I'm about sixty pounds heavier than when we last met, but Aaron's muscles have muscles. The hair beneath his ball cap is braided and runs down the middle of his back. When he slaps my hands, I see his nails are about an inch beyond his fingers. He was locked up for all of the nineties and could not know who I am.

Gaye's so proud to have done something nice for us. She doesn't say it, but I can tell.

But I gotta keep it movin' if I'm gonna see Delbert, so I jump in the Alero and head for Broadway. I'm thinking I can stop at Tower Books and grab a copy of the Sunday *New York Times*. There's a series on race in America that they're running, and I am not trying to read that mess on-line. And I feel so good that I freestyle a rhyme.

The style was mine
On which them motherfuckers dined
I couldn't waste my time
So now I'm cuttin' on a dime
Remember the Titans?
Naw, but I remember the '80s
As long as niggas dyin'
I keep flowin' like Euphrates

Delbert won't get but a minute.

His ancient Mayberry truck's out front of his house on Broadway. One day I'll have to stop and ask him why I've never known him to own a vehicle other than a truck.

I knock on his door and it's all good. He has his teeth in. We hug, keep things movin', and within a few minutes are back outside.

Del's doin' well, working weekends as an in-house caregiver for mentally disabled men. This house he scammed off a hooker who had to go to do time. Maybe he'll be able to get a better truck soon.

"How's this ride do you?" I am edging toward my rental.

"It's very good transportation. Shoot, I've most definitely driven worse, ya see now."

"Oh, no doubt."

"Yeeaah, Son . . ."

"Uh, I think I gotta split."

"Oh."

"Sorry I don't get to stay longer on these things, but I always have a lot going on. Amy and them are waiting for me. And there's all these jobs . . . I'ma do another story for *The Magazine* sometime this fall, maybe Steve McNair."

"What?"

"Yeah, Steve McNair, the quarterback? Plays for Tennessee . . ."

"I know who 'Air' McNair is. I am just amazed that you got it like that. You mean, you can go back up in there and do your thing?"

I'm confused. "Well, how else would I do it?"

Delbert shakes his head just a bit, then he suddenly leans forward, grabs me around the head, and kisses me hard on the left cheek.

"That's what I love about you, man!"

It is at this moment that I begin to wonder profoundly about something. I can't lie, the matter was whether I was holding a loosey and ought to worry about being stopped by airport security. But for the purposes of emotional resonance, let's pretend my concern was, say, spanking. I got spanked maybe a dozen times in my life, and I do sometimes wonder if I'd have been a more overtly useful member of society if there had been more external discipline placed on me. Maybe all I ever needed was a believable character who could tell me no.

Delbert's eyes are misty.

I shrug because I'm cold, even in the June of northern California, and say, "Oh yeah. Sure. Thanks." Dammit, there's no ending to this family mess. I'm going to have to settle for reading that *Times* series on-line. I love the hood, but the hood is mad mailroom, to use my friend Zenobia's expression. Fucking the nanny mailroom. And I still don't really know my father.

And I think not at all about how weird it is to run into long-lost Aaron and long-lost Delbert back-to-back. I think about a lot of things, but I do not think about this and how it might one day be the conclusion of my book. Which is weird, because I'm constantly contriving one part or another of that project. But I know now, as is the case almost always, that my distance is Delbert's punishment for how he did Mom, Gaye, and me. The coldness of my heart is proof, proof, proof.

I'm totally off this as I move through the airport, seeking out the gate for my flight to La Guardia. It is the same Sacramento terminal I flew into from Ohio nearly fifteen years ago, on my very first plane ride, and transformed my life. Sometimes it only takes one bold move.

I began passing through the phalanx of United Airlines gates, and who do I see, standing with slumped shoulders and dressed in baggy shorts and a tilted-forward baseball cap, but CWebb. Of course, he's writing out an autograph for a youth who is awestruck at his feet, staring. Webber, once a media whipping boy, is now winning and a big story. I am truly happy for him.

An aisle away, I drop my suitcase. Seconds later, Webber gets a punch in the arm.

"Whassup, dude?"

The power forward looks over from his pen and paper, and his eyes get that Christmas sparkle. They did this last time I ran into him, at the Garden in the winter. CWebb's expression is unfakeable excitement, as though he's just received an open-court pass from Jason Williams. It is what makes his popularity unsinkable.

"Dog! Whatchu doin'?"

"Not a whole lot. Seein' family. Went to a wedding."

"Hey, you see where they're tryin' to trade Spree? That's unbeliev-able." Webber is giddy.

"I have no idea what you're talking about. Man, start over. The Knicks getting rid of Sprewell? You lyin'!"

"Yes! I mean, no."

"I been outta circulation. What's the deal homey?"

There's animated chat for a few minutes, with CWebb outlining a byzantine plot that I'm not even *trying* to follow, not anymore. But it's great because I'm now acutely aware that there's not the hypeman qual-ity that too often lingers in my verbal exchanges with friends who are famous. Then I remember that wack rap album he made and I'm think-ing something, but only something, like: From the bottom of the ocean to the top of the hill, MCs can't deal with my high-tech skills. They type tight, last all night. Buckle up for safety and prepare to take flight. And I am transported to the party in SoHo, for *Honey* magazine, a few months back. Playa Frank is with me and the scene is kandy-colored, with a bar that's open and efficient. Puffy's on the scene, D'Angelo's in the house, but I hear a publicist whisper that this must really be a major party because Donnell Alexander's here.

Ladies in the spot are as loose as they'll get without being in love or doing E, and some dance on tables with their hips all swishy. And when I zigzag through the densely packed humanity, I'm flicking at a child-proof lighter and the DJ's hitting the 808 drums so that the sub-bass pound gives his mix extra sex and urgency. P-Frank and I step onto the main floor, where the party rages most wild, and somewhere between us a joint gets sparked.

There's a feeling that comes when you hit the chronic and you're already loaded that feels like a raise in salary. Emotions brighten, senses swell. We crabwalk through the sea of people and then come upon a seam. The crowd spreads itself wide and an open hole greets us, introduced by a stilling of the music's throb.

Recognition flashes across the platform of faces. Maybe it's Frank they're concerned with or maybe it's become just that problematic to smoke dope in Manhattan. Regardless, the attention feels righteous. It is at this exact moment that I come to terms with the notion of ghetto celebrity. I'm feeling myself a little bit. Hardly recognize the feeling. I'm not a popcorn pimp, but an earner. Mine is the best way handy for me to put food on the table. I pimps words, kick 'em on the curb. Make 'em do everything I tell 'em; yo, nigga, thought ya heard.

It's easiest to love your ghetto celebrity when you know all you'll ever do is have it and die.

CWebb continues outlining various Sprewell trade scenarios. I dis Knicks management and the New York sporting press, take a look around, and see that a line has formed behind me. There are white folks who cannot possibly be sports journalists. Too many of them are women. Everyone has a pen except for me. I am distinctively lacking even as I'm out of the loop. It is creeping up the back of my neck: the hypeman cometh. I slip aside, give a pound, and tell the baller I'll see him in some city where I know I will not be.

I slip away and settle into a black plastic chair, furniture on a metal chain gang, open up a book, and begin reading. Let's say it's *The Elements of Style,* but, probably, it is not.

Ta-dow!

acknowledgments

Dave Eggers was Rick Rubin to this shit. Chris Jackson played the part of Russell Simmons. Also, I need to give a holler to Julian Rubinstein, because that sort of thing is extremely important to him. But the rest of y'all? Shit, *you* know how you did me!